Literacy Unlocked

Literacy Unlocked

How to Implement the Science of Reading with Young Learners

Amie Burkholder

JB JOSSEY-BASS™
A Wiley Brand

Copyright © 2025 by John Wiley & Sons, Inc. All rights reserved, including rights for text and data mining and training of artificial technologies or similar technologies.

Published by John Wiley & Sons, Inc., Hoboken, New Jersey.
Published simultaneously in Canada.

ISBNs: 9781394285242(Paperback), 9781394285259(ePub), 9781394285266(ePDF)

Except as expressly noted below, no part of this publication may be reproduced, stored in a retrieval system, or transmitted in any form or by any means, electronic, mechanical, photocopying, recording, scanning, or otherwise, except as permitted under Section 107 or 108 of the 1976 United States Copyright Act, without either the prior written permission of the Publisher, or authorization through payment of the appropriate per-copy fee to the Copyright Clearance Center, Inc., 222 Rosewood Drive, Danvers, MA 01923, (978) 750-8400, fax (978) 750-4470, or on the web at www.copyright.com. Requests to the Publisher for permission should be addressed to the Permissions Department, John Wiley & Sons, Inc., 111 River Street, Hoboken, NJ 07030, (201) 748-6011, fax (201) 748-6008, or online at http://www.wiley.com/go/permission.

The manufacturer's authorized representative according to the EU General Product Safety Regulation is Wiley-VCH GmbH, Boschstr. 12, 69469 Weinheim, Germany, e-mail: Product_Safety@wiley.com.

Certain pages from this book (except those for which reprint permission must be obtained from the primary sources) are designed for educational/training purposes and may be reproduced. These pages are designated by the appearance of copyright notices at the foot of the page. This free permission is restricted to limited customization of these materials for your organization and the paper reproduction of the materials for educational/training events. It does not allow for systematic or large-scale reproduction, distribution (more than 100 copies per page, per year), transmission, electronic reproduction or inclusion in any publications offered for sale or used for commercial purposes—none of which may be done without prior written permission of the Publisher.

Trademarks: Wiley and the Wiley logo are trademarks or registered trademarks of John Wiley & Sons, Inc. and/or its affiliates in the United States and other countries and may not be used without written permission. All other trademarks are the property of their respective owners. John Wiley & Sons, Inc. is not associated with any product or vendor mentioned in this book.

Limit of Liability/Disclaimer of Warranty: While the publisher and author have used their best efforts in preparing this book, they make no representations or warranties with respect to the accuracy or completeness of the contents of this book and specifically disclaim any implied warranties of merchantability or fitness for a particular purpose. No warranty may be created or extended by sales representatives or written sales materials. The advice and strategies contained herein may not be suitable for your situation. You should consult with a professional where appropriate. Further, readers should be aware that websites listed in this work may have changed or disappeared between when this work was written and when it is read. Neither the publisher nor authors shall be liable for any loss of profit or any other commercial damages, including but not limited to special, incidental, consequential, or other damages.

For general information on our other products and services, please contact our Customer Care Department within the United States at (800) 762-2974, outside the United States at (317) 572- 3993. For product technical support, you can find answers to frequently asked questions or reach us via live chat at https://support.wiley.com.

If you believe you've found a mistake in this book, please bring it to our attention by emailing our reader support team at wileysupport@wiley.com with the subject line "Possible Book Errata Submission."

Wiley also publishes its books in a variety of electronic formats. Some content that appears in print may not be available in electronic formats. For more information about Wiley products, visit our web site at www.wiley.com.

Library of Congress Control Number is Available

Cover Design: Wiley
Cover Image: © calvindexter/Getty Images
SKY10103721_041725

Contents

Introduction		1
CHAPTER 1	Embarking on Your Reader's Journey	5
CHAPTER 2	Phonemic Awareness in Early Reading Instruction	31
CHAPTER 3	The Role of Handwriting in Early Literacy Development	57
CHAPTER 4	Building the Foundation of Letter-Sound Knowledge	85
CHAPTER 5	From Letter Sounds to Decoding	111
CHAPTER 6	Building Strong Readers Through Systematic Phonics	133
CHAPTER 7	Teaching High-Frequency Words	171
CHAPTER 8	Making Phonics Stick: Application Is Key	191
CHAPTER 9	Background Knowledge and Vocabulary	215

CHAPTER 10	Bringing It All Together: Fostering a Love for Reading and Creating Lifelong Readers	239
	References	247
	Acknowledgments	251
	About the Author	255
	Index	257

Introduction

Welcome! I'm thrilled you've picked up this book and are ready to embark on a journey that I, too, have traveled. For years, I worked in the world of balanced literacy, confident that I was helping my students succeed. But as time went on, I began to notice gaps—students who struggled to become confident, independent readers despite my best efforts. Something wasn't clicking. I realized that if I wanted to truly unlock literacy for all my students, I needed to shift my approach and dig deeper into what the research said about how children learn to read.

That shift—from balanced literacy to structured, research-based practices—was more than a change in teaching methods; it was a turning point that reshaped the entire trajectory of my classroom. As I began to see the impact of using science-backed techniques, it became crystal clear that understanding how the brain processes reading and applying evidence-based strategies could truly unlock the potential in every young learner. The difference in my students' progress was undeniable. Since making this shift, I've committed myself to bridging the gap between research and practice, ensuring that teachers can access and apply what we know about effective literacy instruction.

This book is the result of that journey—a culmination of years spent refining practices, learning from research, and, most importantly, witnessing firsthand how these shifts can transform the lives of young readers. Through these pages, I hope to share what I've learned so that you too can confidently merge research with your daily practice and, in turn, unlock literacy for the students in your care.

As educators, we often hear the notion that kids don't have to love reading—they just have to be able to do it. And, yes, we are facing a literacy crisis in our country, where it is essential that every child learns to read. But I believe that the process of learning to read doesn't have to be a chore. We have the opportunity, as educators, to make reading fun and engaging, even while sticking to the research-based practices that ensure success. The joy of reading should not be lost along the way, and it is our responsibility to help foster that joy, turning reluctant readers into enthusiastic learners.

One thing I want you to know about me is that I am not just a researcher standing on the sidelines—I am a practitioner. I am in classrooms every day, working with students and supporting teachers. I live and breathe this work, just like you. My perspective is rooted in the real-world challenges and triumphs of the classroom. I've walked in your shoes, and it's important to me that you know that this book is written by someone who is right there alongside you, facing the same daily realities.

Each chapter in this book is structured with the same purpose: to give you a clear path from foundational knowledge to practical application. Every chapter includes the following:

- **Introduction:** An overview of the key concepts
- **Research:** A dive into the latest findings and studies that underpin the practice
- **Practical tips for implementation:** Concrete strategies for applying the research in your classroom
- **Classroom implementation actionable steps:** Step-by-step guides and activities to bring these ideas to life

I've also provided companion materials, available at www.literacyedventures.com/literacy-unlocked, to support your journey with additional resources designed to make implementation seamless. You can unlock all the companion resources with the code JOURNEY.

But most important, this book was designed to be more than just something you read once and put on a shelf. It's a daily reference, a guide you can turn to whenever you need support, clarity, or fresh ideas. The strategies and resources here are meant to be low-prep, easy to implement, and immediately useful—so you can take what you learn and put it into practice the very next day.

Think of this book as your literacy coach in your back pocket. My goal is for you to pick it up and think, *"Yes! Now I get it."* I want you to feel empowered—not just with knowledge but also with actionable steps that make a real difference in your teaching.

This book is not just about research—it's about empowering you with the tools, strategies, and confidence to make a difference in your classroom. Together, let's transform literacy instruction for our youngest learners. They deserve to not only learn how to read but also to love the process along the way.

CHAPTER ONE

Embarking on Your Reader's Journey

If you are reading this, you are likely a skilled reader. The words on this page lift easily, and you require little effort to read them. You might not remember how you learned to read, and you're probably not thinking about what's happening in your brain right now as you read these words. However, what's happening in your reading brain is quite impressive.

As educators and literacy teachers, we need to understand this process. Understanding how the brain works and how our students become strong readers is critical to literacy instruction.

Over the years, many cognitive neuroscience studies have offered valuable perspectives on how reading skills develop and function in the brain. This chapter will explore the research on the brain and how we learn to read.

What the Research Says

Thanks to cutting-edge technologies like functional magnetic resonance imaging and electroencephalogram, researchers can peer into the brain and see exactly which areas are active when we read. Moreover, they have discovered that when reading takes place in the brain, it is not confined to just one area. There are actually many areas in the brain that are responsible for reading, and these areas can be found in the left hemisphere. They are responsible for word recognition and understanding speech sounds. These areas facilitate the crucial connections among letters, sounds, words, and language structures.

> **FUN FACT** Did you know our brains aren't naturally wired for reading at birth? Long-term studies following brain development through reading milestones have uncovered some fascinating findings. As children advance from mastering basic reading skills to becoming fluent readers, their brains undergo significant structural and functional changes. These changes typically happen in the brain's language-processing regions. So, the next time you are amazed by your students' reading progress, remember that their brain is evolving alongside their skills!

Our brains are not naturally wired to read, so we have to repurpose parts of them. Just like a rubber band can change and adapt to fit different objects, our brains can adapt to make room for new knowledges and experiences.

Let us take a deeper look at how the brain works. Cunningham and Rose (2010), Turkeltaub et al. (2002), and Hudson et al. (2016) highlight the different regions in the brain and how they work together. There are three central regions responsible for this:

- **The frontal region.** The frontal region is situated at the front of the brain and is responsible for processing speech. It enables us to understand and articulate speech sounds while speaking and listening.
- **The occipital-temporal region.** The occipital region (also known as the letterbox) is positioned at the back of the brain and serves as the space for word appearance and meaning. This area of the brain enables us to recognize letters and words. It is also responsible for automaticity and plays a role in language comprehension.
- **The parietal-temporal region.** Located toward the back of the brain, the parietal-temporal region takes in the written word and dissects it into the individual sounds, analyzes those sounds, and supports decoding.

Let us break it down (see Figure 1.1).

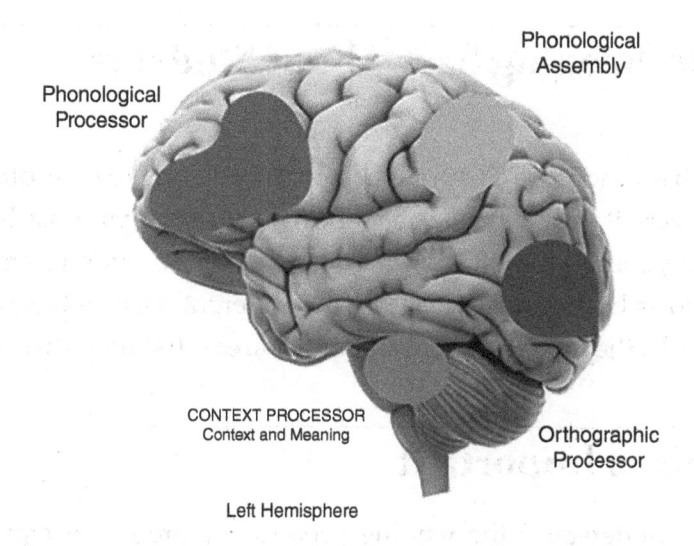

FIGURE 1.1 Reading in the brain.

As children develop reading skills in the primary grades, these regions are trained to become proficient. Brain imaging studies like those by Turkeltaub et al. (2002), as referenced in Turkeltaub et al. (2003), have uncovered notable changes in the structure and function of these brain regions. These findings show how the brain can rewire and improve its neural pathways in reaction to reading instruction. A significant difference in activation patterns depends on a student's reading ability. Early exposure to rich language experiences enhances the brain's receptivity to developing reading skills, such as phonemic awareness, decoding, and word recognition. Notably, beginning readers exhibit increased activity in the parietal-temporal region associated with word analysis, while more experienced readers show heightened activity in the occipital-temporal region linked to word recognition (Keys to Literacy, n.d.).

When we understand how the brain learns to read, we can tailor our instruction to support it. Using evidence-based practices ensures that our instructional methods are grounded in science and that educators use the best techniques for student success.

What the Brain Imaging Says About Students Who Struggle

Cunningham and Rose (2010) suggest that struggling readers often show different activity than strong readers. Their pathways must be developed more, and they must work hard to read. These students are usually referred to as having dyslexia. They use different parts of their brain. In other words, they overcompensate for the areas that they struggle in.

Why All of This Is Important

When we understand the reading process, we are better equipped to support our students as they become readers.

How We Can Support This Rewire

The Simple View of Reading (SVR), developed by Gough and Tunmer in 1986, offers a powerful, straightforward explanation of how reading comprehension is built (see Figure 1.2). The SVR model breaks down reading comprehension into two essential components: decoding and language comprehension. In mathematical terms, it's represented as follows:

Decoding × Language Comprehension = Reading Comprehension

This equation highlights a critical reality: both decoding and language comprehension must be strong for a reader to fully understand a text. If either of these components is weak, overall reading comprehension will suffer. For example, a student may decode fluently but struggle with comprehension due to weak language skills. However, a student with strong language comprehension but weak decoding skills will struggle to unlock the meaning of the printed words.

The Simple View of Reading

word recognition X **language comprehension** = **skilled reading**

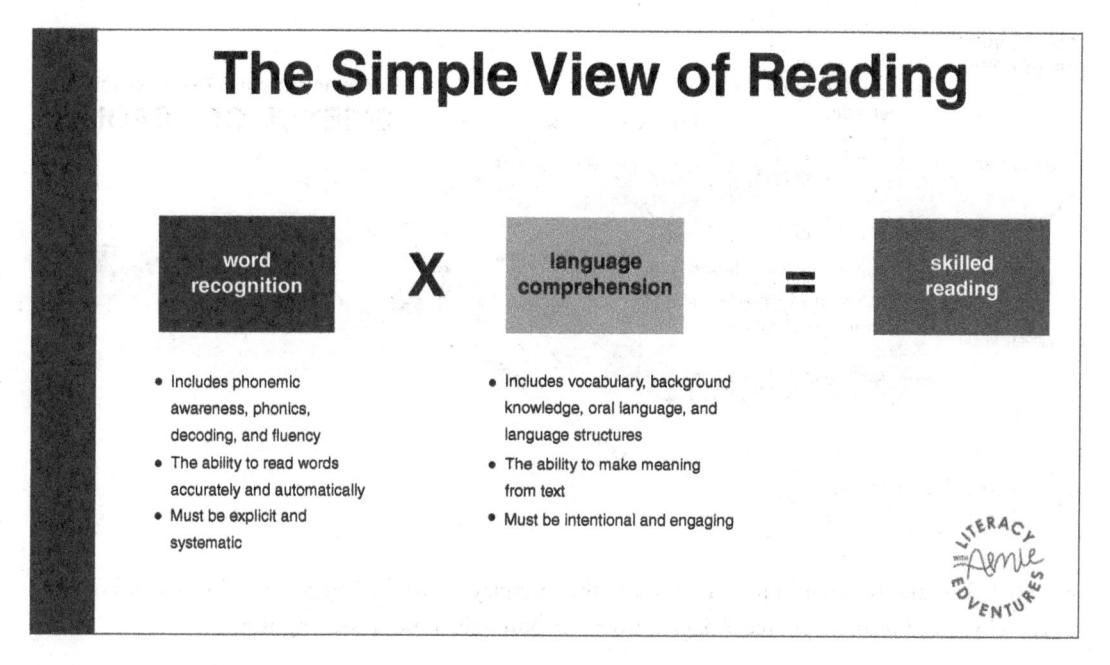

- Includes phonemic awareness, phonics, decoding, and fluency
- The ability to read words accurately and automatically
- Must be explicit and systematic

- Includes vocabulary, background knowledge, oral language, and language structures
- The ability to make meaning from text
- Must be intentional and engaging

FIGURE 1.2 The Simple View of Reading emphasizes the interplay between decoding and language comprehension. Source: Adapted from Gough and Tunmer's (1986) Simple View of Reading model.

The SVR gives us the big picture, emphasizing that for reading comprehension to be successful, both decoding and comprehension must work together. However, it's not enough to simply know the "what." As educators, we also need to understand the "how"—how these components develop, how they interact, and how we can explicitly teach each element in a systematic way. This is where Scarborough's Reading Rope zooms in and deepens our understanding.

Scarborough's Reading Rope: A Closer Look

Developed by Dr. Hollis Scarborough, the Reading Rope, illustrated in Figure 1.3, breaks down decoding and language comprehension into finer strands, showing how each component intricately weaves together to create skilled reading. The beauty of Scarborough's Reading Rope is in its ability to zoom in on each strand within these two primary

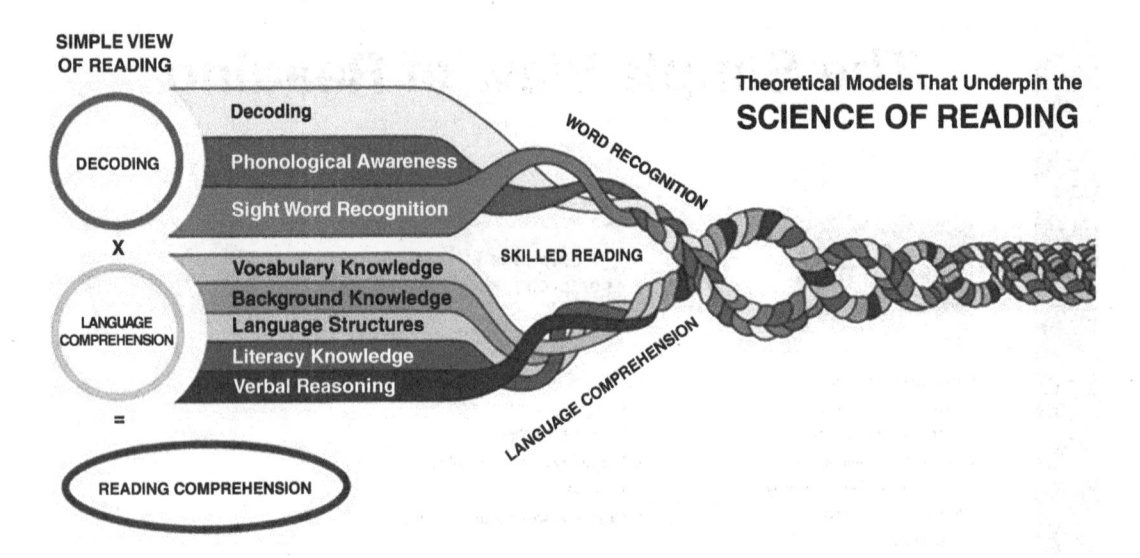

FIGURE 1.3 The Reading Rope demonstrates the interplay of word recognition and language comprehension in skilled reading. Source: Adapted from Scarborough's (2001) Reading Rope.

components, making it clear how different skills support reading development over time.

The lower strands of the rope represent word recognition (decoding), which includes the following components:

- **Phonological awareness:** recognizing and manipulating sounds, which lays the foundation for decoding
- **Decoding and spelling:** understanding letter-sound correspondences and being able to decode unfamiliar words
- **Sight recognition:** automatically recognizing familiar words without needing to sound them out, essential for fluency

The upper strands of the rope focus on language comprehension, which involves the following components:

- **Background knowledge:** knowledge of the world that helps readers make sense of new information
- **Vocabulary:** understanding the meaning of words, crucial for comprehension

- **Language structures:** knowledge of grammar and sentence structure
- **Verbal reasoning:** the ability to make inferences, understand figurative language, and think critically about what's read
- **Literacy knowledge:** familiarity with different text structures and genres

Together, these strands are woven tightly, creating a strong rope that supports skilled reading. If any strand is weak or frayed, it affects the overall integrity of the rope, much like reading comprehension suffers when a student struggles with one or more foundational skills.

Why These Models Matter for Structured Literacy

Both the SVR and Scarborough's Reading Rope reinforce the importance of structured literacy—explicit, systematic instruction in both word recognition and language comprehension. Structured literacy ensures that decoding and comprehension are taught as complementary skills. It's not just about teaching students to read words; it's about ensuring they understand what those words mean within the larger context of the text.

Weakness in any strand of Scarborough's Reading Rope can disrupt the entire reading process.

> **AS SCARBOROUGH** (2001) describes in the Reading Rope framework, weakness in any strand can disrupt reading, and when multiple strands are affected, reading difficulties become even more pronounced. It's not enough to simply say, "This student struggles to read." We must go deeper, asking ourselves, "Why does this student struggle to read?" and identifying the specific road blocks standing in their way.

Here are some guiding questions educators must ask to diagnose and address reading difficulties in their students:

- Do they have a solid understanding of letters and sounds?
- What are their phonemic awareness skills?
- Are they able to decode unfamiliar words?

- Can they comprehend what they are reading?
- Can they comprehend what is read to them?
- What do their phonics skills look like? Are they applying their phonics knowledge to both reading and writing?
- Do they have appropriate background knowledge?

Data-Driven Instruction for Targeted Support

Using data to analyze each component of reading—whether it's decoding, phonemic awareness, comprehension, or vocabulary—enables us to make informed, strategic instructional decisions. This approach ensures we are not guessing at the source of reading difficulties but diagnosing them accurately. Once we understand where the gaps are, we can intervene effectively and provide the necessary support to strengthen those weaker strands.

Scarborough's Reading Rope takes us beyond the overarching structure of the SVR and offers a detailed road map to understanding where a student might be struggling. By focusing on each strand, we can help strengthen weak areas, providing students with the skills they need to read fluently and with deep comprehension.

Practical Tips for Implementation

Now that we have the research behind us, let us look at how we can use that information to support our students on their literacy journey! Before children even encounter printed text, their journey toward literacy starts with oral language development. This is a critical phase, and our role is vital. From the earliest interactions with caregivers, infants begin absorbing the sounds and rhythms of language, laying the foundation for future reading skills. The first step in a reader's journey is phonological awareness.

Phonological Awareness and Letter-Sound Connections: Cracking the Code

The journey toward proficient reading begins not with printed words but with sound. This foundational skill, phonological awareness, is the first step on the path to literacy, encompassing a broad range of sound-related skills that children develop as they listen, play, and interact with language. For many children, this journey begins at home or in preschool, surrounded by songs, nursery rhymes, bedtime stories, and everyday conversations. These experiences help children tune into the rhythm, melody, and sounds of language, long before they pick up a book.

Phonological awareness involves the recognition and manipulation of sounds within spoken language, encompassing larger units like words and syllables down to smaller units like individual sounds or phonemes. During early childhood, children start to develop skills such as alliteration (identifying words that begin with the same sound), rhyming (recognizing and producing words with similar endings), syllable segmentation (breaking words into their syllable parts), and sentence segmentation (identifying the individual words in a sentence). Table 1.1 shows examples of these skills.

Although these abilities can provide insight into a child's language development, they are not necessarily prerequisites for learning to read. The National Institute of Child Health and Human Development (2000)

Table 1.1 Understanding the Larger Components of Phonological Awareness

Skill	Definition	Example
Rhyming	Recognizing and producing words that have the same ending sound	"cat" rhymes with "hat."
Syllables	Breaking words into their individual syllable parts	"butterfly" → but-ter-fly.
Alliteration	Identifying and producing words that begin with the same sound	"Sally sells sea shells by the sea shore."

found that phonemic awareness instruction is most effective when integrated with letters and phonics, rather than focusing solely on broader phonological skills like rhyming. This suggests that although phonological awareness as a whole plays a role in early literacy, instruction should prioritize phonemic awareness—the ability to recognize and manipulate individual phonemes—as this skill directly supports decoding and fluency in reading.

Phonological awareness is also highly interactive; children build these skills by hearing, repeating, and playing with sounds. Singing songs with rhymes or clapping to syllables in words enables children to practice the sounds and rhythms of language in a playful way, helping them become more attuned to the structure of words. For example, as children chant rhymes, they learn to focus on ending sounds and similarities between words. By practicing alliteration, they start to understand that certain sounds occur at the beginning of words. Such playful, low-pressure exposure to sound helps them tune in to the components of words, building a strong foundation for the next phase: phonemic awareness.

Although exposure to spoken language and sound play can contribute to language development, not all phonological skills are necessary precursors to reading. The National Institute of Child Health and Human Development (2000) found that phonemic awareness—specifically the ability to identify and manipulate individual sounds—is the most critical precursor to decoding. Although activities like rhyming and syllable play may support broader language skills, direct instruction in phonemic awareness, especially when integrated with letters, is most effective in preparing children for phonics and decoding.

Rather than being a prerequisite for phonemic awareness, broader phonological awareness skills, such as rhyming and syllable segmentation, may help some children develop an ear for language patterns. However, research suggests that directly teaching phonemic awareness provides the strongest foundation for decoding. Children who struggle with phonemic awareness may face challenges in isolating and manipulating sounds once phonics instruction begins, making it essential to focus on these skills early within a structured literacy approach

Letter Sounds

After developing a sense of phonological awareness, the next step on our readers' journey is understanding the connection between letters and sounds. For many children, this realization—that the language they hear can be represented by symbols—is both exciting and mysterious. These symbols, or letters, represent the sounds they have been listening to, and each letter has a specific sound or set of sounds attached to it. This stage of the journey is critical; it's when they begin to crack the code of written language, laying the foundation for future reading and writing.

Imagine, though, that some children arrive in kindergarten without this prior exposure. For these students, encountering the alphabet might feel like stepping into a foreign land—full of unknown symbols with no clear meaning. Letters may appear as unfamiliar shapes without any relation to the sounds they hear. That's why repetitive, intentional practice is key; children need plenty of opportunities to see, hear, and interact with letters in order to make these connections.

As teachers, our role is to guide students through this discovery. We draw their attention to letters, helping them notice them in meaningful contexts. Perhaps they begin to recognize the first letter of their own name or see letters on signs, labels, and everyday objects. Gradually, children start to understand that these letters and symbols represent the sounds they have already been practicing through phonological awareness activities. The abstract suddenly becomes concrete—letters are not just shapes but carry meaning.

This is when environmental print, like the STOP sign on the street corner or the *M* for McDonald's, becomes incredibly valuable. Children start to notice these prints, identifying letters in familiar names and words around them. Recognizing letters and associating them with sounds helps children move from recognizing the broad sounds of language to connecting specific sounds with specific symbols. They're developing an essential tool for decoding, which will soon enable them to read words independently.

During this stage, children need repeated practice to solidify these connections. We, as teachers, provide countless opportunities for them to interact with letters in various ways—tracing them, saying their names and sounds, seeing them in print, and using them in writing. The journey to literacy is complex, but with each new letter and sound they master, children take one more step toward independent reading.

Phonemic Awareness: Recognizing and Manipulating Sounds

With a foundational understanding of phonological awareness and basic letter-sound relationships, the next critical step in a child's reading journey is developing phonemic awareness. Phonemic awareness is the ability to identify, isolate, and manipulate individual sounds, or phonemes, in spoken words. It goes beyond simply recognizing sounds in language to truly understanding and manipulating them. This skill is crucial because phonemes are the building blocks of words, and recognizing these sounds is essential for decoding and spelling.

In structured literacy, phonemic awareness focuses on helping children become aware that words are composed of separate sounds. For example, in the word "cat," children learn to isolate and recognize the individual sounds /k/, /a/, and /t/. They develop the skills to blend these sounds to form words, segment them into separate phonemes, and even substitute one sound for another to create new words. These activities are essential in helping students unlock words they encounter in text, building confidence as they begin to sound out and recognize words independently.

Phonemic awareness activities are highly interactive and hands on. Children might practice phoneme blending (combining sounds to make a word), phoneme segmentation (breaking a word into its sounds), phoneme deletion (removing a sound to make a new word), and phoneme substitution (replacing one sound with another to create a different word). Each of these activities supports a specific aspect of phonemic awareness, providing students with the flexibility they need to approach unfamiliar words.

One of the key benefits of phonemic awareness is that it enables students to decode words accurately and fluently as they progress. By strengthening phonemic awareness, we help students lay a solid foundation for phonics and build their ability to decode efficiently.

However, a significant disconnect has traditionally existed between teaching phonemic awareness and letter sounds. In many classrooms, these two areas were taught as separate skills, which created a gap in students' understanding. When phonemic awareness (focusing on sounds) is taught in isolation from phonics (focusing on letters), students may struggle to make connections between the sounds they hear and the letters they see in print. This separation can lead to confusion and hinder their ability to decode (see Figure 1.4).

The Connection Between Phonemes and Graphemes

To fully support students, it's essential to integrate phonemic awareness with letter sounds—connecting the abstract sounds they hear (phonemes) with the concrete symbols they see (graphemes). This linkage is critical

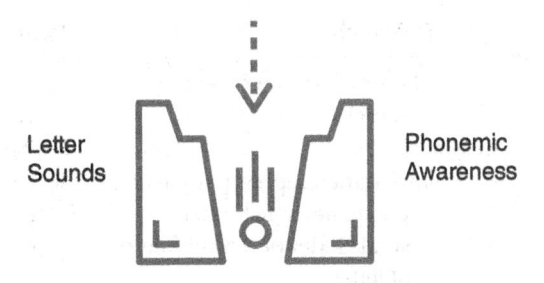

FIGURE 1.4 The disconnect between phonemic awareness and phonics.

because phonemes and graphemes together form the foundation of the alphabetic principle, which states that there is a systematic relationship between sounds and letters. When students understand that each sound corresponds to a letter or group of letters, they gain the tools needed to decode words accurately.

Although we will explore this further in the upcoming chapters, it's important to note that phonemic awareness and phonics (or alphabet knowledge) are often taught separately. Unfortunately, this common practice can create a significant disconnect for students. Spending too much time isolating these two skills can affect students' overall literacy journey. As educators, it is our responsibility to demonstrate

Table 1.2 Phonemic Awareness: Understanding and Manipulating Individual Sounds (Phonemes) in Words

Phonemic Awareness	Definition	Example
Phoneme blending	Combining individual phonemes to form a word	/c/ /a/ /t/ → "cat"
Phoneme segmentation	Breaking a word into its individual phonemes	"cat" → /c/ /a/ /t/
Phoneme deletion	Removing a phoneme from a word to form a new word	"cat" without /c/ is "at"
Phoneme substitution	Replacing one phoneme with another to form a new word	"cat" → replace /c/ with /b/ → "bat"
Phoneme addition	Adding a phoneme to a word to form a new word	"at" → add /c/ → "cat"
Term	**Definition**	**Example**
Phoneme	The smallest unit of sound in speech	/b/, /a/, /t/ (the word "bat" has three phonemes)
Grapheme	The written representation of a phoneme, which can be a single letter or a combination of letters.	b, a, t (the word "bat" has three graphemes)

the connection between sounds and letters, helping students understand that these elements are inherently linked. Phonemic awareness is crucial at the individual sound level, and pairing it with letter sounds in phonics instruction helps students make sense of the code they are learning.

We explore phonemic awareness in greater depth in the upcoming chapters, but it's essential to remember that although separating skills may have its place in early instruction, our goal is to bridge these skills. Phonemic awareness and letter sounds should unite in phonics instruction, providing students with a comprehensive understanding of the language they are learning to read. We'll dive deeper into the practical application of this integration in Chapter 5.

By bridging the gap between phonemic awareness and letter sounds, we equip students with the skills to approach unfamiliar words with confidence, supporting them on their journey to becoming independent readers.

Phonetic Decoding: Building the Bridge to Reading Words

Once students understand phoneme-to-grapheme correspondences—recognizing that sounds (phonemes) are connected to specific letters or groups of letters (graphemes)—they are ready for the next essential step: phonetic decoding. This is the stage where reading truly starts to come alive, as students begin to see how sounds, letters, and words are interconnected in a meaningful system. With this foundation, students can now start to sound out and decode words independently.

Phonetic decoding is the ability to take a series of letters, associate each one with its corresponding sound, and blend those sounds to form a word. For example, in the word "cat," a student would recognize the letters "c," "a," and "t," connect each letter to its sound, and blend them together to pronounce the whole word. Decoding is not simply memorizing words or guessing from pictures or context; it's an active, cognitive process when students apply their phonics knowledge to read each word accurately.

At this stage, students start to blend and segment sounds with purpose. They know that each letter or group of letters in a word has a sound that contributes to the whole word, so they can tackle words sound by sound. This skill becomes especially powerful as they encounter unfamiliar words. Instead of relying on guesswork, they have a systematic approach to decoding, sounding out each phoneme and blending it into a word. This is a critical turning point in the reading journey because it empowers students to read independently, transforming them from passive listeners to active readers.

The Power of Blending and Segmenting

Blending and segmenting are foundational skills that play a pivotal role in phonetic decoding.

Blending involves combining individual phonemes to form a word. For instance, taking the sounds /s/, /a/, and /t/ and blending them to say "sat." This is the heart of reading, enabling students to bring together the sounds they know to form words they understand.

Segmenting is the reverse process, when students break down a word into its individual sounds. This skill is crucial for both reading and spelling, as it helps students analyze and produce words accurately.

As students become more adept at blending and segmenting, they gain the confidence and ability to approach new words. This systematic process enables them to internalize the rules of language, applying their phonics knowledge flexibly across various words. Phonetic decoding opens up the world of text, giving students the freedom to decode words on their own without relying on rote memorization.

Why Phonetic Decoding Is Essential

The ability to decode phonetically is critical because it lays the groundwork for fluent reading. Without phonetic decoding skills, students are likely to face frustration and struggle with comprehension, as they cannot access the meaning of words independently. But once they master phonetic decoding, they can begin to read with accuracy and confidence. This is the foundation for automaticity—the stage when decoding becomes effortless and automatic, freeing up cognitive resources to focus on comprehension.

Phonetic decoding is more than just a skill; it's the gateway to becoming an independent reader. It enables students to see reading as a puzzle they can solve rather than a random sequence of letters they must memorize. With each word they decode, they strengthen their understanding of the alphabetic principle, empowering them to decode more complex words over time. As their decoding skills grow, students are on their way to fluency, setting them up for deeper engagement with text and, ultimately, comprehension.

This step in the reading journey, where phonemes connect with graphemes and decoding begins, marks a critical milestone. The transition from recognizing letters and sounds to actively blending them to form words is a breakthrough moment. Phonetic decoding builds the bridge from early reading skills to fluent, confident reading, preparing students for a lifetime of literacy and learning.

The Pitfalls of Three-Cueing: Why Explicit and Systematic Instruction Is Essential

What happens if we do not teach these foundational steps explicitly and systematically? Instead, if we rely on the three-cueing approach, we may believe we are setting students up for success, but the reality is quite different.

The three-cueing system is a method of reading instruction that encourages students to use meaning (semantic cues), sentence structure (syntactic cues), and visual clues (graphophonic cues) to identify words rather than relying on systematic decoding. In this approach, students are often prompted to guess words based on context rather than decoding them accurately. They might be told to "look at the picture to figure out the word" or "guess based on the first letter." They may memorize a few sight words, and because early reading books are predictable and repetitive, they appear to make progress. But are they truly learning to read?

This approach can create the illusion that students are on grade level, and for a time, they may seem like successful readers. In reality, however, they are becoming overcompensators—relying heavily on guessing strategies rather than solid decoding skills. We've inadvertently given them the tools to become poor readers without equipping them with the actual mechanics of reading.

As these students move up in grade levels, their reliance on guessing and memorization strategies begins to fall apart. By the time they reach second or third grade, they encounter more complex texts, which lack predictable patterns, picture clues, and familiar sight words. This transition is where the gaps in their reading ability become glaringly obvious. They struggle to decode unfamiliar words because they have never been taught to systematically connect phonemes with graphemes. Instead, they have learned to rely on cues that do not hold up with more sophisticated texts.

Overcompensators: The Impact of Ineffective Reading Strategies

Students who have relied on three-cueing often experience a "sight word explosion," where they try to memorize more and more words instead of understanding the code of reading. But as the words become more varied and less predictable, memorization is no longer sustainable. The absence of picture support and predictable text patterns leaves these students floundering, revealing the flaws in their approach. They become overcompensators, struggling to keep up and feeling frustrated because they lack the foundational skills necessary for decoding complex text.

For teachers in second and third grade, this can easily look like a comprehension deficit, because these students seemed to be "reading" in earlier grades. However, the reality is often that they have a phonological or phonics deficit that was masked by three-cueing strategies. The struggles they experience now are not due to a lack of comprehension but a lack of decoding skills, which are essential for accessing more complex texts.

This is why we must think about the journey leading up to this point. To build proficient readers, students need a strong foundation in phonemic awareness, phonics, and decoding skills, which they can apply systematically across any text. Without these tools, we are setting them up for a difficult transition that could have been avoided. By prioritizing explicit and systematic instruction from the beginning, we give students the reliable skills they need to read confidently and independently, empowering them for the challenges of more complex texts later.

Building Fluency: The Journey from Decoding to Automaticity

Now that students are beginning to decode, they are putting their phonics skills into practice in a way that builds on itself. As they move through a carefully structured sequence of phonics instruction, each new skill reinforces the last, creating a solid foundation. The more students decode, the more automatic the process becomes. This gradual shift from effortful decoding to automatic word recognition is essential for developing fluency.

Fluency, in reading, means more than just reading quickly—it involves reading with accuracy, rate, and prosody (expressiveness). True fluency enables students to recognize words effortlessly, which reduces the cognitive load and enables them to focus on the meaning of the text. But how does this transition from decoding to fluency happen?

This progression toward fluency is largely driven by orthographic mapping, a process identified and studied by Linnea Ehri (2004, 2014).

Orthographic mapping is the brain's way of linking sounds to written letters, syllables, and entire words, ultimately making word recognition automatic. With practice, students begin to recognize familiar letters, letter clusters, and even whole words without needing to decode each individual phoneme.

Orthographic Mapping: The Key to Automatic Word Recognition

Orthographic mapping is a sophisticated cognitive process that transforms how we read. When students encounter new words, their brains connect the word's sounds with its written form, forming a mental map for quick retrieval. Each successful decoding experience reinforces this mapping process, enabling students to store words in their long-term memory.

As students continue practicing phonics and decoding skills, they build an ever-growing sight word bank—not merely memorized words, but words that are recognized instantly due to this internal mapping. This recognition happens without conscious effort, similar to how we recognize familiar faces in a crowd without needing to think about each feature.

Orthographic mapping is cumulative: the more students encounter and decode words, the stronger their mental representations become. Soon, these students start recognizing increasingly complex letter combinations and syllable patterns, leading to automaticity.

From Automaticity to Fluent Reading

Once orthographic mapping enables students to recognize words effortlessly, they reach a critical milestone in their reading journey—fluency. Fluent reading combines four essential elements:

- **Accuracy:** reading words correctly without errors
- **Rate:** reading at an appropriate pace, neither too slow nor too fast

- **Prosody:** reading with expression, conveying the natural rhythm and emotion of the text
- **Comprehension:** understanding what is being read

When reading becomes automatic and fluent, the cognitive demand of decoding is lifted. Words begin to lift off the page, enabling students to read in a seamless flow. At this stage, students can channel their mental energy into understanding and interpreting the text, rather than laboriously piecing together each word.

The shift to fluent reading is transformative. Students who can read with fluency are better able to engage with the material, making connections, asking questions, and drawing inferences. They become active readers, not just decoding machines. As reading becomes effortless, students are freed to fully immerse themselves in the text and experience the true joy of reading.

Fluency is essential for comprehension because it creates the mental space needed for processing and interpreting the meaning of the text. With each step toward fluency, students are not only advancing their decoding skills but also developing their ability to engage deeply with the material. This is the moment in the journey when reading turns from a skill into a pathway to learning, exploration, and discovery.

Comprehension: Reading to Learn

Once students are able to read fluently, a new stage in their literacy journey begins—comprehension. This is the moment we, as teachers, have been working toward from day one. We've dedicated ourselves to building foundational skills, helping students piece together phonemic awareness, phonics, and fluency. All of this is in service of one ultimate goal: to guide our students toward reading to learn.

As students develop fluency, they are no longer focused on decoding each word or understanding every letter-sound relationship. The cognitive load of decoding has been lifted, enabling their minds to shift from *how* to read to *what* they are reading. This transition frees up mental energy to fully engage with the text, to grasp its meaning, make connections, and think critically. The words on the page no longer feel like puzzles to decode—they become tools for understanding ideas, stories, and information.

The Role of Background Knowledge and Vocabulary in Comprehension

All along, we have been laying the groundwork for comprehension through rich, intentional read-alouds, vocabulary development, and background knowledge building. These practices are critical because comprehension is not just about recognizing words; it's about connecting those words to a larger framework of understanding.

Background knowledge enables students to make sense of what they are reading by linking new information to what they already know. For example, if a student reads a passage about ecosystems, they are more likely to understand it if they have prior knowledge about plants, animals, and environmental systems. Vocabulary, similarly, gives students the language they need to interpret new ideas. A word-rich environment, full of diverse vocabulary, helps students grasp the meaning of complex texts with confidence.

The Two Elements Come Together: Understanding the Text

When background knowledge and vocabulary start to merge with fluency, comprehension emerges. Students can engage with the text, ask questions, make inferences, and draw conclusions. They begin to recognize main ideas, identify details that support those ideas, and connect new information with what they know.

These are the moments teachers cherish—the times when we witness the work we have put in come to life. The students are no longer just reading; they are understanding, learning, and growing through what they read. They are building a foundation for deeper thinking, and every book or passage becomes an opportunity to explore the world and expand their horizons.

Comprehension as the Culmination of the Reading Journey

Comprehension is the culmination of all the skills we have taught, woven together to help students become independent, lifelong learners. Reading is no longer a series of skills they practice—it is a vehicle for discovery. With each story they read, each concept they explore, students develop a greater understanding of the world around them and their place within it. They're no longer just learning to read; they are reading to learn, fulfilling the ultimate purpose of literacy.

As we progress in this book, we'll explore more strategies for supporting comprehension and delve into ways to enhance critical thinking, encourage questioning, and foster a love for reading that will carry students forward. For now, it's important to recognize that comprehension is not a stand-alone skill. It is the seamless integration of all the skills we have developed, brought to life through each book, passage, and conversation.

Bringing It All Together: The Focus of This Book

As we wrap up this introduction to the science of reading, it's essential to bring the focus back to why we are here: to guide young learners at the very start of their journey to reading. Using evidence-based practices grounded in the science of reading, we have the incredible opportunity to build a strong foundation for every student, no matter where they begin.

Phonemic awareness and phonics play a critical role in this journey. They are the foundation stones on which we build students' ability to decode and ultimately read fluently with comprehension. I want you to imagine the reading journey as a hill a runner must tackle. You're one of two runners, and you are approaching the base of this steep incline. One runner is confident, thinking, "I can tackle this hill—let's go!" They're ready to take on the challenge because they know the value of what lies beyond the peak. The other runner is unsure, thinking, "I don't really like running, I'm not very good at it. Maybe I'll just walk away."

These are the very students who walk into our classrooms every day. We have those who come from rich print environments, immersed in books and language from early on, confidently ready to begin their reading journey. And then we have those who have had less exposure and are hesitant, nervous about stepping into the world of words. They may not feel like runners, but they will attempt the hill, no matter how daunting, because they have teachers like you pushing them forward, supporting them with every step.

Now, let us think back to the critical skills of phonemic awareness—specifically blending and segmenting sounds—and decoding. This stage is the peak of the hill for many students. This is where they start to lose steam, where the struggle becomes real. They're putting in effort, and it's hard. Their legs start to burn, and they are not sure if they want to keep going. For some, this is the moment they want to give up. It's uncomfortable, and progress can be slow.

But as teachers, this is when we step in with determination and patience. We allow this productive struggle, understanding that this is the very foundation they need. We sit with them through the awkward moments of decoding, through the hesitations, the mistakes, and the pauses. We do not rush them. We let them take the time they need to sound out each letter, to blend sounds, to break down words. And we celebrate each small success along the way because we know this is what builds resilient readers (see Figure 1.5).

In the chapters to come, we are going to dive deep into how to support our students as they begin this journey to becoming proficient readers. We'll explore practical strategies for teaching phonemic awareness

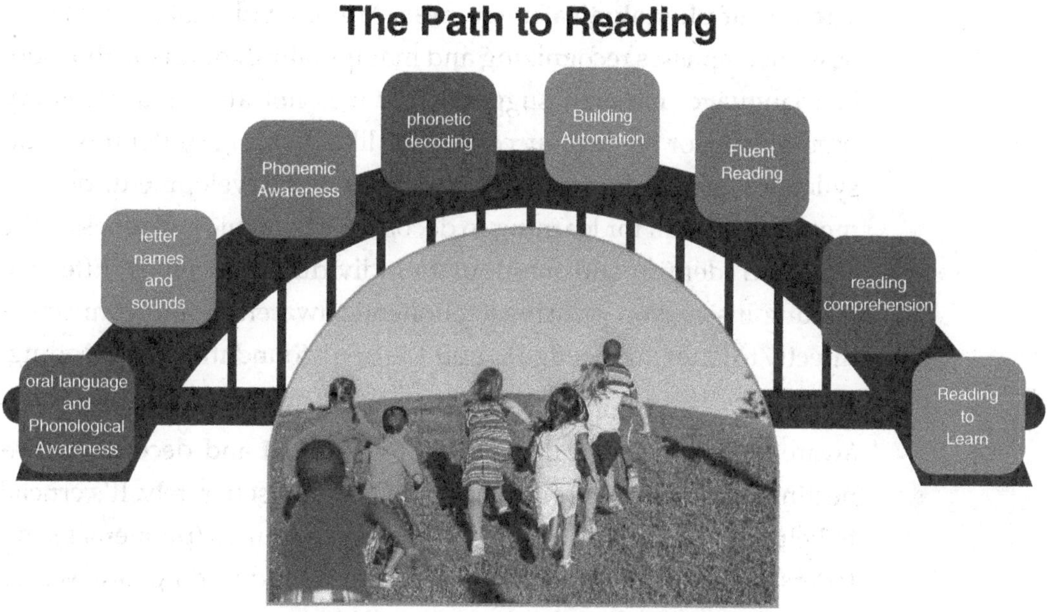

The Path to Reading

FIGURE 1.5 The path to reading: A progression from foundational skills to higher-level skills, building toward skilled reading.

and phonics, build on each step they take, and help them gain the confidence to tackle that hill on their own. Together, we'll create a path for our young learners, ensuring that every student—regardless of where they start—has the tools to not only read but also to learn and grow as readers for life.

Five Key Takeaways from Chapter 1

- **The brain's role in reading.** Reading is a complex process that involves multiple regions of the brain working together. Key areas such as the frontal, occipital-temporal, and parietal-temporal regions play critical roles in recognizing sounds, processing speech, and decoding words. Understanding how these regions contribute to reading helps educators tailor instruction that supports these neurological functions.

- **The role of phonological awareness.** Although phonological awareness encompasses recognizing and manipulating sounds within spoken language, research suggests that it is not always a necessary prerequisite for reading success. Skills like rhyming, alliteration, and syllable segmentation can support language development, but the most critical skill for learning to decode is phonemic awareness—the ability to identify and manipulate individual phonemes. Effective reading instruction prioritizes phonemic awareness and connects it directly to letter knowledge to build a strong foundation for decoding.

- **Decoding and phonemic awareness are inseparable.** Phonemic awareness (understanding individual sounds) and decoding (connecting sounds to letters) should not be taught separately. It's crucial to help students see the connection between sounds (phonemes) and letters (graphemes), building a foundation for decoding new words and achieving reading fluency.

- **Orthographic mapping and fluency.** Orthographic mapping, the process of connecting sounds to written letters, enables students to recognize words automatically. Fluency is built on the foundation of decoding and orthographic mapping, enabling students to read effortlessly, freeing up cognitive resources for comprehension.

- **Reading comprehension is the ultimate goal.** The end goal of reading instruction is comprehension—reading to learn. Fluency, background knowledge, and vocabulary are all essential components that enable students to understand, interpret, and engage with the text. These skills combine to help students transition from learning to read to reading to learn.

CHAPTER TWO

Phonemic Awareness in Early Reading Instruction

Phonemic awareness (PA) is a foundational skill that is critical to our students' reading success. It is the understanding that words are made of individual sounds. Those sounds come together to create the words we read every day. In this chapter, we explore PA and its importance. We will look at research as well as effective teaching strategies to support that research.

PA

Phonemic awareness is the ability to hear, perceive, and manipulate the individual sounds (phonemes) that make up the words we speak, read, and write. PA differs from phonics because PA involves the sound (phoneme), and phonics involves both the sound and the printed form (grapheme). In other words, phonics is more about knowing how letters represent the sounds in written words. Both are necessary for reading to take place. For example, If I say the word "cat" and then break it into its sounds, it has three separate sounds: /c/ /a/ /t/. Those sounds (phonemes) map onto letters or graphemes that form the printed word "cat."

Layers of PA

There are many layers of PA. Your students probably fall into one of these layers depending on their knowledge and experiences. It is important to note that you do not need to teach these layers in order, but you should ensure that your students have a solid understanding of each.

Phoneme Isolation

- Phoneme isolation involves identifying and isolating individual sounds in spoken words. For example, in the word "fan," the initial sound is /f/, the medial sound is /a/, and the final sound is /n/.

| fan |

Blending

- Blending is the process of combining individual sounds to form words. Students listen to separate phonemes like /r/, /ă/, and /g/, then blend them quickly to read or say the word "rag."

| r-a-g ⟹ rag |

Segmenting

- Segmenting is breaking down a spoken word into its distinct sounds. For example, when given the word "sip," students would segment it into /s/, /i/, and /p/.

```
sip ⟹ s-i-p
```

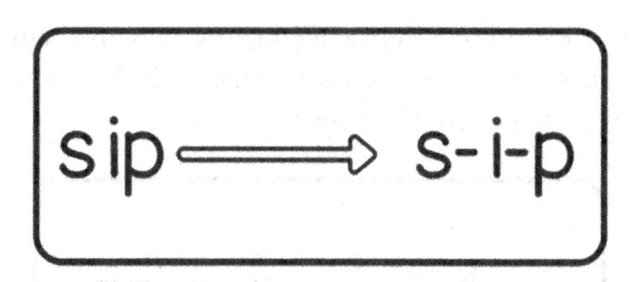

Phoneme Manipulation, Addition, Deletion, and Substitution

- Phoneme manipulation is the ability to manipulate phonemes effectively. Students must be able to hold sounds in their working memory long enough to add, delete, or substitute them, then blend these sounds to form new words.
- Phoneme addition is adding a sound to an existing word to create a new one. For example, by adding /s/ to "nap," the word becomes "snap."

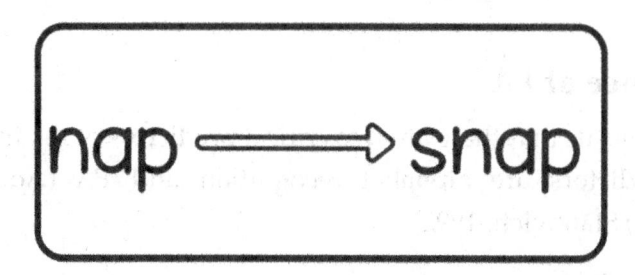

```
nap ⟹ snap
```

- Phoneme deletion is removing a sound from a word. For instance, taking away /s/ from "sway" results in "way."

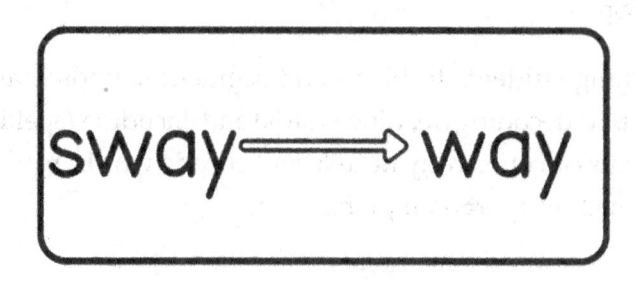

```
sway ⟹ way
```

- Phoneme substitution is replacing one sound with another to form a new word. An example would be changing /t/ in "cat" to /p/, transforming the word into "cap."

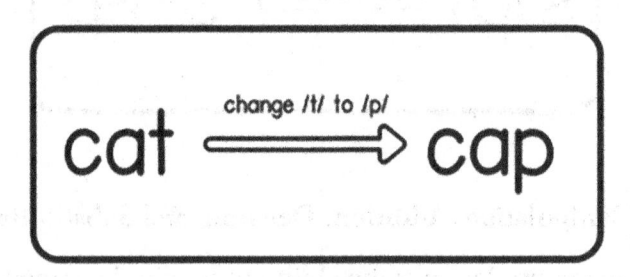

cat ⟹ cap (change /t/ to /p/)

This higher level of PA involves the modification of phonemes within words. Research suggests that although we can teach PA orally, it is more beneficial to add print to this instruction as soon as possible.

> **ORAL PA** is a critical component, but for shorter spurts of time: approximately six minutes per day for kindergarten and first-grade students or any student with a deficit in this area.

Importance of PA

Research tells us that there are two critical predictors of reading success. Those predictors are alphabet recognition and PA (Adams, 1990; Chall, 1996; Stanovich, 1992).

> **EXPERTS TELL** us that PA plays a critical role in children's ability to learn to read proficiently in the early years of school. Effective PA instruction, specifically the sub-skills of blending and segmenting, significantly affects the development of reading and writing.

By teaching students to blend and segment sounds orally, we can directly support decoding (reading words) and encoding (spelling words). When students can effectively decode and encode words, reading fluency increases, which supports comprehension.

What the Research Says

Rice et al. (2022) conducted a meta-analysis combining findings from 49 studies on PA instruction. The goal was to determine whether PA instruction alone or with added print support was more effective. Their analysis of 16 studies found that initial PA instruction without including letters led to significant growth in PA skills. However, the research also showed that incorporating letter instruction with PA activities over time supported reading gains. After approximately 16 hours of PA instruction that included letters, students demonstrated noticeable improvement in their reading skills.

This suggests that PA instruction is highly effective even before students are introduced to letters. However, once students have a foundation of letter knowledge, combining PA activities with letter instruction significantly enhances reading progress. This finding is critical for early educators who may need to balance PA activities with letter-sound instruction, knowing that both approaches yield strong results when applied systematically.

Webber et al. (2024) conducted an experimental study comparing the effects of PA, letter-sound knowledge, and decoding interventions on struggling beginning readers. The study involved 222 participants who received targeted instruction to improve their reading skills. Initially, there was no significant improvement in the students' decoding abilities. However, closer examination revealed that students made better progress decoding words they had previously learned, particularly in the group receiving combined PA and decoding instruction.

This data suggests that focusing on PA alongside decoding can be particularly effective for struggling readers. When these skills are taught together, students can better apply their understanding of sounds to printed words, leading to improved reading outcomes over time.

Both studies highlight the importance of integrating PA instruction into early literacy programs. Although PA skills can be developed without letters in the early stages, incorporating letters as early as possible is vital for reading achievement. These findings emphasize the need for a balanced, systematic approach to teaching PA and decoding in early education settings.

Wrap-Up of the Research

Rice et al. (2022). "Phonemic Awareness: A Meta-Analysis for Planning Effective Instruction."

- **PA is powerful even without letters.** Early PA instruction without letters leads to significant gains in PA skills, which are essential for developing early reading abilities.
- **Adding letters boosts reading gains.** Incorporating letter instruction after initial PA work amplifies reading success, with noticeable improvements after about 16 hours of combined instruction.
- **Balanced PA and letter instruction.** Teachers should prioritize PA and letter-sound teaching to support long-term reading development.

Webber et al. (2024). "An Experimental Comparison of Phoneme Awareness, Letter-Sound Knowledge and Decoding for Struggling Beginner Readers."

- **Combining PA and decoding is key.** Struggling readers benefit the most from simultaneous PA and decoding practice, which helps them apply phonemic skills to real reading tasks.
- **Reinforcement through practice.** Students showed better decoding abilities for words they had previously learned, highlighting the importance of review and repeated practice in literacy instruction.
- **Effective for struggling readers.** Integrating PA and decoding strategies helps early readers who face difficulties improve their phonics and reading skills.

Practical Tips for Implementation

As educators, we constantly navigate the challenge of balancing foundational skills with the ever-present demands of the classroom. PA is one of those skills that often sparks questions: *When should I teach it? How do I fit it in?* This section offers practical insights into the timing and importance of PA instruction, helping you identify when to prioritize it in your teaching and how to align it with your students' needs. By understanding its role in reading development, you'll be better equipped to support your students and integrate these critical skills seamlessly into your daily practice.

When Should I Teach PA?

PA and letter recognition are readiness skills. This means we should be hyper-focused on these skills in kindergarten and grade one. Louisa Moats (2023, p. 3) says, "One of the most important jobs for the teacher of beginning reading or the teacher of students with reading problems is to foster awareness of phonemes (speech sounds) in words and to help children acquire the ability to articulate, compare, segment, and blend those phonemes."

Still, we must remember to assess struggling readers to ensure they do not have gaps or deficiencies in their reading due to a lack of PA. Students of any age could have phonological deficits.

How Should I Teach PA?

We now know that research indicates that a combination of letter sounds and PA is powerful. The goal of PA instruction is to make sure students understand how words work. But sometimes, it can be hard to know where to start. Although it can be tempting to spend more time on the larger units of phonological awareness, such as rhyming, syllables, onset rhyme, and so on, students must focus their time and energy on the individual sound level. This means we should combine PA and phonics as early as possible. I like to practice larger units of phonological awareness early on and in a whole-group setting. Students usually pick this up quickly, and it is easy to do during the first few weeks of kindergarten as I establish routines.

What Do I Do If My Students Struggle to Help with PA at the Individual Sound Level?

> **ALTHOUGH OUR** ultimate goal is to get our students to the individual phoneme level as soon as possible, there are times when we have to provide a scaffold to get them there.

Have you ever sat down at the table with a child and said, "Listen carefully, I am going to sound out a word very slowly, and I want you to tell me what word is /b/ /a/ /t/" and the student says something off the wall like "CUPCAKE?" Or have you ever asked them to segment a word, they do it beautifully, and then say a completely different word? Chances are, if you have students who respond this way, they need extra support to get to the phoneme level. That's when we need to work backward a bit. I suggest returning to each below-level level until you hit that sweet spot. But do not stay too long; once they understand one level, move to the next until they reach the individual phoneme level. Students often just need a quick refresh on how sounds work. They will catch on pretty quickly. Figure 2.1 shows an easy flow chart for scaffolding phoneme instruction. If a student is struggling at the phoneme level, start by working backward to identify the specific area where they need support. Then, gradually progress back toward blending at the phoneme level. Figure 2.1 and Table 2.1 show a progression of activities to support students in developing blending skills, starting with compound words and advancing to individual phoneme blending.

Phonemic Awareness in Early Reading Instruction

```
Scaffolded Phoneme Blending Instruction
       Individual Phoneme Blending
                  ⇩
          Onset-Rime Blending
                  ⇩
           Syllable Blending
                  ⇩
         Compound Word Blending
```

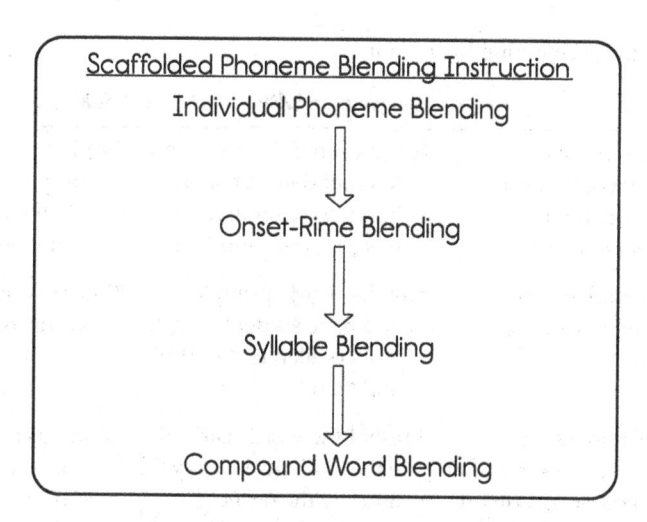

FIGURE 2.1 Scaffolding phoneme instruction.

Table 2.1 Scaffolded Phoneme Blending Instruction

Level	Focus	Example Activity	Goal
Compound word blending	Teaching students to blend whole words to form compound words	Present the words "sun" and "set" separately, then have students blend them to say "sunset."	Students can blend whole words to form compound words.
Syllable blending	Teaching students to blend syllables to form words	Break the word "pumpkin" into syllables "pump" and "kin," then have students blend the syllables to say "pumpkin."	Students can blend syllables to form multisyllabic words.
Onset-rime blending	Teaching students to blend the onset (initial consonant or consonant cluster) and the rime (vowel and following consonants) of a word	Present the onset "m" and the rime "ap" separately, then have students blend them to say "map."	Students can blend onsets and rimes to form words.
Individual phoneme blending	Teaching students to blend individual phonemes (sounds) to form words	Show students the letters "c," "a," and "t" separately and have them blend the sounds /c/ /a/ /t/ to say "cat."	Students can blend individual phonemes into words.

Table 2.2 Scaffolded Phoneme Segmenting Instruction

Level	Focus	Example Activity	Goal
Compound word segmenting	Teaching students to segment compound words into their component words	Say the word "sunset" and have students break it into the component words: "sun" and "set."	Students can segment compound words into their component words.
Syllable segmenting	Teaching students to segment words into syllables	Say the word "pumpkin" and have students break it into syllables: "pump" and "kin."	Students can segment words into syllables.
Onset-rime segmenting	Teaching students to segment the onset (initial consonant or consonant cluster) and the rime (vowel and following consonants) of a word	Present the word "cat" and have students identify and say the onset "c" and the rime "at" separately.	Students can segment words into onsets and rimes.
Individual phoneme segmenting	Teaching students to segment individual phonemes (sounds) in words	Say the word "map" and have students identify and say each sound separately: /m/ /a/ /p/	Students can segment words into individual phonemes.

How Much Time Should Be Dedicated to PA Instruction Each Day?

Many programs might encourage you to spend excessive time practicing oral phonemic awareness. To this, I say, be smarter than the programs. Follow the research and understand the needs of your students. Research suggests that although phonemic awareness is crucial, it is most effective when integrated with letters rather than being taught in isolation for extended periods (National Institute of Child Health and Human Development, 2000). Some programs emphasize oral phonemic awareness activities—such as listening-only segmentation or manipulation tasks—without connecting them to print. However, studies indicate that phonemic awareness instruction is more impactful when paired with graphemes, as this reinforces the connection between sounds and letters, a key component of decoding (Ehri et al., 2001).

Rather than treating phonemic awareness as a separate skill taught in isolation, it should be incorporated into phonics instruction. This approach ensures that students immediately apply their phonemic awareness skills to reading and writing, reinforcing the sound-symbol relationships essential for decoding and spelling.

> **THE NATIONAL** Institute of Child Health and Human Development (2000) recommends dedicating approximately 20 hours of PA instruction over the course of a school year, spread out over daily sessions. The average school year is about 180 days. If we divide that by 20 hours, it comes out to about six minutes daily.

I do an even faster oral PA warm-up (three minutes) and then incorporate the rest of the time with print activities. Once it's added to print, I include a little more time in my phonics lesson through activities like word chaining, sound mapping, and "tap it, write it" activities, all of which we'll dive into in Chapter 6 of this book.

You might be wondering what those brief three-minute activities look like. Let us explore that next.

Classroom Implementation Actionable Steps

Now that we have a better understanding of PA, what it is, why it's important, and how we should and should not teach it in our classrooms, let us dive into some ways you can begin incorporating it in your classroom tomorrow!

Lesson Plan 1   Blend It! Flip It!

Do you want to see this activity in action and grab the resources that go with it?
Go to `http://www.literacyedventures.com/literacy-unlocked`.

Objective
Students will blend words from individual phonemes to reinforce PA.

Materials Needed
- Consonant vowel consonant (CVC) picture cards for each word: map, dad, wag, cat, fan, sad, hat. Each student should have two to four different picture cards in front of them.

Scripted Lesson Plan

1. Introduction (One Minute)
Teacher: "Today, we are going to play a game called 'Blend it! Flip it!' I'm going to say some sounds, and you are going to put those sounds together to make a word. When you blend the sounds and hear a word that matches one of your pictures, say the word out loud and flip over the picture card."

(Place two picture cards in front of you, such as "map" and "dad.")

Teacher: "Let me show you how it works. (Point to each picture and say the word.) Listen carefully as I say one of these words breaking it into individual sounds."

Teacher: "Let us start with /m/ /a/ /p/. Now, listen carefully and blend those sounds together. /m/ /a/ /p/... what word does that make?"

Teacher (modeling): "Map! The word is 'map'! So, I'll flip over the picture of the map because that's the word I just blended."

Teacher: "Do you see how that works? When you blend the sounds together and they make a word that matches a picture you have, say the word and flip over that card."

(Wait for any questions and ensure students have their picture cards ready. You may give students the same picture cards or different cards depending on the needs of your small group. Ensure students know what each picture is before starting the activity.)

Teacher: "Alright, it's your turn! Listen carefully to the sounds I say. When you hear a word that matches a picture in front of you, blend the sounds into the word, say it out loud, and flip it over!"

2. Blending Practice (Two to Three Minutes)

Teacher: "Let us get started! I'll say the sounds in a word, and you'll blend them together. Listen closely! Here we go."

Teacher: /m/ /a/ /p/
Students: "Map!" (Students with the "map" picture flip it over.)
Teacher: "Great! Let us try another one."

Teacher: /d/ /a/ /d/
Students: "Dad!" (Students with the "dad" picture flip it over.)
Teacher: "Nice blending!"

Teacher: /w/ /a/ /g/
Students: "Wag!" (Students with the "wag" picture flip it over.)
Teacher: "Fantastic!"

Teacher: /c/ /a/ /t/
Students: "Cat!" (Students with the "cat" picture flip it over.)
Teacher: "You're getting it! Let us keep going."

Teacher: /f/ /a/ /n/
Students: "Fan!" (Students with the "fan" picture flip it over.)
Teacher: "Excellent work! Let us do another."

(Continued)

Teacher: /s/ /a/ /d/
Students: "Sad!" (Students with the "sad" picture flip it over.)
Teacher: "Good job listening and blending."

Teacher: /h/ /a/ /t/
Students: "Hat!" (Students with the "hat" picture flip it over.)
Teacher: "Wow, that was smooth! You're blending like pros!"

Teacher: "Alright, let us go through those words one more time to see if we can blend them even faster!"

Teacher: /m/ /a/ /p/
Students: "Map!"

Teacher: /d/ /a/ /d/
Students: "Dad!"

Teacher: /w/ /a/ /g/
Students: "Wag!"

Teacher: /c/ /a/ /t/
Students: "Cat!"

Teacher: /f/ /a/ /n/
Students: "Fan!"

Teacher: /s/ /a/ /d/
Students: "Sad!"

Teacher: /h/ /a/ /t/
Students: "Hat!"

3. Conclusion (One Minute)

Teacher: "Great job, everyone! You listened carefully, blended sounds, and flipped over the right cards. I'm so proud of how well you blended each word."

   Teacher: "Remember, blending sounds to make words is a big step in learning to read. Keep practicing, and soon you'll be blending words even faster! Amazing job today, everyone!"

Lesson Plan 2   Race Car Dash

Do you want to see this activity in action and grab the resources that go with it?
   Go to `http://www.literacyedventures.com/literacy-unlocked`.

Objective

Students will enhance their PA by segmenting and blending sounds in a fun and engaging way.

Materials Needed

- Small toy cars (one for each student or group)
- CVC picture cards for each word: pig, sit, mix, wig, six, bin, fin, dip
- Paper with a race track drawn on it

Scripted Lesson Plan

1. Introduction (30 Seconds)

Teacher: "Today, we are going to play a fun game called 'Race Car Dash!' You'll each get a little race car, and we'll use it to help us practice blending sounds. I'll show you how to 'drive' your car along a track, moving it for each sound in a word until you blend the sounds together into a whole word."

(Continued)

(Hold up the toy car and place it on the start of the race track on a piece of paper with a picture card of "pig" nearby.)

Teacher: "I'm going to take my car, move it along the track, and say each sound slowly. Like this ... /p/... /i/... /g/. Now, when my car reaches the finish line, I blend those sounds together to say the word: 'pig'!"

Teacher: "So, as you move the car along the track, each stop is a sound, and at the finish line, you blend the sounds together to make a word. Let us get our cars ready to race and practice blending sounds!"

2. Segmenting and Blending Practice (Two Minutes)

Teacher: "Now that you know how to drive your car on the track and blend sounds, let us take turns with different words. I'll place a picture card on your track, and you'll drive your car along the track, saying each sound until you reach the finish line and blend it into the word."

Teacher: "Here's our first word!"
   (Teacher places "pig" card on the track.)
Student moves car: /p/... /i/... /g/.
Student at finish line: "pig!"
Teacher: "Perfect! You reached the finish line with 'pig'!"

Continue with:
- "sit" → /s/ ... /i/ ... /t/ → "sit!"
- "mix" → /m/ ... /i/ ... /x/ → "mix!"
- "wig" → /w/ ... /i/ ... /g/ → "wig!"
- "six" → /s/ ... /i/ ... /x/ → "six!"
- "bin" → /b/ ... /i/ ... /n/ → "bin!"
- "fin" → /f/ ... /i/ ... /n/ → "fin!"
- "dip" → /d/ ... /i/ ... /p/ → "dip!"

3. Conclusion (30 Seconds)

Teacher: "Great job, everyone! You all did fantastic driving your cars along the track and blending each sound into a word!"

Teacher: "Remember, blending sounds together is a big part of learning to read. Keep practicing, and you'll get even faster! Amazing work, racers!"

Lesson Plan 3 Penelope the Pig

Do you want to see this activity in action and grab the resources that go with it?
Go to http://www.literacyedventures.com/literacy-unlocked.

Objective

Students will practice segmenting and blending phonemes using a character to make it engaging.

Materials Needed

- A stuffed pig toy (Penelope)
- CVC picture cards for each word: vet, bed, leg, pen, red, hen, web, ten

Scripted Lesson Plan

1. Introduction (30 Seconds)

Teacher: "Today, we have a special visitor in our classroom—meet Penelope the Pig! Penelope is a little different from us. She's not a human, so she often has a hard time speaking like one. When Penelope tries to say words, she says them very slowly, sound by sound."

(Hold up Penelope the Pig and wave her around playfully.)

(Continued)

Teacher: "Penelope needs our help to say words a little faster. Your job is to listen closely to the sounds Penelope says, blend them together, and say the word for her."

Teacher: "Are you ready to help Penelope speak faster? Let us help her say her words!"

2. Segmenting and Blending Practice (Two Minutes)

Teacher: "Alright, Penelope is going to try her first word. Let us listen closely and help her!"

Teacher (pretending to be Penelope): /v/ ... /e/ ... /t/.

Students: "vet!" (Students blend the sounds to form "vet.")

Teacher: "Yes! Penelope says, 'vet.' Great job helping her!"

Teacher: "Let us try another word. Here's the next one!"

Teacher (pretending to be Penelope): /b/ ... /e/ ... /d/.

Students: "bed!" (Students blend the sounds to form "bed.")

Teacher: "Awesome! You helped Penelope say 'bed!'"

Continue with:
- "leg" → /l/ ... /e/ ... /g/ → "leg!"
- "pen" → /p/ ... /e/ ... /n/ → "pen!"
- "red" → /r/ ... /e/ ... /d/ → "red!"
- "hen" → /h/ ... /e/ ... /n/ → "hen!"
- "web" → /w/ ... /e/ ... /b/ → "web!"
- "ten" → /t/ ... /e/ ... /n/ → "ten!"

3. Conclusion (30 Seconds)
Teacher: "Great job, everyone! You did an amazing job helping Penelope the Pig say her words faster. She's so happy she had your help!"

Teacher: "Blending sounds together to make words is such an important skill, and you all did it so well! Keep practicing, and you'll be blending even faster. Great job, helpers!"

Lesson Plan 4   Mystery Bag

Do you want to see this activity in action and grab the resources that go with it?
Go to http://www.literacyedventures.com/literacy-unlocked.

Objective
Students will practice blending phonemes.

Materials Needed
- Small bag (I use a brown lunch bag and draw question marks all over it to spark suspense.)
- CVC picture cards or word list for each word: mop, top, log, pot, hop, dot, fox, pop

Activity

1. Introduction (30 Seconds)
Explain the activity and demonstrate picking a picture card from the bag, not allowing students to see it. Segment the sounds in that word and ask the students to blend it back together.

(Continued)

2. Segmenting Practice (Two Minutes)
Repeat this step, calling on different students each time.

3. Conclusion (30 Seconds)
Review the activity and together and segment some of the words they blended.

Lesson Plan 5   Phoneme Segmenting with Sticky Notes

Do you want to see this activity in action and grab the resources that go with it? Go to `http://www.literacyedventures.com/literacy-unlocked`.

Objective
Students will practice segmenting words into phonemes using sticky notes.

Materials Needed
- Sticky notes
- Marker

Scripted Lesson Plan

1. Introduction (30 Seconds)
Teacher: "Today, we are going to practice breaking words into their sounds using these sticky notes! I'll say a word, and we'll listen carefully to hear each sound in the word separately. Then, we'll use sticky notes to tap out each sound as we say it."

(Hold up a picture card of "mop" as an example.)

Teacher: "Let us look at this word, 'mop.' When we say it slowly, we hear each sound: /m/ ... /o/ ... /p/. Watch as I tap each sound, and let us say them together!"

Teacher: "Are you ready to try this with some new words and help me segment each sound on its own sticky note? Let us go!"

2. Segmenting Practice (Two Minutes)

Teacher: "Now, I'll say a word, and I want you to listen carefully and tap each sound using your sticky notes."

Teacher: "Our word is 'top.' Let us say it slowly: /t/ ... /o/ ... /p/."

(Tap a sticky note for each sound while saying the sounds aloud together.)

Teacher: "Great! Let us try another word."
- "log" → /l/ ... /o/ ... /g/
- "pot" → /p/ ... /o/ ... /t/
- "hop" → /h/ ... /o/ ... /p/
- "dot" → /d/ ... /o/ ... /t/
- "fox" → /f/ ... /o/ ... /x/
- "pop" → /p/ ... /o/ ... /p/

Teacher: "Fantastic job! Now let us go through each of those words one more time to see if we can tap out the sounds even faster."

3. Conclusion (30 Seconds)

Teacher: "You all did a great job listening to each sound in the words and tapping them out on sticky notes!"

(Continued)

Teacher: "Before we wrap up, I'd like each of you to share one word you segmented today using sticky notes. [Student's Name], what word did you work with?"

(Have each student to share a word, tapping it out one more time.)

Teacher: "Segmenting sounds helps us understand words better, and you all did an amazing job today! Keep practicing, and soon you'll be able to tap out sounds even faster. Great work, everyone!"

Lesson Plan 6   Segment the Sounds

Do you want to see this activity in action and grab the resources that go with it?
Go to `http://www.literacyedventures.com/literacy-unlocked`.

Objective
Students will practice segmenting words into phonemes and blending them back together.

Materials Needed
- Elkonin boxes
- CVC picture cards for each word: cat, dog, sun, bed, fox, bug, cup, pig
- Tokens (one for each phoneme in the words)

Scripted Lesson Plan

1. Introduction (30 Seconds)
Teacher: "Today, we are going to play with sounds by using Elkonin boxes! Each box will hold one sound, and we'll use these tokens to help us hear each

sound in a word. I'll say a word, and as we say each sound, we'll place a token in a box."

(Hold up a sound box and three tokens. Place a picture card of "cat" in front of you.)

Teacher: "Let us try it together with the word 'cat.' I'll say each sound and move a token for each one. /c/ ... /a/ ... /t/. When I put a token in each box, I hear all the sounds in the word. Now, I'll say them quickly to blend them back together: 'cat'!"

Teacher: "Are you ready to try it yourselves? Let us get started!"

2. Segmenting Practice (Two Minutes)

Teacher: "I'm going to give each of you a picture card. Look at the picture and say the word it shows. Then, place a token in a box for each sound you hear in the word. Finally, push each token up to blend the sounds back together."

(Teacher shows "dog" picture card.)

Students: /d/ ... /o/ ... /g/ (The students push one token in each box for each sound.)
Teacher: "Great! Now blend those sounds together."
Student: "dog!"
Teacher: "Awesome work with 'dog'!"

Continue with:
- "sun" → /s/ ... /u/ ... /n/ → "sun!"
- "bed" → /b/ ... /e/ ... /d/ → "bed!"
- "fox" → /f/ ... /o/ ... /x/ → "fox!"
- "bug" → /b/ ... /u/ ... /g/ → "bug!"
- "cup" → /k/ ... /u/ ... /p/ → "cup!"
- "pig" → /p/ ... /i/ ... /g/ → "pig!"

(Continued)

Teacher: "Let us go through each word quickly to make sure we are all confident with segmenting and blending. Listen closely and blend the sounds back together."

- "dog" → /d/ ... /o/ ... /g/
- "sun" → /s/ ... /u/ ... /n/
- "bed" → /b/ ... /e/ ... /d/
- "fox" → /f/ ... /o/ ... /x/
- "bug" → /b/ ... /u/ ... /g/
- "cup" → /k/ ... /u/ ... /p/
- "pig" → /p/ ... /i/ ... /g/

3. Conclusion (30 Seconds)

Teacher: "Fantastic work, everyone! You all did an amazing job sounding out each word and blending it back together. I'm so proud of you!"

Teacher: "Before we finish, let us do one last round together with the word 'cat.' Let us segment the sounds, say each one as we place a token, and then blend it back to say 'cat.' Ready?"

(Guide the students through segmenting /c/ ... /a/ ... /t/ with tokens and then blending to say "cat.")

Teacher: "Blending and segmenting sounds helps us with reading and understanding words. Keep practicing, and soon you'll be pros at it! Wonderful job today, everyone!"

Five Key Takeaways from Chapter 2

1. **Importance of PA.** Understand that PA is a crucial foundational skill for reading and spelling, directly affecting students' literacy development. It is extremely important to provide this instruction in K–1 and for students who need intervention in this area.

2. **Daily practice.** Daily PA activities can significantly enhance students' reading and spelling abilities. Remember, six minutes a day is all you need!

3. **Integration with phonics.** Combining PA with phonics instruction helps reinforce the connection between sounds and letters, making reading and spelling more accessible for students. Remember: decoding is the goal, not PA.

4. **Variety of activities.** Using a range of engaging activities, such as blending, segmenting, and interactive games, will help keep students engaged.

5. **Scaffolded instruction.** Providing scaffolded instruction tailored to students' current levels of PA ensures that they receive the appropriate support to progress from simpler tasks to more complex ones. But the key is to get to the individual phoneme level as soon as possible.

CHAPTER THREE

The Role of Handwriting in Early Literacy Development

Handwriting and letter formation are both critical literacy instruction components that often get left out. When students learn proper letter formation, they can not only print legibly but also connect letter names, shapes, and sounds. Fluent letter formation also supports encoding. In this chapter we will explore the importance of handwriting and proper letter formation. I will share some of my tried-and-true teaching strategies to help students as they master this skill.

Handwriting in Literacy

Handwriting in the context of literacy refers to the ability to form letters correctly, fluently, and legibly. When students can do this with very little thought, they have mastered the art of letter formation. Although it might seem that letter formation is simply about neat handwriting, it's actually much deeper than that. Handwriting plays a crucial role in reinforcing the alphabetic principle—the understanding that letters represent sounds in spoken language. This connection between written and spoken language enables students to link letter shapes, names, and sounds seamlessly, supporting their ability to decode and encode words effectively. By integrating handwriting instruction with a focus on the alphabetic principle, we lay the foundation for strong reading and writing skills.

LETTER FORMATION is directly linked to a child's ability to recognize and recall letter sounds and shapes. When we provide handwriting instruction early on, we are helping our students solidify their understanding of letter names and sounds, which is directly supporting their ability to read and spell accurately.

Although handwriting is connected to letter names, sounds, and shapes, it is also closely connected to fine motor skills and cognitive development. As children practice forming letters, they strengthen the muscles in their hands and fingers, which improves coordination and control.

What the Research Says

Handwriting is more than just a motor skill—it's a critical component of literacy development. Research consistently demonstrates a strong correlation between handwriting practice and letter recognition. Studies show that children who practice writing letters while learning their sounds and names develop a deeper understanding of those letters, which is essential for early reading success.

Explicit and systematic instruction in letter formation is particularly effective. Teaching the correct strokes and sequences for each letter, paired with visual aids and repeated practice, helps students build the motor skills required for fluent handwriting. This fluency enables students to write letters effortlessly, freeing up cognitive resources for more complex literacy tasks, like spelling and composition.

The connection to the Simple View of Writing underscores why handwriting instruction is so important. Skilled writing requires both transcription (the ability to write fluently and legibly) and composition (the ability to generate and organize ideas). When too much effort is spent on forming letters, students' overall writing abilities can suffer. By ensuring that handwriting becomes an automatic process, we support not only transcription but also students' capacity to focus on composition, enabling them to develop as skilled writers. Let us take a closer look at the research that reinforces the case for explicit handwriting instruction.

Ray et al. (2022) conducted a systematic review that examined the relationship between handwriting ability and literacy development in kindergarten students. Their analysis found that letter-writing fluency is a critical component of early literacy and directly influences vital skills such as writing composition and letter knowledge. The study found that children who develop fluency in handwriting tend to perform better in these areas, as they are able to more efficiently and effectively translate their thoughts into written form. This in turn leads to improved writing outcomes. The research also highlighted that handwriting fluency significantly affects spelling and word reading. The findings from this study emphasize the importance of integrating handwriting instruction into early education curriculums.

In a study by Santangelo and Graham (2016), researchers examined the effectiveness of handwriting instruction to determine its impact on writing quality and fluency. This analysis found that explicit instruction in handwriting, especially when teaching correct stroke formation, significantly enhances students' overall writing abilities. They found that a structured approach improves the speed and legibility of handwriting and supports many literacy skills, including but not limited to spelling and reading comprehension.

This meta-analysis also highlighted that handwriting instruction is most effective when it is systematic and consistent, with teachers providing explicit modeling, guided practice, and immediate feedback. These practices help students develop the motor and cognitive skills necessary to write fluently. The findings suggest that educators should prioritize handwriting instruction in the early grades (K–2).

Graham et al. (2000) conducted a study that explored the importance of handwriting instruction in early literacy development. This study focused on grades kindergarten through second grade. Their research found a need for daily handwriting practice, especially in the younger grades. They recommend spending at least 10–15 minutes per day on direct handwriting instruction. This consistent and routine practice is crucial for developing handwriting automaticity. This automaticity enables students to write fluently without being hindered by the mechanics of letter formation, Once students achieve fluency in handwriting, they can focus their cognitive resources on higher-level writing tasks like spelling, organization, and sentence construction. Researchers have concluded that daily, focused handwriting instruction in the early grades is essential for building the motor skills and automaticity that support successful writing and academic achievement.

Wrap-Up of the Research

Ray et al. (2022). "The Relationship of Handwriting Ability and Literacy in Kindergarten: A Systematic Review."

- **Handwriting is a core literacy skill.** Handwriting fluency is linked to critical literacy skills such as letter knowledge, spelling, and writing composition.
- **Impacts on spelling and reading.** This research showed moderate positive effects on spelling and word reading, suggesting that handwriting plays a supportive role in other areas of literacy.
- **Integration in early education.** Early handwriting instruction should be systematic and explicit. It should be integrated into curricula to strengthen foundational literacy skills and ensure long-term academic success.

Santangelo and Graham. (2016). "A Comprehensive Meta-Analysis of Handwriting Instruction."

- **Explicit instruction is key.** Teachers should prioritize explicit, systematic handwriting instruction, including proper stroke formation. This approach significantly improves the quality and fluency of students' handwriting.

- **Integration with literacy instruction.** Handwriting instruction should be integrated with broader literacy activities like letter-sound instruction. This integration helps reinforce letter recognition, spelling, and reading comprehension, leading to stronger literacy outcomes.
- **Consistent practice and feedback.** Teachers must provide consistent, guided practice with immediate feedback. This helps students develop the motor skills necessary for fluent writing, which frees up their cognitive load.

Graham et al. (2000). "Is Handwriting Causally Related to Learning to Write?"

- **Daily practice is crucial.** Teachers should allocate 10–15 minutes daily to handwriting instruction, especially in the early grades (K–2). This daily practice is essential for developing the automaticity that enables students to write fluently without focusing on the mechanics of handwriting.
- **Foundational skill for literacy.** Regular practice of handwriting fluency reduces the cognitive load during writing tasks, enabling students to concentrate more on content and higher-level writing processes.
- **Early and regular intervention.** Teachers should implement regular handwriting instruction early in the educational process. This early intervention builds the motor skills and automaticity necessary for academic success in writing and beyond.

Practical Tips for Implementation

Teaching handwriting effectively requires more than just introducing letters—it involves building a solid foundation of skills, routines, and strategies that align with students' developmental needs. As educators, we often wonder, *When should I start? How do I balance fine motor skill development with letter formation? What are the best practices for ensuring consistency across classrooms?*

The next sections provide practical tips for implementing handwriting instruction that supports all learners. From identifying readiness to introducing routines and strategies for posture and pencil grip, you'll find actionable insights to enhance your practice. Whether you are teaching prekindergarten students to master the basics or helping older students refine their handwriting, these considerations will help set your students up for success.

Considerations for Effective Handwriting Instruction

Teachers often face questions regarding the best practices for teaching handwriting, such as when to begin formal instruction and whether to start with uppercase or lowercase letters:

- **Age and readiness for handwriting.** The ideal time to begin teaching proper letter formation is generally during prekindergarten through first grade. During this period, children's physical and visual motor coordination aligns with their developing letter knowledge. They begin to move from scribbles to understanding the alphabetic principle. However, readiness can vary, and some children may need more support with pencil grip or fine motor skill development before starting formal handwriting instruction.

- **Uppercase versus lowercase letters.** Although lowercase letters should be the primary focus of instruction, uppercase letters are also important and should not be overlooked. In fact, LETRS Early Childhood (LETRS EC) recommends teaching the formation of both uppercase and lowercase letters together during alphabet instruction. Lowercase letters are typically prioritized because they make up about 80% of the text students encounter in reading and writing, but incorporating uppercase letters alongside lowercase ensures students develop a comprehensive understanding of the alphabet. This balanced approach supports reading and writing fluency while preparing students for real-world applications of both letter forms.

Prerequisites for Effective Handwriting Instruction

Before diving into letter formation, there are several foundational skills that students need to develop:

- **Fine motor skills.** Strong fine motor skills are necessary for proper pencil grip, posture, and paper positioning. Activities supporting hand strength and coordination include playing with Play-Doh, threading beads, or using tongs to pick up smaller objects. Since the early 2020s, I have seen a decline in students' fine motor abilities when entering kindergarten. Knowing this, my teachers and I made literacy stations that really supported this fine motor development at the beginning of the year. I have linked many of these for you on the companion site (`http://www.literacyedventures.com/literacy-unlocked`).

- **Understanding writing lines.** Students must understand the parts of their writing paper. They need to know where to locate the paper's top, middle, and bottom lines. Understanding these lines helps them correctly position letters and ensure neat and legible handwriting.

```
TOP    ─────────────────
DOTTED - - - - - - - - -
BOTTOM ─────────────────
```

- **Pencil grip and posture.** Proper pencil grip and posture are essential for efficient and comfortable writing. Teaching students to hold a pencil correctly and sit with good posture can prevent fatigue and improve handwriting quality. Next are some tips and tricks for nailing this down with your students.

Daily Routines for Pencil Grip

Incorporating a daily routine with a fun song or chant can be a simple yet effective way to reinforce proper pencil grip and posture in young learners. Start each writing session with a posture chant to remind students about their body alignment. For example, a chant like "Bottom to bottom, back to back, feet flat on the floor" helps students sit up straight, with their bottom at the back of the chair, back against the chair, and feet flat on the floor.

Follow this with a "Pencil Grip Song" to guide students in holding their pencils correctly. I found this song on YouTube and give full credit to the great Linda Laporte Torres! This daily routine will help build strong habits while making learning fun.

Daily Routine with the "Pencil Grip Song"

Posture chant. Begin each writing session with a chant that reminds students to sit up straight, with their bottom on the chair, their back against the chair, and their feet flat on the floor, such as chanting "Bottom to bottom, back to back, feet flat on the floor."

"Pencil Grip Song." Next, guide students to place their pencil flat on the desk, point facing them. Teach them to make an "okay" sign with their fingers and how to pinch the pencil tip, and flip it into the correct writing position. A great way to practice this is by singing a catchy song, such as this one:

> Everything was A-OK, A-OK, A-OK until my fingers fell asleep ZZZZZZ.
>
> Then a little crab came out, crab came out, crab came out.
>
> Then a little crab came out and pinched my pencil tip—FLIP!

When students flip their pencils, they should rest with an appropriate pencil grip and positioning. If you choose to use this chant, it is important to be consistent and use it every time you begin to write until students are using the appropriate grip frequently without prompting.

Consistency Across Teachers

Given the variety of educators—such as special education teachers, speech language pathologists, instructional assistants, reading interventionists, and even parent volunteers—who might work with a student throughout the day, everyone must use the same terms when teaching letter formation. For example, consistently referring to elements like "tall stick," "short stick," "circle back," and "slanted line" ensures that students internalize the correct techniques for forming letters, leading to better handwriting skills. In Table 3.1 I share my letter-sound chants. You can grab a copy of these on the companion website (http://www.literacyedventures.com/literacy-unlocked).

AS EDUCATORS, we all know how important consistency and routine is. The same is true for handwriting. Having a consistent method for teaching handwriting and letter formation is essential.

Table 3.1 Letter Formation Chants

Tall Letters	
l	Start at the top line, straight stick down.
t	Start at the top line, straight stick down, cross on the dotted line.
f	Start at the top line, hook it down, cross on the dotted line.
h	Start at the top line, straight stick down, bounce up to the dotted line and around.
b	Start at the top line, straight stick down, bounce up to the dotted line and all the way around.
Short Letters	
i	Start at the dotted line, short stick down, a small dot on top.
u	Start at the dotted line, short stick down, curve up, and right back up to the dotted line.
r	Start at the dotted line, short stick down, bounce up to the dotted line and just a little around.

(Continued)

Table 3.1 (*Continued*)

Short Letters	
m	Start at the dotted line, bounce up and around, bounce up and around.
n	Start at the dotted line, bounce up and around.
p	Start at the dotted line, short stick down, down below the bottom line, bounce up to the dotted line and around.
j	Start at the dotted line, short stick down, down below the bottom line and curve to the left.
Circle Back Letters	
c	Start at the dotted line, circle back.
o	Start at the dotted line, circle back, and all the way around.
a	Start at the dotted line, circle back, up to the dotted line, and short stick down.
d	Start at the dotted line, circle back ("c" before "d"), up to the top line and straight stick down.
e	Start just below the dotted line, go out of the middle, and circle back
g	Start at the dotted line, circle back, up, short stick down, down below the bottom line and curve to the left.
q	Start at the dotted line, circle back up, short stick down, down below the bottom line and down, down.
s	Start at the dotted line, circle back, go to the right, curve to the left.
Slanted Line Letters	
x	Start at the dotted line, slanted line down, pick up your pencil, slanted line down make an "x."
v	Start at the dotted line, slanted line down, pick up your pencil, slanted line down make a "v."
w	Start at the dotted line, slanted line down, slanted line up to the dotted line, slanted line down, slanted line up to the dotted line.
y	Start at the dotted line, slanted line down, pick up your pencil, slanted line down, slanted line down, down below the bottom line and stop.
z	Start at the dotted line, cross to the right, slanted line down, cross to the right.
k	Start at the top line, straight stick down, pick up your pencil, start at the dotted line, slant to the middle, slant to the bottom line and stop.

Combining Letter Formation with Literacy Development

Letter formation and practice should be integrated into your daily literacy block.

> **AS STUDENTS** learn letter names and sounds, they should also practice writing those letters. When we combine the two, our students' understanding of the alphabetic principle strengthens.

Students are more likely to internalize the connection between spoken and written language by engaging in phonemic awareness and letter formation activities. This practice enhances their decoding skills, supports spelling accuracy, and fosters fluency in reading and writing. Moreover, integrating handwriting with literacy activities encourages active engagement and makes learning more meaningful and effective. This holistic method ensures that students are not memorizing letters in isolation but are developing a deeper, more functional literacy skill set that will benefit them throughout their educational journey.

Classroom Implementation Actionable Steps

Now that we have a solid grasp of letter formation, its significance, and the best practices for teaching it effectively, let us explore some practical strategies you can implement in your classroom immediately!

Lesson Plan 1   Pencil Grip and Posture

Objective
Students will learn the correct pencil grip and writing posture using a fun and interactive song.

Materials Needed
- Pencils
- Paper

Activity

1. Introduction (30 Seconds)
Explain the importance of holding the pencil correctly and sitting with good posture while writing.

2. Posture Practice (One Minute)
Chant to remind students to sit up straight with their feet flat on the floor and their backs against the chair. "Bottom to bottom, back to back, feet flat on the floor!"

3. "Pencil Grip Song" (One Minute)
Teach students the "Pencil Grip Song." Show them how to make an "okay" sign with their fingers, pinch the pencil tip, and flip the pencil into the correct writing position. Then, sing the "Pencil Grip Song."

4. Conclusion (30 Seconds)
Review the pencil grip and posture. Ask students to demonstrate the correct grip and posture.

Lesson Plan 2   Introduction to Handwriting Lines

Objective
Students will learn to identify and practice forming the basic handwriting lines: tall stick, short stick, slanted line, and circle back. These foundational lines are the building blocks for forming letters.

Materials Needed
- Writing paper with wide lines
- Pencils
- Visual aids displaying examples of each line (tall stick, short stick, slanted line, circle back)
- Whiteboard and markers for demonstration

Activity

1. Introduction (One Minute)
Begin by explaining that all letters in the alphabet can be made with a few simple lines. Tell the students that today, they will learn about the different types of lines that help form letters. Demonstrate each line on the whiteboard as you describe it.

2. Tall Stick (One Minute)
Explain that a tall stick is a straight line that starts at the top line and goes down to the bottom. Draw the line several times, saying the chant, "Start at the top line, straight stick down."

- **Student Practice (One Minute):** Have students practice drawing tall sticks on their paper, ensuring they start at the top and pull straight down.

(Continued)

3. Short Stick (One Minute)

Describe the short stick as a smaller version of the tall stick, starting at the middle (dotted line) and going down to the bottom. Draw the line several times, saying the chant, "Start at the dotted line, straight stick down."

- **Student Practice (One Minute):** Students practice drawing short sticks, focusing on starting at the middle line and pulling down.

4. Slanted Line (One Minute)

Introduce the slanted line as a line that slants down from the dotted line. Draw the line several times, saying the chant, "Start at the dotted line, slanted line down."

- **Student Practice (One Minute):** Students practice drawing slanted lines (slanting both ways on their paper).

5. Circle Back (One Minute)

Explain the circle back as a curved line that forms a part of a circle, Draw the "c" several times, saying the chant, "Start at the dotted line, and circle back."

- **Student Practice (One Minute):** Students practice drawing circle backs, starting from the dotted line and curving around.

6. Guided Line Formation Practice (One Minute)

Lead the students through drawing each type of line on their paper. Call out a line type (e.g., "Tall stick!") and have students draw it on their paper as you draw it on the board. Repeat with a short stick and a slanted line and circle back, alternating between them.

7. Conclusion (One Minute)

Review the four basic lines they practiced today. Ask students to identify which line they found easiest and the most challenging. Find ways to incorporate at least one form daily.

> **Teacher Tip:** There are five days in your school week. Create a calendar. On Monday, practice tall stick letters, on Tuesday practice short stick letters, on Wednesday practice circle back letters, on Thursday practice slanted line letters, and on Friday, do a mix of letters that you notice your students might be struggling with. Grab this calendar and sheets to support this practice on the companion website (`http://www.literacyedventures.com/literacy-unlocked`).

Lesson Plan 3   Short Line Practice

Objective
Students will practice forming letters with short lines.

Materials Needed
- Writing paper with lines
- Pencils
- Visual aids showing short line letters: i, u, r, m, n, p, and j

Scripted Lesson Plan

1. Introduction (30 Seconds)
Teacher: "Today, we are going to practice writing letters that are made using short lines, or what we sometimes call 'sticks.'"

Teacher: "Some letters use these short lines, and it helps us write them neatly and correctly."

(Draw a short line on the board to demonstrate.)

Teacher: "See this short line? We're going to use lines like this to make letters like 'i' and 'r.' I'll show you each one, and then you'll have a chance to try it on your own. Are you ready to make some short lines with me?"

(Continued)

2. Guided Practice (Two Minutes)

Teacher: "I'll show you how to make each letter using short lines. Watch closely, and then we'll practice together."

Letter i

Teacher: "Let us start with the letter 'i.' Start at the dotted line, make a short stick down, and then add a small dot on top. Let us try that together. Watch me first."

(Demonstrate drawing the letter "i" on the board, then invite students to trace and write it themselves.)

Teacher: "Now, trace the 'i' on your paper. Once you feel ready, write it five more times on your own. Remember: short stick down, dot on top."

Letter u

Teacher: "For the letter 'u,' start at the dotted line, make a short stick down, curve up, and go right back up to the dotted line."

(Demonstrate and guide students to trace and then write "u" independently.)

Teacher: "Great! Now, write the letter 'u' five more times on your own."

Letter r

Teacher: "For 'r,' start at the dotted line, make a short stick down, then bounce up to the dotted line and make a little curve."

(Model and have students trace and then write "r.")

Teacher: "Now, write 'r' five more times. Take your time and keep the lines nice and short."

Letter m

Teacher: "For the letter 'm,' we start at the dotted line, bounce up and around, then bounce up and around again. Let us do it together."

The Role of Handwriting in Early Literacy Development 73

(Demonstrate and let students trace, then write "m" on their own.)

Teacher: "Excellent! Now try writing 'm' five more times."

Letter n

Teacher: "For the letter 'n,' start at the dotted line, bounce up and around once. It's like half of 'm.'"

(Model and have students trace and then write "n.")

Teacher: "Now write 'n' five more times on your paper."

Letter p

Teacher: "For 'p,' start at the dotted line, make a short stick that goes below the bottom line, bounce up to the dotted line, and make a little loop around."

(Demonstrate and encourage students to trace and then try "p" independently.)

Teacher: "Great job! Now write the letter 'p' five more times, focusing on those neat short lines."

Letter j

Teacher: "Finally, for 'j,' start at the dotted line, make a short stick down, below the bottom line, and curve to the left. Then add a dot on top."

(Model for students, then have them trace and write "j.")

Teacher: "Now write 'j' five more times on your paper, and do not forget that little dot on top!"

3. Independent Practice (One Minute)

Teacher: "Now that you have practiced each letter with me, it's time to try them all on your own. Focus on making your short lines nice and neat. I'll come around to give you feedback as you practice."

(Allow students a minute to write the letters independently, focusing on neatness and correct form. Provide immediate feedback as you observe their work.)

(Continued)

Conclusion (30 Seconds)

Teacher: "You all did a fantastic job practicing your short-line letters! Remember, short lines help us write these letters neatly. Keep practicing, and soon, you'll be able to write them perfectly every time."

Teacher: "Can anyone show me one of the letters they feel most proud of? Let us share a couple of examples before we finish!"

(Invite a few students to share, providing praise and encouragement for their efforts.)

Teacher: "Great work today, everyone! Keep practicing those short lines, and you'll see how much easier it becomes to write neatly."

Lesson Plan 4 Tall Line Practice

Objective
Students will practice forming letters with tall lines.

Materials Needed
- Writing paper with lines
- Pencils
- Visual aids showing tall line letters: l, t, f, h, and b

Scripted Lesson Plan

1. Introduction (30 Seconds)

Teacher: "Today, we are going to practice writing letters that are made with tall lines, or what we call 'sticks.'"

Teacher: "Some letters use these tall lines, and it helps us write them neatly and correctly."

(Draw a tall line on the board to demonstrate.)

Teacher: "See this tall line? We're going to use lines like this to make letters like 'l' and 't.' I'll show you each one, and then you'll have a chance to try it on your own. Are you ready to make some tall lines with me?"

2. *Guided Practice (Two Minutes)*
Teacher: "I'll show you how to make each letter using tall lines. Watch closely, and then we'll practice together."

Letter l
Teacher: "Let us start with the letter 'l.' Start at the top line and draw a straight stick down. Let us try that together. Watch me first."

(Demonstrate drawing the letter "l" on the board, then invite students to trace and write it themselves.)

Teacher: "Now, trace the 'l' on your paper. Once you feel ready, write it five times as you practice on your own.

Teacher: "Remember: start at the top line and make a straight stick down."

Letter t
Teacher: "For the letter 't,' start at the top line, make a straight stick down, and cross it on the dotted line."

(Demonstrate and guide students to trace and then write "t" independently.)

Teacher: "Great! Now, write the letter 't' five times as you practice on your own."

Letter f
Teacher: "For 'f,' start at the top line, hook it down, and cross it on the dotted line."

(Model and have students trace and then write "f.")

Teacher: "Now, write 'f' five times as you practice on your own. Take your time to get that nice hook shape and neat cross."

(Continued)

Letter h
Teacher: "For the letter 'h,' start at the top line, draw a straight stick down, then bounce up to the dotted line and around."

(Demonstrate and let students trace, then write "h" on their own.)

Teacher: "Excellent! Now try writing 'h' five times as you practice on your own."

Letter b
Teacher: "For the letter 'b,' start at the top line, make a straight stick down, bounce up to the dotted line, and go all the way around to form a loop."

(Model and have students trace and then write "b.")

Teacher: "Now write 'b' five times as you practice on your own."

3. Independent Practice (One Minute)
Teacher: "Now that you have practiced each letter with me, it's time to try them all on your own. Focus on making your tall lines nice and neat. I'll come around to give you feedback as you practice."

(Allow students a minute to write the letters independently, focusing on neatness and correct form. Provide immediate feedback as you observe their work.)

Conclusion (30 Seconds)
Teacher: "You all did a fantastic job practicing your tall-line letters! Remember, tall lines help us write these letters neatly. Keep practicing, and soon, you'll be able to write them perfectly every time."

Teacher: "Can anyone show me one of the letters they feel most proud of? Let us share a couple of examples before we finish!"

(Invite a few students to share, providing praise and encouragement for their efforts.)

Teacher: "Great work today, everyone! Keep practicing those tall lines, and you'll see how much easier it becomes to write neatly."

Lesson Plan 5   Circle Back Practice

Objective
Students will practice forming letters with circle-back lines.

Materials Needed
- Writing paper with lines
- Pencils
- Visual aids showing circle-back letters: c, o, a, d, e, g, q, and s

Scripted Lesson Plan

1. Introduction (30 seconds)
Teacher: "Today, we are going to practice writing letters that start with a circle-back motion."

Teacher: "Some letters, like 'c' and 'o,' are made by circling back, which helps us write them neatly."

(Demonstrate a circle-back motion on the board.)

Teacher: "This circle-back motion is what we'll use to write these letters. I'll show you each one, and then you'll have a chance to practice it on your own. Ready to circle back with me?"

2. Guided Practice (Two minutes)
Teacher: "I'll show you how to make each letter using a circle-back line. Watch closely, and then we'll practice together."

Letter c
Teacher: "Let us start with the letter 'c.' Start at the dotted line and circle back. Let us try that together. Watch me first."

(Demonstrate drawing the letter "c" on the board, then invite students to trace and write it themselves.)

(Continued)

Teacher: "Now, trace the 'c' on your paper. Once you feel ready, write it five times as you practice on your own."

Letter o
Teacher: "For the letter 'o,' start at the dotted line, circle back, and go all the way around to complete the circle."

(Demonstrate and guide students to trace and then write "o" independently.)

Teacher: "Great! Now, write the letter 'o' five times as you practice on your own."

Letter a
Teacher: "For 'a,' start at the dotted line, circle back, go up to the dotted line, and then make a short stick down."

(Model and have students trace and then write "a.")

Teacher: "Now, write 'a' five times as you practice on your own."

Letter d
Teacher: "For the letter 'd,' start at the dotted line, circle back as if making a 'c,' then go up to the top line and make a straight stick down."

(Demonstrate and let students trace, then write "d" on their own.)

Teacher: "Excellent! Now try writing 'd' five times as you practice on your own."

Letter e
Teacher: "For the letter 'e,' start just below the dotted line, go out from the middle, and then circle back."

(Model and have students trace and then write "e.")

Teacher: "Now write 'e' five times as you practice on your own."

Letter g
Teacher: "For 'g,' start at the dotted line, circle back up, short stick down, down below the bottom line and curve to the left."

(Demonstrate and encourage students to trace and then try "g" independently.)

Teacher: "Great job! Now write the letter 'g' five times as you practice on your own."

Letter q

Teacher: "For 'q,' start at the dotted line, circle back up, short stick down, down below the bottom line and down, down."

(Model for students, then have them trace and write "q.")

Teacher: "Now write 'q' five times as you practice on your own."

Letter s

Teacher: "Finally, for 's,' start at the dotted line, circle back, curve right, then curve it left. This letter has a nice wave to it."

(Model and guide students through tracing, then writing "s.")

Teacher: "Now write 's' five times as you practice on your own."

3. Independent Practice (One Minute)

Teacher: "Now that you have practiced each letter with me, it's time to try them all on your own. Focus on making your circle-back lines smooth and neat. I'll come around to give you feedback as you practice."

(Allow students a minute to write the letters independently, focusing on neatness and correct form. Provide immediate feedback as you observe their work.)

Conclusion (30 Seconds)

Teacher: "You all did a fantastic job practicing your circle-back letters! Remember, the circle-back motion helps us form these letters smoothly. Keep practicing, and soon, you'll be able to write them perfectly every time."

Teacher: "Can anyone show me one of the letters they feel most proud of? Let us share a couple of examples before we finish!"

(Continued)

(Invite a few students to share, providing praise and encouragement for their efforts.)

Teacher: "Great work today, everyone! Keep practicing those circle-back letters, and you'll see how much easier it becomes to write them neatly."

Lesson Plan 6   Slanted Line Practice

Objective
Students will practice forming letters with slanted lines.

Materials Needed
- Writing paper with lines
- Pencils
- Visual aids showing slanted line letters: x, v, w, y, z, and k

Scripted Lesson Plan

1. Introduction (30 Seconds)

Teacher: "Today, we are going to practice writing letters that use slanted lines, which help give letters like 'x' and 'v' their unique shapes."

(Draw a slanted line on the board as a demonstration.)

Teacher: "See this slanted line? We're going to use lines like this to make letters. I'll show you each one, and then you'll have a chance to try it on your own. Are you ready to start making some slanted lines with me?"

2. Guided Practice (Two Minutes)

Teacher: "I'll show you how to make each letter using slanted lines. Watch closely, and then we'll practice together."

Letter x

Teacher: "Let us start with the letter 'x.' Start at the dotted line, make a slanted line down, pick up your pencil, and make another slanted line down. Let us try that together. Watch me first."

(Demonstrate drawing the letter "x" on the board, then invite students to trace and write it themselves.)

Teacher: "Now, trace the 'x' on your paper. Once you feel ready, write it five times as you practice on your own."

Letter v

Teacher: "For the letter 'v,' start at the dotted line, make a slanted line down, pick up your pencil, and make another slanted line down to complete the letter."

(Demonstrate and have students trace and then write "v" independently.)

Teacher: "Great! Now, write the letter 'v' five times as you practice on your own."

Letter w

Teacher: "For the letter 'w,' start at the dotted line, make a slanted line down, slanted line up to the dotted line, slanted line down again, and slanted line up to the dotted line. Watch closely and let us practice together."

(Model the letter and guide students to trace and write "w.")

Teacher: "Excellent! Write 'w' five times as you practice on your own."

Letter y

Teacher: "For the letter 'y,' start at the dotted line, make a slanted line down, pick up your pencil, make another slanted line down below the bottom line, and stop. Watch me, then we'll try together."

(Demonstrate and have students trace and then write "y.")

Teacher: "Now, write 'y' five times on your own, focusing on neat slanted lines."

(Continued)

Letter z
Teacher: "To form the letter 'z,' start at the dotted line, cross to the right, slant down, and cross to the right again. Watch as I demonstrate."

(Demonstrate and let students trace, then write "z" on their own.)

Teacher: "Excellent! Now try writing 'z' five times."

Letter k
Teacher: "For the letter 'k,' start at the top line, make a straight stick down, pick up your pencil, start at the dotted line, slant to the middle, and then slant down to the bottom line. Let us practice together."

(Demonstrate and guide students as they trace and write "k.")

Teacher: "Now, write 'k' five times on your own."

3. Independent Practice (One Minute)
Teacher: "Now that you have practiced each letter with me, it's time to try them all on your own. Focus on making your slanted lines nice and neat. I'll come around to give you feedback as you practice."

(Allow students a minute to write the letters independently, focusing on neatness and correct form. Provide immediate feedback as you observe their work.)

Conclusion (30 Seconds)
Teacher: "You all did a fantastic job practicing your slanted-line letters! Remember, neat, slanted lines make these letters stand out. Keep practicing, and soon, you'll be able to write them perfectly every time."

Teacher: "Can anyone show me one of the letters they feel most proud of? Let us share a couple of examples before we finish!"

(Invite a few students to share, providing praise and encouragement for their efforts.)

Teacher: "Great work today, everyone! Keep practicing those slanted lines, and you'll see how much easier it becomes to write neatly."

Five Key Takeaways from Chapter 3

- **Handwriting is a core literacy skill.** Handwriting fluency is essential for developing critical literacy skills such as letter and sound knowledge, spelling, and writing composition. It's not just about neatness; it's about building the cognitive connections necessary for literacy.

- **Daily practice is essential.** Regular handwriting practice, with at least 10–15 minutes per day dedicated to this skill, is crucial in the early grades. This consistent practice develops the automaticity that enables students to write fluently without being bogged down by the mechanics of letter formation.

- **Integration with literacy instruction.** Combining handwriting instruction with literacy activities, such as phonemic awareness and letter-sound correspondence, strengthens understanding of the alphabetic principles and supports literacy journeys.

- **Explicit and systematic instruction.** Handwriting instruction is most effective when explicit, systematic, and includes correct stroke formation. This approach helps students develop the motor and cognitive skills needed for fluent writing, enhancing their overall literacy outcomes.

- **Consistency across educators.** Consistency in language and instructional methods across all educators working with students is vital for reinforcing learning. Using uniform terminology and routines ensures that students internalize the correct techniques for forming letters, leading to better handwriting skills and literacy development.

CHAPTER FOUR

Building the Foundation of Letter-Sound Knowledge

The alphabetic principle is the cornerstone of literacy, providing the understanding that written letters and letter combinations represent the sounds of spoken language. It's the foundational concept that empowers students to decode words by recognizing the sounds behind letters and letter patterns. For instance, the word "cat" is broken down into the sounds /k/, /a/, and /t/, represented by the letters "c," "a," and "t." Mastery of the alphabetic principle enables students to decode and spell new words independently, setting the stage for fluent reading and comprehensive literacy development.

In this chapter, we'll explore the research behind the alphabetic principle, examining how teaching letter names and sounds together can significantly enhance students' literacy skills. We will dive into practical tips for classroom implementation, focusing on strategies for teaching letter sounds effectively and ensuring students not only learn the alphabetic principle but apply it confidently. Let us unlock the key to helping our students become independent readers and writers by mastering this essential literacy skill.

What the Research Says

In a study by Piasta, Purpura, et al. (2010), preschool-aged children were randomly assigned to receive small-group instruction in either letter names and sounds (as a treated control group). The study evaluated the effectiveness of two approaches commonly used in early childhood classrooms: combined letter name and sound instruction or letter sound only instruction. The instruction consisted of 34 15-minute lessons, with children pre- and post-tested on various emergent literacy skills, including alphabet knowledge, phonological awareness, letter-word identification, emergent reading, and developmental spelling. The study's results suggested combining letter names and sound instruction significantly benefits children's acquisition of letter sounds.

Piasta, Wagner, et al. (2010) explored the critical factors involved in letter-sound acquisition among 653 English-speaking kindergarten students at the beginning of the school year. The study specifically examined the role of letter name knowledge and phonological awareness in facilitating letter-sound learning. The researchers investigated two key aspects: (1) how phonological awareness contributes to letter-sound acquisition from letter names and (2) the likelihood of letter-sound acquisition based on the characteristics of different letters, such as consonant vowel letters (e.g., "b" and "d"), vowel consonant letters (e.g., l and m), letters with no sound cues (e.g., "h" and "y"), and vowel letters.

The findings revealed that letter name knowledge had a significant impact on letter-sound acquisition. Phonological awareness was more substantial in letter-sound knowledge when the students already knew the letter names. Additionally, the study found that students were more likely to understand the sounds of consonant vowel letters compared to vowel consonant letters and letters with no sound cues. The likelihood of knowing the sounds for letters with no sound cues was lowest, but this varied depending on the students' levels of phonological awareness and letter name knowledge.

In the study by Treiman et al. (2008), the researchers explored how children use letter names to learn letter sounds and whether this ability is influenced by phonological awareness. The study found that children, including those with speech sound disorders, performed better on letter-sound tasks with letters where the sound appears at the beginning of the letter's name (e.g., "v" in "vi") compared to letters where the sound appears at the end (e.g., "m" in "em") or not at all (e.g., "h" in "aitch"). The results suggest that many children, including those with speech sound disorders, use letter names as a cue to learn letter sounds, even if they have limited phonological awareness.

Wrap-Up of the Research

Piasta, Purpura, et al. (2010). "Preschool-Aged Children's Letter-Sound Acquisition: The Role of Instruction in Letter Names and Sounds."

- **Combined instruction benefits.** Teaching letter names and sounds together significantly enhances children's ability to learn letter sounds.
- **Targeted outcomes.** The benefits of combined instruction were specific to letter-sound acquisition and did not generalize to other emergent literacy skills, such as phonological awareness or developmental spelling.
- **Instructional approach.** The findings support using a combined instructional approach in early childhood settings to promote letter-sound knowledge effectively.

Piasta, Wagner, et al. (2010). "The Role of Phonological Awareness in Letter-Sound Acquisition: Evidence from Kindergarten Students."

- **Letter name knowledge.** A strong foundation in letter name knowledge significantly enhances letter-sound acquisition.
- **Phonological awareness.** Phonological awareness positively affects letter-sound knowledge when students already know the letter names.
- **Letter characteristics.** Students are more successful in learning the sounds of consonant vowel letters than vowel consonant letters or letters with no sound cues, mainly when letter names and phonological awareness are both accounted for.

(Continued)

Challenges with no sound cues. Letters with no sound cues in their names (such as "h," "w," and "y") present the most significant challenge for sound acquisition, particularly for students with lower levels of phonological awareness. Because their letter names do not provide clear hints to their corresponding sounds, students may require additional explicit instruction and practice to master these associations.

Treiman et al. (2008). "Which Children Benefit from Letter Names in Learning Letter Sounds?"

- **Children's use of letter names.** Children often use letter names to help learn the sounds, especially when the sound is at the beginning of the name.
- **Performance differences.** Children perform better on letter-sound tasks when the sound is at the beginning of the letter's name (e.g., "v") rather than at the end (e.g., "m") or not in the name at all (e.g., "h").
- **Impact of phonological awareness.** Children with low phonological awareness can use letter names to learn letter sounds, suggesting that explicit phonological awareness may not be necessary for this task.
- **Speech sound disorders.** Children with speech sound disorders show similar patterns, though they generally perform worse on letter-sound tasks than typically developing children.

Practical Tips for Implementation

In this section, I'll be diving into practical tips planning and implementing letter-sound learning in your classroom. We will explore some important things to consider as you begin preparing your lesson plans as well as effective ways to execute those lesson plans in your classroom.

Preparing to Teach Letter Sounds

Teaching letter sounds is one of the most foundational aspects of early literacy instruction. However, preparing to teach these critical skills

Building the Foundation of Letter-Sound Knowledge

goes beyond simply introducing letters and their corresponding sounds. Thoughtful planning, intentional strategies, and a deep understanding of how students learn sounds are essential for effective instruction.

Picture Representation

Being intentional with the pictures we choose to represent sounds is important. The pictures we choose should allow for the purest form of the sound. Take the following pictures in Figures 4.1 and 4.2, for example. In Figure 4.1, when we say the word "grape" the /r/ blend overpowers the /g/ sound. When we say the word "goat" we can clearly hear the /g/ sound in its purest form. Therefore, choosing the picture of a "goat" to represent the /g/ would be a better choice. In Figure 4.2, when we say the word "elephant" the /l/ sound overpowers the /e/ sound, but when we say "edge," we can hear the short /e/ sound in its purest form. Therefore, "edge" would be a better picture representation for the short /e/ sound.

FIGURE 4.1 Comparing picture representations for teaching the /g/ sound.

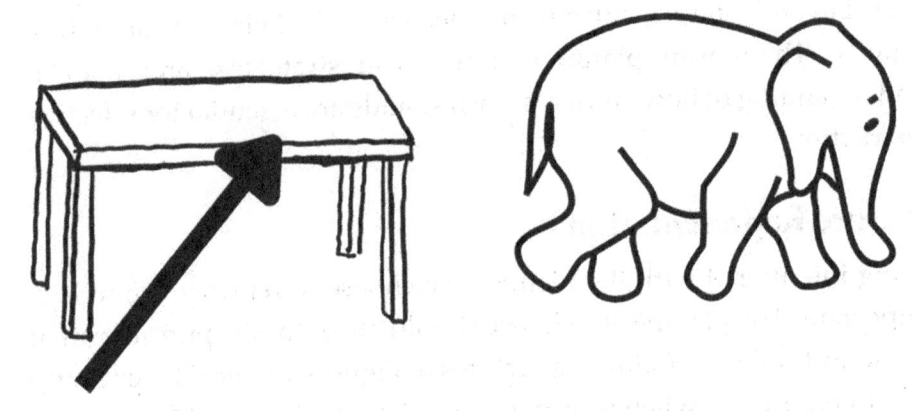

FIGURE 4.2 Comparing picture representations for teaching the /e/ sound.

Consider a Thoughtful Scope and Sequence

Although there is no universally agreed-on scope and sequence for teaching letter-sound relationships, a good sequence will introduce high-utility letters first and encourage word reading as early as possible. A thoughtful scope and sequence ensures that letters are introduced in a way that maximizes students' ability to decode words early in their reading journey. It's crucial to select a scope and sequence that you and your team can agree on. This will ensure consistency across the grade level for students. Next, I'll share some very important things to consider when deciding on or creating a scope and sequence.

Understanding Voiced and Unvoiced Sounds

Voiced sounds occur when your vocal cords vibrate. For example, when saying the sound "g" (as in "go"), placing fingers on the throat will reveal a vibration. Other voiced sounds include "b," "d," "v," and "z."

Unvoiced sounds are made without vocal cord vibration. The letter "f" (as in "fan") is unvoiced. Students can place their hands on their vocal cords to observe the absence of vibration when making this sound. Other unvoiced sounds include "p," "t," "k," and "s" (see Table 4.1).

Table 4.1 Alphabet Voiced and Unvoiced Sounds

Letter	Sound
a	voiced
b	voiced
c (soft)	unvoiced
c (hard)	unvoiced
d	voiced
e	voiced
f	unvoiced
g (soft)	voiced
g (hard)	voiced
h	unvoiced
i	voiced
j	voiced
k	unvoiced
l	voiced
m	voiced
n	voiced
o	voiced
p	unvoiced
q	unvoiced
r	voiced
s	unvoiced
t	unvoiced
u	voiced
v	voiced
w	voiced
x (ks)	unvoiced
x (gz)	voiced
y	voiced
z	voiced

Addressing Voiced and Unvoiced Sounds

Understanding the difference between voiced and unvoiced sounds is crucial for emerging readers. Some letter sounds share almost identical mouth positions. The only difference between these sounds is whether the vocal cords vibrate or not. These are often called "consonant pairs" or "consonant cousins." A student just learning letter sounds can easily confuse these pairs. It is important to remember this when choosing or creating a scope and sequence because teaching sounds with similar articulation close together could confuse students. However, later in instruction, if students are still confusing these consonant pairs, it is essential to help them recognize that the difference in the sounds lies within the vibration of their vocal cords. In Lesson Plan 2, I show how to help students who confuse consonant pairs. Let us take a look at some of these consonant pairs.

Similar Mouth Movements, Different Outcomes

Take a look at some of the consonant pairs shown in Figure 4.3. The tongue, lips, and airflow positions are the same, but the difference lies in whether the vocal cords vibrate. Explicitly teaching students to place their hands on their vocal cords while making these sounds can help them differentiate between voiced and unvoiced sounds. This practice reduces confusion and enhances phonemic awareness, which is critical for recognizing and manipulating individual sounds in words, and makes it easier for them to connect letter names with their corresponding sounds.

Focus on Continuous and Stop Sounds

Instruct students on the difference between continuous sounds (e.g., "m," "s") and stop sounds (e.g., "b," "t") (see Table 4.2). Continuous sounds can be stretched out, which makes them easier for students to hear and manipulate, and stop sounds are more abrupt. Starting with continuous sounds and then gradually introducing stop sounds can help students develop a better understanding of how different sounds function in words. This approach enhances students' phonemic awareness and aids in their ability to blend and segment sounds in words, which is essential for reading and spelling.

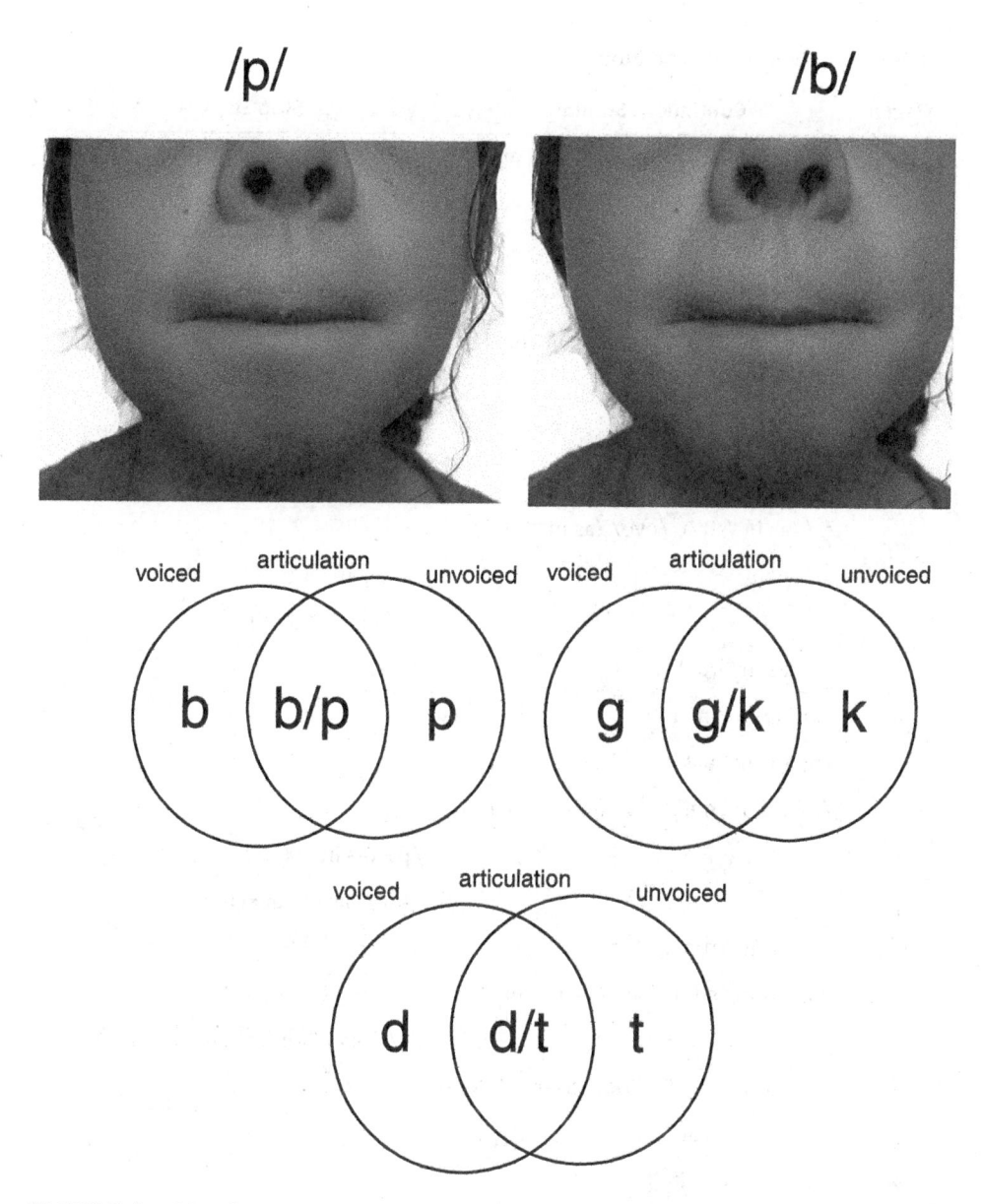

Building the Foundation of Letter-Sound Knowledge

FIGURE 4.3 Mouth movements for consonant pairs.

Table 4.2 Continuous and Stop Sounds

Letter	Continuous Sounds	Stop Sounds
a	/a/ (as in "apple"), /a/ (as in "ape")	
b		/b/ (as in "bat")
c	/s/ (as in "city")	/k/ (as in "cat")
d		/d/ (as in "dog")
e	/e/ (as in "bed"), /ee/ (as in "he")	
f	/f/ (as in "fun")	
g	/zh/ (as in "genre")	/g/ (as in "goat")
h	/h/ (as in "hat")	
i	/i/ (as in "sit"), /eye/ (as in "kite")	
j		/j/ (as in "jump")
k		/k/ (as in "kite")
l	/l/ (as in "lip")	
m	/m/ (as in "man")	
n	/n/ (as in "net")	
o	/o/ (as in "not"), /o/ (as in "go")	
p		/p/ (as in "pan")
q		/kw/ (as in "queen")
r	/r/ (as in "run")	
s	/s/ (as in "sit"), /sh/ (as in "ship")	
t		/t/ (as in "top"), /ch/ (as in "chair")
u	/u/ (as in "cup"), /oo/ (as in "flute")	
v	/v/ (as in "van")	
w	/w/ (as in "win")	
x	/z/ (as in "xylophone") /ks/ (as in "box")	
y	/y/ (as in "yes")	
z	/z/ (as in "zoo")	

Start with High-Utility Letters

As we plan out which letters to introduce and when it's essential to consider high-utility letters (see Table 4.3). High-utility letters like "a," "m," "s," and "t" are letters that students will frequently encounter in the words they read. If we can prioritize these letters early on, we can help ensure students are able to recognize common words quickly and efficiently. This approach enables students to apply what they have learned to real reading situations right away, building confidence and reinforcing the connection between letter-sound knowledge and actual text. Integrating high-utility letters early creates opportunities for immediate success, helping students feel more motivated and engaged as they begin to see their progress in real time.

Group Letters Strategically

Although research has not settled on a specific scope and sequence, it is safe to assume that we need to start simple and move to more complex

Table 4.3 High-Utility Letters Grid

High-Utility Letter	Common Words	Notes
a	cat, hat, bat, mat	Common vowel sound; used in many simple consonant vowel consonant (CVC) words
m	man, mat, map	Commonly used at the beginning of words; easy to blend
s	sat, sun, sip	Often used in early words; provides a clear, continuous sound
t	top, tap, tan	Common in CVC words; stop sound that is easily identified
b	bat, bag, big	Common initial consonant in simple words; easy to blend
r	run, rat, red	Commonly used in early words; continuous sound
n	nap, net, nod	Appears in many simple words; continuous sound
p	pat, pen, pit	Commonly used initial sound; stop sound that is easily identified

patterns. A solid scope and sequence builds the foundation with letter sounds and considers the following:

- **Voiced and unvoiced sounds.** Understanding the difference between voiced and unvoiced sounds (e.g., /b/ versus /p/) is crucial. Teaching consonant pairs carefully can prevent confusion. Help students differentiate these sounds by feeling the vibrations in their vocal cords.
- **Continuous versus stop sounds.** Introducing continuous sounds, like /m/ and /s/, first helps students hear and manipulate sounds more easily. Stop sounds, like /b/ and /t/, are more abrupt, so gradually introducing them helps build phonemic awareness.
- **High-utility letters.** Start with letters that appear frequently in words students will encounter, such as "a," "m," "s," and "t," to encourage early word recognition and reading success.

By keeping these factors in mind, you can create a scope and sequence that lays a strong foundation for students' reading development. I have compiled all that we have discussed in Table 4.4 as a quick reference.

Table 4.4 Strategic Grouping of Letters

Letter Group	Reasons to Group or Avoid Grouping	Examples
Visually similar letters	Avoid introducing them together to prevent visual confusion	b, d, p, q
Phonetically similar letters	Avoid introducing together to prevent auditory confusion	b, p, k, g, v, f
Continuous sounds	Can be held longer, easier for students to hear and manipulate; consider adding continuous sounds in earlier on your scope and sequence	m, s, r, n, l
Stop sounds	Sounds are quick and more abrupt; helps students understand different types of sounds when mixed with continuous sounds	t, b, d, p, k
Mixed grouping	Combines continuous and stop sounds to enhance phonemic awareness	m, t, s, b, r, a

Tips for Teaching Letter Sounds

Teach All Aspects of a Letter Together

When teaching a letter, it's important to cover the letter name, sound, and formation simultaneously. This approach engages multiple parts of the brain, helping students learn letters more quickly and solidify their understanding. By integrating letter-sound instruction with letter formation and articulation (more on that next), students can better connect the sounds they hear with the print on the page, enhancing both their reading and writing skills. This comprehensive approach ensures that students develop a well-rounded understanding of each letter, which is crucial for their overall literacy development (see Figure 4.4).

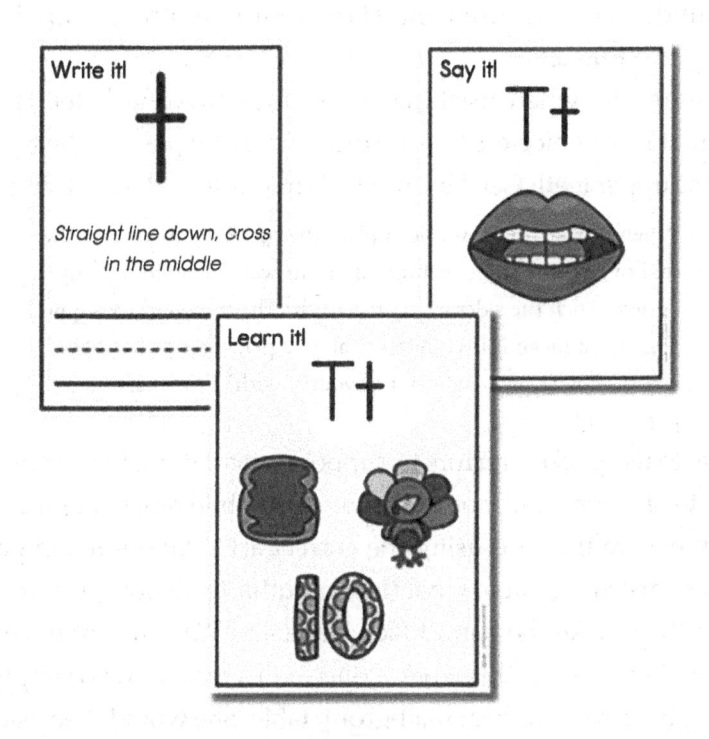

FIGURE 4.4 Integrating letter-sound instruction with letter formation and articulation.

Teach Articulation

When teaching letter sounds, it's crucial for teachers to emphasize articulation—how the mouth, tongue, and lips should move to correctly produce each sound. If students do not learn proper articulation, they may develop habits like adding a *schwa* sound (the "uh" sound) at the end of letters, making sounds like "b" and "t" come out as "buh" and "tuh." This can confuse students when blending sounds later on. Some students may enter our classrooms having already formed this bad habit. This is why it is critical to teach the proper articulation of each sound.

Providing a visual model or picture of the correct mouth position for each sound can make a big difference. When students can see what their mouths are supposed to do—whether it's the placement of the tongue, teeth, or lips—they are better able to produce the sound accurately. This visual aid, combined with clear articulation instruction, helps students form sounds correctly from the start, setting a strong foundation for decoding and fluency.

For example, when teaching the sounds that the letter "t" makes, explain that it is a voiceless "pop" sound made by placing the tongue just behind the upper teeth (see Figure 4.5). It might sound something like this:

> When I make the /t/ sound, I place the tip of my tongue on the roof of my mouth just behind my front teeth. The sides of my tongue touch the sides of my top teeth. The /t/ sound feels quiet. That must mean it is voiceless. Can you give it a try? (/t/.) Do you see how it pops right out of your mouth? That makes it a pop sound!

I love to use pocket mirrors to support articulation. When students are allowed to observe their mouth movements while practicing the sound, it will help ensure they are using the correct articulation. It's important to draw students' attention to what their mouths, teeth, tongues, and lips are doing as they make the sound (see Table 4.5). You do not have to have pocket mirrors to make this work. I once had a teacher who simply placed a full length mirror near her small-group table. She would then ask the kids to practice making the sound one at a time on the day that she introduced it.

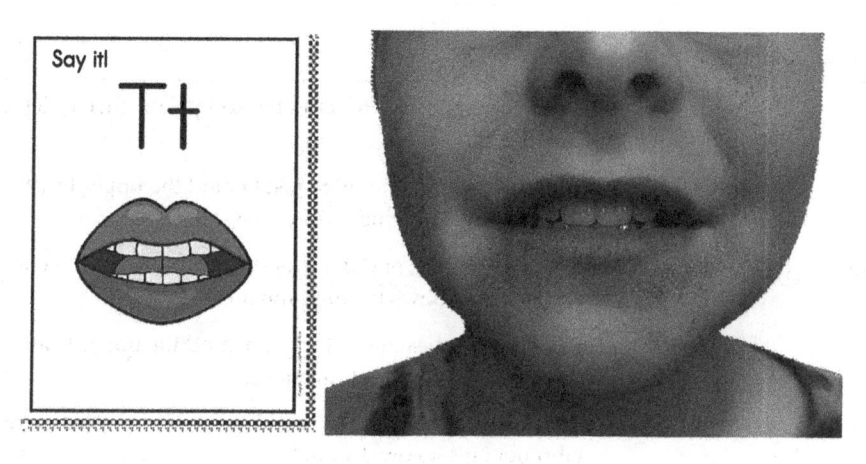

Building the Foundation of Letter-Sound Knowledge   99

FIGURE 4.5 Articulation of the letter sound /t/.

Table 4.5 Letters, Sounds, and Articulation

Letter	Sound	Articulation Description
a	/a/ as in "cat"	The sound is produced by opening the mouth wide; it's a vowel sound, and the air flows freely.
b	/b/ as in "bat"	Lips come together and then release, creating a quick burst of sound.
c	/k/ as in "cat"	The back of the tongue touches the soft palate, then quickly releases.
d	/d/ as in "dog"	The tongue touches the ridge just behind the upper front teeth, then quickly releases.
e	/e/ as in "bed"	The tongue is positioned in the middle of the mouth; it's a vowel sound with free airflow.
f	/f/ as in "fish"	The bottom lip touches the upper teeth, and air is forced out through the gap.
g	/g/ as in "go"	The back of the tongue touches the soft palate, then releases to produce the sound.
h	/h/ as in "hat"	Air flows freely through the open vocal tract; it's a soft, breathy sound.
i	/i/ as in "sit"	The tongue is high in the mouth; it's a vowel sound, and the air flows freely.
j	/j/ as in "jam"	The sound is produced by the tongue touching the ridge just behind the upper front teeth and releasing.

(Continued)

Letter	Sound	Articulation Description
k	/k/ as in "kite"	The back of the tongue touches the soft palate, then quickly releases.
l	/l/ as in "lamp"	The tongue touches the ridge just behind the upper front teeth, with air flowing around the sides.
m	/m/ as in "man"	Lips come together, and the sound is made with vocal cord vibration; air flows through the nose.
n	/n/ as in "net"	The tongue touches the ridge just behind the upper front teeth; air flows through the nose.
o	/o/ as in "not"	The mouth is open, and the sound is made with vocal cord vibration; it's a vowel sound.
p	/p/ as in "pat"	Lips come together and then release, creating a quick burst of sound.
q	/kw/ as in "queen"	The back of the tongue touches the soft palate, then quickly releases, usually combined with a "w" sound.
r	/r/ as in "run"	The tongue is close to the roof of the mouth but not touching; air flows freely.
s	/s/ as in "sit"	The tip of the tongue is close to the ridge just behind the upper front teeth; air flows out sharply.
t	/t/ as in "top"	The tongue touches the ridge just behind the upper front teeth, then quickly releases.
u	/u/ as in "cup"	The tongue is in a central position in the mouth; it's a vowel sound, and the air flows freely.
v	/v/ as in "van"	The bottom lip touches the upper teeth, and air is forced out through the gap.
w	/w/ as in "wet"	Lips are rounded, and the back of the tongue is raised; the sound is a glide.
x	/ks/ as in "box"	The back of the tongue touches the soft palate, then quickly releases, followed by an "s" sound.
y	/y/ as in "yes"	The middle of the tongue is raised toward the roof of the mouth; the sound is a glide.
z	/z/ as in "zip"	The tip of the tongue is close to the ridge just behind the upper front teeth; air flows out sharply.

Establish a Daily Routine

Routine is critical in early literacy instruction. Students and teachers alike thrive with a good routine. The same is true for teaching letter sounds. Establishing a plan for teaching each letter will help ensure everyone is on the same page and that explicit, systematic instruction is taking place. Breaking down your lesson plan into manageable chunks is key. I typically break my phonics lessons into three parts:

1. **Warm-up/cumulative.** This section includes phonemic awareness practices, visual drills, auditory drills, and a vowel intensive.
2. **Explicit teaching.** This section includes direct instruction of the letter sound and ample time to practice.
3. **Application.** This section enables students to apply what they have learned. This can be through games, dictation, reading words in isolation, and so on.

I explore this further in the upcoming chapters. For now, consider what routines you will establish as you begin planning.

Build in Cumulative Review

Building in time for cumulative review is essential. As students are introduced to new sounds, they must continue revisiting the ones they have already learned. This repetition strengthens their ability to recall and apply those sounds when reading and writing. Students may struggle to retain earlier sounds without regular review, which can hinder their ability to blend or decode words effectively. When cumulative review is incorporated daily, students maintain a strong foundation, enabling them to progress confidently through more challenging phonics skills. Cumulative review can be as simple as taking a few minutes to review the sounds your students have learned on flash cards. Simply show students a letter card and ask for the sound.

Apply Student Knowledge

Beyond recognizing individual letter sounds, students need frequent opportunities to apply what they have learned meaningfully. Students can apply their learning through decoding words with the sounds they have learned or using those sounds in writing activities. It is within this practical application where mastery happens. When students use letter sounds to blend words in reading or break apart words during dictation, they are solidifying their understanding of how these sounds work together.

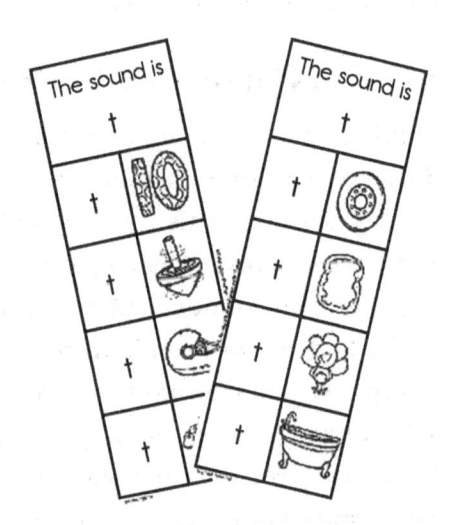

Use Consistent Terminology

Throughout this book, I have discussed the importance of consistency. The same is true for teaching letter sounds. In Table 4.5, I shared some common terms a child might hear during a lesson while learning letter sounds.

If a student is struggling, inconsistent language can add to their confusion. For example, if one teacher says, "This is a voiced sound," and another says, "This is a motor-on sound," it can make the learning process even more challenging for a child struggling to grasp a new concept. Consistency in terminology helps avoid confusion and provides students with a transparent and predictable framework, making learning more accessible and practical. I encourage you to discuss topics like this with your team and parents. Take the following script, for example. This provides explicit instruction for the letter "t." Grade levels, schools, and districts using the same script to introduce letter sounds will build cohesiveness across the board.

> "The letter "Tt" makes the /t/ sound. When I make the /t/ sound, I place the tip of my tongue on the roof of my mouth just behind my front teeth. The sides of my tongue touch the sides of my top teeth. The /t/ sound feels quiet. Can you give it a try?" Give each student a pocket mirror and have them practice making the sound. Correct any incorrect articulation, mispronunciation, or added schwa /tuuuu/.

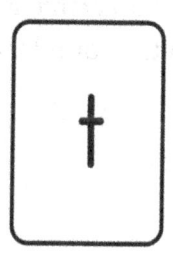

t

Encourage Active Engagement

Engagement is critical to effective learning, especially for young learners. Use active and interactive methods to keep students involved in their learning process. Whether through hands-on activities, games, or multisensory approaches, keeping students engaged helps reinforce their understanding and retention of letter sounds. Active participation in learning activities makes abstract concepts more concrete and accessible, which is crucial for developing foundational solid literacy skills.

In summary, effective letter-sound instruction is grounded in thoughtful planning, consistent practice, and engaging activities that connect learning to real-world reading and writing experiences. By following these practical tips, educators can create a learning environment where students not only learn their letter sounds but also apply them to become proficient readers and writers.

Classroom Implementation Actionable Steps

Lesson Plan 1   Letter Tt

Objective

Students will learn to identify, say, and write the letter "Tt."

Materials Needed

- Visual and sound cards
- Mirrors (for articulation)
- Writing paper, pencils
- Picture cards (objects starting with "t")
- Magnetic letters

Daily Lesson Outline

Warm-Up

Teacher (phoneme blending): "Listen carefully as I say a word slowly. I want you to listen to each sound and then say my word fast—like this: t-i-p. Are you ready?"

(Repeat using words from a growing word list. These words will consist of words made with known letter sounds.)

Visual/Auditory Drill (Choose One)

Visual drill. Show students a stack of known letter sounds. Ask them to say the sound that matches the grapheme on each card. Note: these cards/sounds will be previously taught sounds.

Auditory drill. Tell students to write the letter that corresponds with the sound you make. Example: The sound is /m/ and students write the letter "m." As they are writing the letter "m" they will say "m" /mmmmm/.

(Continued)

Teacher (vowel intensive): "Let us practice our vowel sounds. Point to each sound as we say it together."

Students: a /a/ e /e/ i /i/ o /o/ u /u/

(Then move into the vowel intensive. Use the teacher cheat sheet to support.)

Explicit Teaching

1. **Letter ID.** "Today we are going to learn about the letter 't.'" Show students the Letter ID Visual Card and say, "This is the uppercase 'T' and this is the lowercase 't.' 'T' for /t/ /t/ /toast/." Draw students' attention to the alphabet chart or arch and say, "Can you find this letter on the chart?"

2. **Letter ID.** Lay out several letter tiles or write letters on a whiteboard and say, "Can you help me say this letter three times as we point to it?" Have students point to the letter "Tt" cards and say it three times.

3. **Articulation.** Say, "The letter 'Tt' makes the /t/ sound as in 'toast.' When I make the /t/ sound, my teeth and lips are slightly open and my tongue hits the top of my mouth and pops down right behind my teeth. If I touch my throat, I cannot feel a vibration. /t/ is a stop sound, which means it pops and stops. We call them pop sounds. Can you give it a try?" Give each student a pocket mirror and have them practice making the sound. Correct any incorrect articulation, mispronunciation, or added schwa.

4. **Sound ID.** Sort pictures to find the ones that begin with the /t/ sound. Show students several pictures and say: "Let us listen to see if we hear the /t/ sound in any of these pictures." Model the first few. "This is a picture of a box. Do you hear the /t/ sound at the beginning?" Have students answer. If they hear the sound at the beginning, place it under /t/. If the picture does not have the /t/ sound, place it in the trashcan (trashcan template provided at literacyedvnetures.com/literacy-unlocked).

5. **Find letter sounds.** Say "Let us practice some more." Give students the sound practice strip and ask them to touch each picture as they practice the sound.

6. **Letter formation.** Say "Now, let us practice writing this letter. Did you know that the way we write our letters is very important? It's true! Watch as I write this letter. I came up with a little chant to help us remember how to write it. Start at the top line, straight stick down, cross on the dotted line." Model letter formation a few times and then ask students to practice. Provide multiple opportunities that apply to the senses (table writing, sand writing, sky writing, etc.) as students are practicing, and have them repeat the chant. Then provide students with piece of paper and have them practice writing the letter this time and as they form the letter ask them to say the sound.

Application of Skills
Fluency sound practice. Ask students to point to the letters and say each sound (/i/, /t/, /n/).
Dictation sound practice. Ask students to write the letters that represent the following sounds (/i/, /t/, /n/).

Lesson Plan 2   Articulation Confusion

Objective
Students will learn to discriminate among consonant pairs.

Materials Needed
- Pocket mirrors
- Articulation cards
- Picture cards

(Continued)

Lesson Outline

Consonant pairs (g/k—p/b—t/d—s/z—v/f) can be tricky for students. We often see this confusion when blending and writing. If you notice that students are confusing these sounds, try this lesson.

Teacher: "Today, we will talk about two very similar sounds. These two sounds feel alike when we say them. The difference is that one vibrates our vocal chords, and the other does not. We are going to practice telling the difference today. Say /f/."

Students: /f/

Teacher: "Great! Now, look in the mirror, what are your lips, mouth, teeth, and tongue doing when you make that sound?"

(Have students notice the articulation.)

Teacher: "The /f/ sound is continuous, which means that it is a sound you can hold on to it. Let us feel our vocal chords. Is our motor on or off when we make the /f/ sound?"

(You can also say "stretch" and model with a slinky or something stretchy while saying the sound to model that hold.)

Students: "Now say /v/."

Teacher: /v/

(Repeat the previous steps. Students should notice they make the same articulatory gesture, but when they feel the vocal cords, they vibrate. It might be helpful to have a visual like the following to help students notice the difference.)

> (Once students understand the two sounds move to a phonemic awareness lesson.)
>
> *Teacher:* "Say 'live' (long 'i') now say 'life.'"
> *Students:* "live, life"
> *Teacher:* "What's the difference?" (Draw their attention to the difference.) "Let us sound it out: /l/ /i/ /v/.
> *Student:* /l/ /i/ /v/
> *Teacher:* "What sound do you hear at the end?"
> *Students:* /v/
> *Teacher:* "Yes! What makes the /v/ sound?" (Refer to the pictures and say:) "Write the sound you hear at the end of the word live /v/."
>
> (Continue as needed.)

Five Key Takeaways from Chapter 4

- **The alphabetic principle is the cornerstone of literacy.** Mastery of the alphabetic principle is essential for early reading success. It equips students with the understanding that letters and letter combinations represent sounds in spoken language, enabling them to decode and spell words independently.

- **Research supports combining letter name and sound instruction.** Studies show that teaching letter names and sounds together significantly enhances letter-sound acquisition. This combined approach strengthens students' ability to connect letters to their sounds and accelerates their literacy development.

- **Intentional planning and scope matter.** A thoughtful and strategic scope and sequence for introducing letter-sound relationships ensures that students can begin decoding words early. Prioritizing high-utility letters and teaching voiced/unvoiced and continuous/stop sounds in a systematic way prevents confusion and builds a strong foundation.

- **Phonemic awareness enhances letter-sound learning.** Phonemic awareness plays a vital role in helping students learn letter sounds, especially when paired with knowledge of letter names. Explicit teaching of articulation, such as distinguishing voiced and unvoiced sounds or continuous and stop sounds, reinforces students' understanding of how sounds function in words.
- **Consistent and engaging instruction is key.** Effective letter-sound instruction relies on explicit, systematic teaching paired with active engagement. Using consistent terminology, visual aids, and multisensory techniques across educators ensures students internalize letter-sound relationships, setting them up for reading and writing success.

CHAPTER FIVE

From Letter Sounds to Decoding

In previous chapters, we laid a strong foundation in letter-sound knowledge and phonemic awareness, which are essential for reading success. However, recognizing letter names and sounds is not the ultimate goal—decoding words is where real reading begins. The transition from learning letter sounds to blending words like simple consonant vowel consonant (CVC) words can be challenging at first, but it is a crucial step in students' literacy journey.

Moving from reading sounds in isolation to reading CVC words fluently requires a combination of phonemic awareness and systematic phonics instruction. In this chapter, we explore the importance of phonemic awareness and letter-sound mastery and how to apply these skills to begin decoding words. We'll also dive into research-based strategies for helping students make this critical transition.

The Research

Decades of research highlight the critical role of systematic phonics instruction in early literacy development. When done well, phonics instruction helps students understand the relationship between the sounds they hear and the letters they see.

Ehri (2004) emphasizes that teachers need a strong understanding of letter sound knowledge, phonemic awareness, and word reading to provide effective instruction. Letter-sound knowledge is the cornerstone of early literacy, enabling children to connect written symbols (letters) to their corresponding sounds. This understanding is crucial for decoding unfamiliar words, which builds word recognition over time and lays the foundation for fluency. Ehri (2004) stresses that phonemic awareness—the ability to hear, manipulate, and isolate sounds—enables students to grasp how sounds map to letters, supporting reading and spelling.

Ehri (2004) advocates for explicit, systematic phonics instruction, in which letter-sound correspondences are taught sequentially, progressing from simpler to more complex patterns. This structured approach ensures that students build a strong foundation by first mastering basic sounds and then advancing to more complex letter combinations like blends and digraphs. Additionally, Ehri (2004) highlights the importance of practice through meaningful reading and writing activities, reinforcing students' ability to decode and spell words and transitioning them toward fluency.

Erbeli et al. (2023) conducted a meta-analysis on the optimal cumulative dose of early phonemic awareness instruction. Their research shows that a specific amount of instruction is critical to ensuring students master letter-sound correspondences. Erbeli et al. (2023) discovered a threshold after which students show significantly better reading outcomes. The research suggests that consistent, moderate doses of phonemic awareness instruction, spread over time, are more effective than condensed, intensive bursts. This cumulative approach provides students the practice they need to internalize and apply skills in reading and writing contexts.

These studies underscore the importance of explicit, systematic instruction in letter-sound knowledge and phonemic awareness, coupled with consistent practice and optimal instruction dosage, to support early literacy development.

Wrap-Up of the Research

Ehri. (2004). "What Teachers Need to Know and Do to Teach Letter-Sounds, Phonemic Awareness, Word Reading, and Phonics."

- **Systematic instruction.** Teach phonics in a logical order, starting with simple sounds and moving to more complex patterns like blends and digraphs.
- **Letter-sound knowledge.** Build a strong foundation by ensuring students know their letter sounds inside and out—it's the first step to fluent reading.
- **Phonemic awareness.** Teach students how to break words into sounds and manipulate those sounds. This helps them understand how letters and sounds fit together, making reading and spelling easier.
- **Practice makes perfect.** Give students plenty of opportunities to apply what they learn through reading and writing activities. The more practice, the better they'll get at decoding words.

Erbeli et al. (2023). "A Meta-Analysis on the Optimal Cumulative Dosage of Early Phonemic Awareness Instruction."

- **Optimal dosage.** Do not overwhelm students with too much phonemic awareness practice at once. Instead, sprinkle it into your daily routine, giving students regular practice over time.
- **Consistent practice.** Focus on cumulative practice. Students need to revisit and strengthen skills to internalize them fully.
- **Reading outcomes.** There's a sweet spot for how much phonemic awareness instruction works best. When students get the right amount of consistent practice, their reading skills skyrocket!

Practical Tips for Implementation

Transitioning from recognizing individual letter sounds to blending CVC words is crucial in early literacy development. This process requires more than just letter recognition; it involves the ability to hear and manipulate sounds at the phonemic level. Phonemic awareness practice—such as isolating, segmenting, and blending sounds—lays the foundation by helping students understand how sounds work together to form words. Without these strong phonemic awareness skills, students may struggle to blend the sounds together while decoding.

At the same time, systematic phonics instruction also plays an essential role in guiding students through applying sound knowledge to print. Phonics instruction introduces the predictable relationships between letters and sounds, helping students recognize patterns such as CVC structures. By integrating these two approaches—explicit phonemic awareness activities alongside structured phonics lessons—students can move from simply identifying sounds to confidently blending them into words. This combination of skills is essential for building a strong foundation in decoding and word recognition.

Moving Beyond Letter Sounds

As students begin to make the sound-to-symbol connection, they need to practice blending these sounds to form simple consonant vowel (CV), vowel consonant (VC), and CVC patterns. The focus during this phase is to help students become aware of the individual phonemes in words they have learned and recognize that these sounds combine to form meaningful words they can understand and use.

The key to a successful transition from letter sounds to word formation is making the process natural and engaging for students. As teachers, we can model decoding through blending techniques to demonstrate how individual sounds come together to make up the words we speak. We can begin by practicing familiar words or chunks and gradually introduce more challenging ones. With consistent practice and modeling, students will develop the ability to decode words independently.

Strategies to Support the Connection

Blending sounds into words is a cornerstone of early reading success, but it can be a challenging skill for many young learners. With thoughtfully designed scaffolds, we can guide students step-by-step from recognizing individual sounds to fluently blending them into words. This resource provides a comprehensive framework for mastering blending through effective techniques like VC blending, CV blending, successive blending with word pyramids, and continuous blending.

Each method is designed to meet students where they are, addressing common challenges while building confidence and fluency. By incorporating explicit modeling, scaffolded instruction, and plenty of practice, these techniques equip teachers to support every learner on their journey to becoming a proficient reader.

Sound Boxes for Phoneme Segmentation

Sound boxes are an excellent tool for teaching students to segment and blend sounds in a structured and visual way. To begin, it's helpful to start with oral practice. Ask students to push a manipulative, like a chip or counter, into a box for each sound they hear in a word. For example, in the word "cat," students would push one chip for each sound: /c/, /a/, and /t/. This exercise helps students focus on hearing and identifying individual phonemes in a word, reinforcing their phonemic awareness skills. It also gives them a hands-on way to engage with sound segmentation, making the abstract concept of phonemes more tangible.

The six-box grid is designed to help students segment words into individual sounds. This grid provides a visual and tactile way to reinforce phoneme awareness. Here are the instructions for how to use the grid:

1. Ask students to place one chip in each bottom box of the grid.
2. Say a word, such as "cat."

3. As students hear each sound, they push one chip into the corresponding top box:
   - /c/ → Push the first chip up into the first top box.
   - /a/ → Push the second chip up into the middle top box.
   - /t/ → Push the third chip up into the final top box.
4. After all chips have been moved, students blend the sounds together to say the full word: "cat."
5. As students progress, they can begin replacing the chips with letters, writing each sound in the bottom boxes to reinforce letter sound connections.

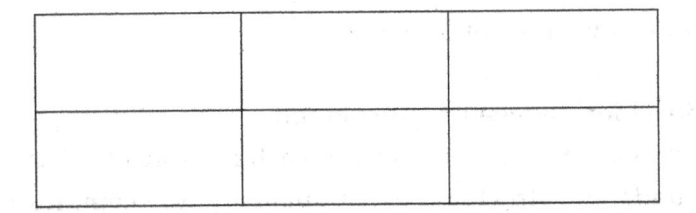

Once students are confident in their ability to orally segment sounds using the boxes, you can introduce magnetic letters to connect these sounds to print. This next step helps students see the relationship between the sounds they are hearing and the letters that represent those sounds. By placing the corresponding letters in the boxes, students begin to understand the link between phonemes and graphemes, moving from sound segmentation to word building. Using manipulatives to build phonemic awareness and then transitioning to magnetic letters can help young learners connect sounds to letters, supporting their move from phonemic awareness to decoding.

Model Blending
Blending is a crucial skill in early reading that requires explicit modeling. Blending activities help students understand how sounds come

together to form words. When introducing new words, it's important to break down each sound slowly and distinctly. For example, with the word "ran," you would sound out each phoneme—/r/ ... /a/ ... /n/—pausing between each one.

As you repeat the process, gradually speed up the pace until the full word is blended smoothly. This method enables students to hear and see the blending process in action, giving them a clear and concrete example to imitate. Modeling this step-by-step approach is key for students to understand how individual phonemes merge to form a whole word.

Once students have observed the blending process, chorally blend words to help solidify their understanding. Start by blending sounds slowly, and progressively speed up as they become more comfortable. Repeated practice will help them internalize the rhythm and flow of blending, eventually leading to automaticity in word recognition. This gradual release reinforces their confidence in blending sounds, making the transition to fluent reading smoother and more natural. Providing students with ongoing opportunities to practice blending not only strengthens their decoding skills but also sets the foundation for future reading success.

VC Blending

VC blending begins by focusing on the vowel sound and blending it into the following consonant, such as combining "a" and "t" to form "at" in the word "bat." This approach is especially helpful for students who struggle with vowels, as it enables them to focus on common and familiar VC patterns like "at" or "up." By breaking the word into manageable chunks, students can more easily see how vowels work in combination with consonants, which can be challenging for early readers. This technique provides a solid foundation for recognizing word patterns and building confidence in blending sounds.

Once students have mastered the basic VC pattern, you can challenge them to add an initial consonant to complete the word. For example, after blending "at," students can add the /b/ sound to create "bat." This step helps them apply their knowledge of blending in a more complex context and introduces them to the concept of word families. Word families such as "cat," "bat," and "sat" enable students to practice VC blending in multiple words, reinforcing the patterns they are learning. Through repetition and practice, students gain fluency in blending and become more comfortable decoding words independently.

Blend these word parts				
ag	ip	ed	ot	eb

CV Blending

CV blending is an effective technique in which students first focus on blending a consonant with a following vowel to form a simple syllable, such as "ba" or "ma." This approach simplifies the blending process by introducing sound pairings frequently occurring in words, making it more intuitive for early readers. By concentrating on just the initial consonant and vowel, students can grasp the concept of blending without being overwhelmed by a full word.

Once students become confident with these CV pairings, they can blend in the final consonant, completing words like "bat" or "map." This gradual approach, from CV blending to full word blending, allows for manageable steps that build students' fluency and confidence.

Research supports CV blending, especially in the early stages of reading instruction, because it aligns with how the brain processes speech sounds and syllable structures. Studies in phonological awareness and early reading development emphasize the importance of focusing on smaller sound units before advancing to more complex patterns. According to Ehri's phases of word recognition development, teaching students to blend CV units supports their transition from partial alphabetic to full alphabetic reading, where they can decode entire words fluently (Ehri, 1995, 2004).

Blend these word parts				
ma	pi	ve	do	hu

Successive Blending

Successive blending is an effective strategy that simplifies the blending process by breaking it down into smaller, more manageable steps. This method involves presenting a word in a pyramid form, starting with just the first sound of the word. For example, if teaching the word "cat," you would begin with the /c/ sound. Once the student is comfortable with the initial sound, you add the second sound, blending the first two sounds together (e.g., /ca/). Finally, the student blends all the sounds to form the complete word, "cat." By breaking down the word in this step-by-step manner, successive blending helps students focus on one part of the word at a time, making the process less overwhelming.

This scaffolding approach is particularly beneficial for struggling readers who may find it difficult to blend all the sounds at once. By gradually building the word from smaller segments, successive blending enables students to develop their blending skills incrementally, leading to greater accuracy and confidence. As students gain more practice with this technique, they will eventually be able to blend sounds more fluidly, improving their ability to decode words independently. Successive blending provides the support that struggling readers need to master this critical reading skill in a way that feels manageable and achievable.

Blend these words				
c	h	r	p	b
ca	hi	re	po	bu
cat	hip	red	pod	bug

Continuous Blending

Continuous blending is a technique where each sound in a word is stretched out and blended smoothly without any pauses between the sounds. For example, when teaching the word "mat," the teacher would model by saying "mmmmmaaaaat" in a continuous flow, rather than breaking up the sounds. This approach helps students hear how the sounds blend together into a complete word, making it easier for them to understand the flow of phonemes. By eliminating pauses, continuous blending prevents students from forgetting the first sound or losing track of the word's structure as they move through each phoneme. It's a particularly helpful method for beginners or students who struggle with traditional blending techniques.

Starting with simple CVC words is key to mastering continuous blending. Teachers should exaggerate the sounds initially, stretching them out to give students a clear understanding of how the sounds flow together. As students become more comfortable and familiar with the blending process, the exaggeration can gradually be reduced until they can blend the sounds fluently without needing to slow down as much. Continuous blending not only reinforces phonemic awareness but also strengthens students' ability to decode words more smoothly, ultimately contributing to their overall reading fluency.

Blend these words				
map	pin	vet	dog	hut

Helping students transition from recognizing individual letter sounds to blending CVC words is critical in developing early reading skills. This process requires a thoughtful combination of phonemic awareness practice and systematic phonics instruction. Phonemic awareness helps students understand how sounds work together in spoken language, and phonics instruction teaches them to connect those sounds to letters and blend them into words. Together, these approaches provide a solid foundation for reading fluency. By focusing on these blending techniques, teachers can help students develop the ability to smoothly and confidently blend sounds, a key skill needed for early reading success. Each method targets different challenges students may face when learning to decode words, making the process accessible and effective for all learners.

The importance of explicit modeling cannot be overstated. When teachers model blending techniques—such as CV, VC, and CVC patterns—they demonstrate how sounds come together to form words. This step-by-step demonstration is particularly valuable for students who struggle with decoding, as it makes the abstract process of blending more concrete. For example, breaking down words like "bat" or "cat" into their individual sounds (/b/ /a/ /t/ or /c/ /a/ /t/) and blending them together provide a clear visual and auditory example for students to imitate. Students will begin to internalize these processes with consistent practice and become more confident in blending sounds independently.

Through consistent practice, scaffolded instruction, and explicit modeling, teachers can provide all learners with the support they need to master the essential skill of blending sounds into words. Each technique—whether VC, CV, or CVC blending; Elkonin boxes; or successive and continuous blending—serves as a stepping stone toward fluent reading. By addressing the individual challenges students may face and offering targeted instruction, teachers can help students bridge the gap between sound recognition and automatic word reading, ultimately setting the foundation for long-term reading success. Students will gain the confidence and skills needed to become proficient readers with patience, repetition, and the right strategies.

Lesson Plan 1   Continuous Blending

Objective
Students will practice continuous blending of CVC words to develop smooth decoding skills.

Materials Needed
- Picture cards with simple CVC words (e.g., map, sat, can, fad, nap)
- Whiteboard and markers

Scripted Lesson Plan

1. Introduction (One Minute)

Teacher: "Today, we are going to practice something called 'continuous blending.' This means we'll blend sounds slowly, moving from one sound to the next without a pause, to help us read words smoothly."

Teacher: "Let me show you how it works. I'm going to use the word 'map' as an example. Listen carefully as I blend the sounds together without stopping between them."

(On the board, write the word "map" and point to each letter as you blend the sounds.)

Teacher: "Watch and listen: 'mmmmmaaaap.' Notice how I move from one sound to the next slowly and smoothly. This helps us hear how the sounds connect to form the word. Now, you'll get to try it with some words of your own!"

2. Blending Practice (Two Minutes)

Teacher: "I'm going to show you a picture card, and we'll practice continuous blending together. Let us start with the word 'sat.'"

(Hold up a picture card with "sat" and write the word on the board. Point to each letter as you blend the sounds.)

Teacher: "Let us stretch each sound slowly, connecting them like this: 'ssssaaaat.' Notice how I did not stop between the sounds. Now it's your turn!"

(Choose a student to pick a picture card and read the word using continuous blending.)

Teacher: "Great job! Remember to stretch the sounds smoothly without rushing. Who's next?"

(Continue with each student, guiding them through the process, and providing gentle reminders to connect sounds continuously without pauses.)

Example words and prompts:

- "map"—"mmmmmaaaap"
- "sat"—"ssssaaaat"
- "can"—"cccaaaan"
- "fad"—"fffaaad"
- "nap"—"nnnnaaap"

Teacher: "Remember, keep moving from one sound to the next without any breaks!"

3. Conclusion (One Minute)

Teacher: "You all did an amazing job with continuous blending! Can anyone share one of the words they practiced blending today?"

(Continued)

(Have a few students share and provide praise for their efforts.)

Teacher: "Stretching the sounds slowly and continuously helped us hear the entire word without stopping. This will make reading easier and smoother. Keep practicing, and soon you'll be blending words with confidence."

Teacher: "Fantastic work, everyone! Continuous blending is a great skill that will help you read more and more words smoothly."

Lesson Plan 2   VC Blending

Objective
Students will practice blending vowels with final consonants to build fluency with VC word parts.

Materials Needed
- Word part cards with simple VC patterns (e.g., ap, ad, it, etc.)

Word Parts for Practice
ap, ad, it, in, et, ed., og, op, un, ud

Scripted Lesson Plan

1. Introduction (One Minute)
Teacher: "Today, we are going to practice blending word parts by focusing on just two sounds at a time. Instead of blending three sounds, we'll start by blending the vowel with the last sound."

(Show students the word part card "at" and point to each letter as you blend the sounds.)

Teacher: "Listen as I blend this word part. I'll hold onto the vowel sound and move smoothly into the last sound: /aaaaat/ . . .'at.' Did you hear how the sounds connected together without stopping? This makes blending a little easier."

(Demonstrate with a few other word part cards, such as "ap" and "ad," blending slowly and emphasizing the smooth connection between the vowel and consonant.)

Teacher: "Now, I'm going to give each of you a set of word part cards to practice blending. You'll practice stretching the vowel into the ending sound, just like I did."

2. Blending Practice (Three Minutes)

Teacher: "I'll start by showing a word part card, and we'll blend the sounds together slowly and smoothly. Let us take it one step at a time!"

1. Word Part: "ap"

Teacher: "Let us start with the word part 'ap.' I'll say each sound slowly, and I want you to listen carefully. Ready? /aaaa … p/. Did you hear how I stretched out the 'a' sound and smoothly joined it with the 'p' sound?"

(Hold up the "ap" word part card and point to each letter as you blend.)

Teacher: "Now, let us try it together. Stretch out the 'a' sound and connect it with the 'p': /aaaa … p/. Good! Say it with me again: /aaaa … p/."

(Students echo the blending as you say it slowly.)

2. Word Part: "ad"

Teacher: "Now, let us move on to 'ad.' I'll start first: /aaaa … d/. Notice how I did not stop between sounds? I went straight from the 'a' sound to the 'd' sound."

(Hold up the "ad" word part card and model the blending again.)

Teacher: "Your turn! Stretch out the 'a' sound and slide it right into the 'd': /aaaa … d/. Let us try it together a few times—/aaaa … d/."

(Repeat with students, ensuring they blend smoothly without pausing.)

3. Word Part: "in"

Teacher: "Here's the next one: 'in.' I'll go first—/iiii … n/. Notice how the 'i' sound keeps going right into the 'n' without stopping."

(Continued)

(Model with the "in" word part card.)

Teacher: "Now your turn! Let us stretch out the 'i' sound and blend it into the 'n': /iiii ... n/. Great! One more time together: /iiii ... n/."

(Encourage students to focus on the smooth connection between sounds.)

Note: Have students practice blending the remaining word parts (et, ed, og, op, un, ud) on their own or with a partner, focusing on keeping the blending smooth and continuous.

3. Conclusion (One Minute)

Teacher: "You all did a fantastic job blending word parts today! Blending the vowel and final consonant helps us hear the sounds clearly, making reading smoother.

Can anyone share one word part they blended today? What sounds did you blend together?"

(Have a few students share their word parts, providing positive reinforcement for their efforts.)

Teacher: "Great work, everyone! Practicing with word parts is a helpful way to get better at blending. Keep practicing, and soon blending will feel even more natural!"

Lesson Plan 3   Modeling Blending

Objective

Students will observe and practice modeling the blending process to decode CVC words.

Materials Needed

- Whiteboard and markers
- Letter cards for each sound in CVC words (e.g., b, i, n, a, t, m, e, p, g, r)

Scripted Lesson Plan

1. Introduction (One Minute)

Teacher: "Today, we are going to learn a way to blend sounds together to read words. First, you'll watch me model the blending process so you can see how I do it. After that, you'll get to try it on your own!"

Teacher: "I'll show you how to slowly blend the sounds in a word, connecting each one until we can read the whole word smoothly. Watch and listen closely, because soon it'll be your turn!"

2. Blending Practice (Three Minutes)

Teacher: "Let us start with a word. I'll pick the word 'bin.' Watch as I say each sound one by one, and then blend them together."

(On the whiteboard, write the letters "b," "i," and "n" or use letter cards for each sound. Point to each letter as you say the sounds.)

Teacher: "/b/... /i/... /n/... Now, I'll put them together a little faster: 'bin.' See how I started slow and then brought the sounds together to make the word?"

Teacher: "Now, I'll make just one change to the word. Let us turn 'bin' into 'ban' by changing the middle sound. Watch carefully: /b/... /a/... /n/... And now faster: 'ban.' Can you hear the difference?"

(Move to the next word, "bat," and repeat the process of changing just one sound each time.)

3. Practice Words Sequence (Three Minutes)

- bin → ban → bat → mat
- mat → met → men → pen
- pen → pin → pig → rig

Teacher: "Each time, I'm changing just one sound, which helps us hear how the word changes. Now it's your turn! I'll pass out some letter cards. Choose a

(Continued)

word from the cards, say each sound slowly just like I did, and then blend them together to say the full word."

(Have students work with letter cards, guiding them through blending sounds and reminding them to change only one sound at a time as they practice.)

4. Conclusion (One Minute)
Teacher: "Great job, everyone! Let us talk about how modeling helped us. Did watching me blend the sounds slowly and then speed up help you understand the process?"

(Encourage a few students to share how the modeling helped them, and provide positive reinforcement for their insights.)

Teacher: "Breaking down the sounds and then bringing them together helps us read words more easily. Keep practicing this method, and soon you'll be blending words on your own with confidence!"

Lesson Plan 4   Sound Boxes for Phoneme Segmentation

Objective
Students will practice phoneme segmentation by using sound boxes to map sounds to letters.

Materials Needed
- Sound boxes (one set per student)
- Chips or counters
- Magnetic letters or letter tiles
- Dry erase boards and markers

Scripted Lesson Plan

1. Introduction (One Minute)

Teacher: "Today, we are going to use sound boxes to help us break words into individual sounds. This will help us hear each sound in a word clearly."

Teacher: "Watch as I show you how to do this with the word 'cat.' I'll say each sound in the word and pull a chip into each box for every sound."

(Demonstrate by saying /c/ /a/ /t/ while pulling a chip down into each box for each sound.)

Teacher: "See how I moved a chip into a box for each sound? Now you'll get to try this with your own sound boxes and chips."

2. Phoneme Segmentation Practice (Two Minutes)

Teacher: "Let us practice with another word. This time, I'll use the word 'dog.' Watch as I say each sound and pull down a chip for each one."

(Say the word "dog" slowly and pull a chip down for each sound: /d/ ... /o/ ... /g/.)

Teacher: "Now, I want you to try this with your sound boxes and chips. Choose a word from the list, say each sound slowly, and pull down a chip for each sound."

(Give students time to practice with their own boxes and chips, providing guidance and feedback as they segment words like "dog," "sun," or "top.")

3. Sound-to-Letter Mapping (Two Minutes)

Teacher: "Now that we have practiced breaking words into sounds, let us take it one step further by replacing each chip with a letter. This will help us see how each sound is connected to a letter."

Teacher: "Watch as I replace the first chip in 'dog' with the letter 'd' for the sound /d/. Then I'll replace the next chip with 'o' for /o/, and the last one with 'g' for /g/."

(Continued)

(Replace each chip in "dog" with the corresponding lowercase letters, saying the sound as you place each letter.)

Teacher: "Now, try this on your own sound boxes. Replace each chip with the lowercase letter that matches the sound you hear. For example, if your word is 'cat,' you'd replace the chips with 'c', 'a,' and 't.' Let us go through a few more words together."

(Guide students through replacing chips with lowercase letters for words like "cat," "bat," and "rug," reinforcing the sound-to-letter connection.)

4. Conclusion (One Minute)

Teacher: "You all did an excellent job breaking words into sounds and mapping those sounds to letters! Can anyone share one of the words they segmented today?"

(Have a few students share a word they worked on and provide positive reinforcement.)

Teacher: "Using sound boxes to map sounds to letters helps us read and write words. Every time you practice, you are building strong reading skills!"

Teacher: "Great work today! Keep practicing, and soon these sounds and letters will feel natural."

Transitioning Students from Letter Sounds to Reading Words

Moving students from recognizing letter sounds to confidently reading CVC words is a critical step in early literacy development. Teachers play a key role in this process by combining phonemic awareness and systematic phonics instruction with effective blending strategies and consistent practice. These elements work together to ensure that all students, including those who may struggle, are supported in their literacy journey.

Five Key Takeaways from Chapter 5

- **Phonemic awareness is foundational.** Helping students isolate, blend, and manipulate sounds builds the foundation for decoding words. This prepares them to connect sounds to written text.

- **Explicit and systematic phonics instruction.** Introducing letter-sound correspondences in a logical sequence enables students to apply their phonemic awareness skills directly to reading.

- **Blending techniques bridge the gap.** Strategies like continuous blending, successive blending, and VC blending provide practical tools for transitioning from sounds to words.

- **Modeling and consistent practice reinforce skills.** Demonstrating blending and decoding shows students how sounds combine to form words. Tools such as Elkonin boxes and word pyramids offer structured practice to build fluency.

- **Scaffolding for struggling students.** Differentiated instruction, such as breaking blending into smaller steps or focusing on word families, makes the process accessible and builds confidence for all learners.

CHAPTER SIX

Building Strong Readers Through Systematic Phonics

Research has shown that phonics instruction must be explicit, systematic, and cumulative for students to develop strong decoding skills. According to the National Institute of Child Health and Human Development (2020), explicit phonics instruction teaches the rules and patterns of the English language, helping students understand how sounds are represented by letters and how to apply these patterns when reading words. A systematic approach begins with simple phonics patterns, such as consonant vowel consonant (CVC) words, and gradually moves to more complex ones, ensuring that foundational skills are mastered before introducing new concepts.

RESEARCH INDICATES that early reading instruction should place a stronger emphasis on the code (phonics) before focusing on meaning-based approaches.

Studies have shown that focusing on phonics in the early stages of reading development leads to better outcomes by fourth grade. When students have a strong foundation in phonics and are able to decode words fluently, they can shift their attention to comprehension and tackle more complex text with ease.

In this chapter, we'll explore strategies that will support students and their ability to decode, offering research-based methods for phonics instruction that are practical and easy to implement.

We'll examine what the research says about systematic phonics instruction and why it's critical to student success. We'll also dig into the nuts and bolts of implementation, answering questions like these:

- What activities will engage my students?
- How can I make lessons effective and efficient?
- What does research say about best practices for teaching phonics?

What the Research Says

The foundation of effective reading instruction lies in evidence-based practices that support the development of foundational literacy skills. Decades of research have demonstrated that explicit, systematic instruction is essential for helping students develop the ability to decode words, comprehend text, and achieve reading fluency. By focusing on approaches backed by scientific studies, educators can provide all students, including those at risk for reading difficulties, with the tools they need for success.

Systematic phonics instruction, in particular, has emerged as a critical component of early literacy development. Studies consistently highlight its effectiveness in teaching students to recognize letter-sound correspondences, decode unfamiliar words, and build the skills necessary for independent reading. This research not only informs best practices for classroom instruction but also underscores the importance of a structured, sequential approach to teaching foundational reading skills.

The National Reading Panel of the National Institute of Child Health and Human Development (2000) conducted a comprehensive review of evidence-based research to assess the effectiveness of various reading instructional methods, including systematic and explicit phonics instruction. The study analyzed how these methods influence students' reading achievement and literacy development. The findings revealed that explicit and systematic phonics instruction significantly benefits early reading development, particularly for beginning readers and at-risk students. The panel reviewed both synthetic phonics (teaching students to blend individual letter sounds to form words) and analytic phonics (teaching students to analyze whole words and recognize patterns without isolating individual sounds) and found that systematic phonics instruction, whether synthetic or analytic, leads to better reading outcomes than methods relying on incidental or opportunistic instruction.

The results highlight the importance of using systematic instruction that builds on students' existing knowledge (e.g., progressing from simple consonant vowel consonant words to more complex patterns) and follows a sequential, structured progression designed to enhance mastery over time.

Linnea Ehri et al. (2001) evaluated numerous studies on systematic phonics instruction to determine its effectiveness compared to other methods. They found that phonics instruction had a robust positive impact on reading skills, especially for young learners and struggling readers. It examined how systematic phonics programs, when taught explicitly, helped students in learning to decode unfamiliar words and develop better reading comprehension.

The study reinforced the idea that a structured approach to phonics, which involves teaching letter-sound correspondences in a sequential and systematic manner, leads to significant gains in literacy achievement, particularly for students in kindergarten and first grade.

Foorman et al. (1998) focused on at-risk children and compared different methods of reading instruction, including systematic and explicit phonics instruction. The results revealed that children who received systematic phonics instruction showed greater gains in word reading, spelling, and overall literacy development than those taught through other methods, such as whole-language approaches. The study particularly emphasized the effectiveness of early intervention with systematic phonics instruction for preventing reading difficulties in students who are at risk of failure. The study provided clear evidence that systematic phonics is not only beneficial for average students but also crucial for supporting those who struggle with early reading.

Wrap-Up of the Research

National Institute of Child Health and Human Development. (2000). *Report of the National Reading Panel.*

- **Explicit instruction.** Systematic phonics instruction explicitly teaches the relationship between letters and sounds, making it easier for children to decode words.
- **Better outcomes.** Students receiving systematic phonics instruction showed significant improvements in decoding, spelling, and reading comprehension.
- **Structured approach.** The most effective programs were those that followed a clear, structured sequence of phonics skills, moving from simple to more complex.
- **Practice makes perfect.** Give students plenty of opportunities to apply what they learn through reading and writing activities. The more practice, the better they'll get at decoding words.

Ehri et al. (2001). "Systematic Phonics Instruction Helps Students Learn to Read."

- **Positive impact.** Systematic phonics instruction is highly effective, especially for younger students and struggling readers.
- **Boosting decoding skills.** This approach helps students decode new words and build reading fluency.
- **Long-term benefits.** Systematic phonics is a critical early reading intervention that can help prevent reading difficulties later on.

Foorman et al. (1998). "The Role of Instruction in Learning to Read: Preventing Reading Failure in At-Risk Children."

- **Support for at-risk learners.** Systematic phonics instruction helps prevent reading failure in students who are at risk, particularly in the early years.
- **Word reading and spelling.** Students receiving systematic instruction outperformed peers on measures of decoding, spelling, and reading comprehension.
- **Early intervention.** Systematic phonics should be a key focus in early reading interventions, especially for students showing signs of struggle.

Practical Tips for Implementation

This section offers practical strategies to help you integrate these foundational skills into your instruction. From explicit modeling to engaging activities, these tips will guide you in creating lessons that empower students to decode confidently and fluently. Whether you are working with beginning readers or those needing additional support, these actionable ideas will help you make phonics instruction meaningful and impactful.

Understanding the complexities of the English language can be a daunting task, but it's essential for us as teachers to feel confident when sitting down at the small group table and teaching phonics.

> **PHONICS IS** the gateway to decoding and reading fluency, and by knowing the rules and generalizations, we can teach them explicitly and systematically.

These rules not only help our students with decoding but also provide them with the understanding of why words are spelled and pronounced in specific ways. In the following sections, I have compiled a comprehensive overview of the rules and generalizations that form the backbone of effective phonics instruction.

Short Vowel Sounds and CVC Patterns

Short vowel sounds are some of the first sounds students are introduced to when learning to read. Typically, these are found in closed syllables, where a vowel is followed by one or more consonants, as in the simple CVC patterns such "map," "pig," "red," "lot," and "mug" (see Figure 6.1). In closed syllables, the vowel sound is short, and students begin to understand that vowels can change their sounds depending on the pattern in which they are placed.

map	pig	red	lot	mug

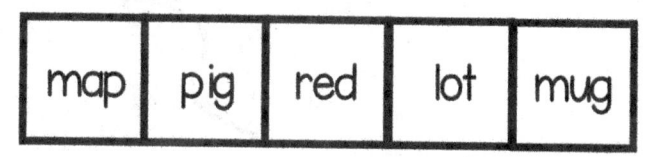

FIGURE 6.1 Short vowel sounds in closed syllables.

The "C" and "K" Generalization

The consonants "c" and "k" often confuse young readers because both can make the same /k/ sound at the beginning of a word. A helpful mnemonic is to teach students that "c" is usually followed by the vowels "a," "o," or "u" (as in "cat," "cop," "cut"), and "k" is followed by "e" or "i" (as in "kit" or "kept"). Visual aids, such as the image of a cat with "c" and a kite with "k," as shown in Figure 6.2, are particularly helpful for reinforcing this concept.

Ending "-ck" and Other Doubled Consonants

A common challenge with short vowel sounds comes in spelling patterns, particularly with final consonant combinations like "-ck." When a word has a short vowel sound and ends with the /k/ sound, it is typically spelled with "-ck" (e.g., "back"), whereas words with a long vowel sound or vowel teams (e.g., "oak," "peak") end with a simple "-k." This concept can be simplified for students with the chant, "Long spelling after a short vowel," helping them remember that "-ck" follows a short vowel, and "-k" follows a long vowel or vowel team.

FIGURE 6.2 Visual mnemonics for "c" and "k."

Another layer to this rule is the so-called floss rule, which explains that if a one-syllable word ends in "f," "s," or "z" (and occasionally "l"), you double the final consonant, as in "buzz," "pass," and "fill." This rule solidifies students' understanding of how specific endings work, giving them more control over their spelling decisions.

Digraphs and Blends: Understanding the Difference

A common area of confusion is the distinction between digraphs and blends. A digraph is when two letters combine to make a single, new sound, like "sh" in "ship" or "ch" in "chat." Digraphs are treated as one sound, and when using tools like Elkonin boxes, they occupy a single box. By contrast, blends are two or more consonants that come together while maintaining their individual sounds, such as "sl" in "slip" or "sh" in "ship." Because both sounds are heard, blends take up separate boxes (see Figure 6.3).

Additionally, digraphs like "th" can make two sounds: the voiced sound (as in "them") and the unvoiced sound (as in "thin"). Teaching students the difference through mouth placement and physical cues (like touching their throat to feel the vibration of the voiced "th") can help them distinguish between these sounds.

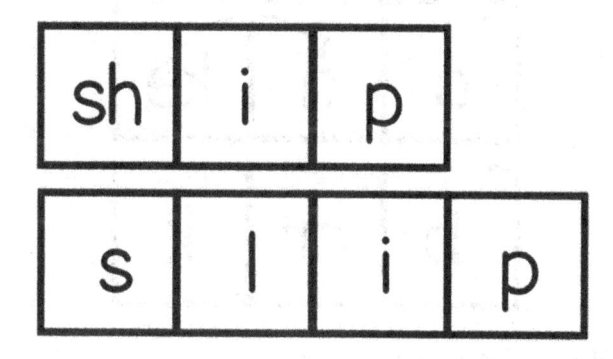

sh	i	p

s	l	i	p

FIGURE 6.3 Digraphs versus blends.

The Power of Silent "E" and "R"-Controlled Vowels

A phonics skill that students often struggle with is the silent "e" rule, also known as the vowel consonant "e" pattern (VCE). This rule changes short vowel sounds to long ones, as in "cape" (from "cap") or "bite" (from "bit"). A simple way to explain this is that the silent "e" "jumps" over the consonant to make the vowel say its name. Silent "e" has additional roles, like ensuring English words do not end in "i," "u," or "v"—hence, words like "have" and "give" require the final "e," even though it does not change the vowel sound (see Figure 6.4).

"R"-controlled vowels are another key area that deserves attention. When a vowel is followed by an "r," its sound changes, as in "car," "bird," or "fur." Although "r"-controlled vowels are not digraphs, combining two letters to make a new sound is still relevant. Introducing these vowels early on, especially common combinations like "er," is important because students will encounter them frequently.

Vowel Teams, Trigraphs, and Other Patterns

Vowel teams like "ai" and "ay," as well as trigraphs like "igh," are crucial for building students' understanding of how letters work together to represent long vowel sounds. A chant like "'Ai' in the middle, 'ay' at the end" helps students remember when to use each combination. Similarly,

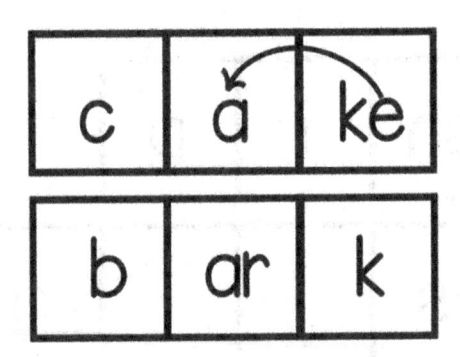

FIGURE 6.4 Silent "e" and "r"-controlled vowels.

```
┌───┬────┬───┐
│ p │ ai │ n │
└───┴────┴───┘

┌───┬───┬────┐
│ p │ l │ ay │
└───┴───┴────┘
```

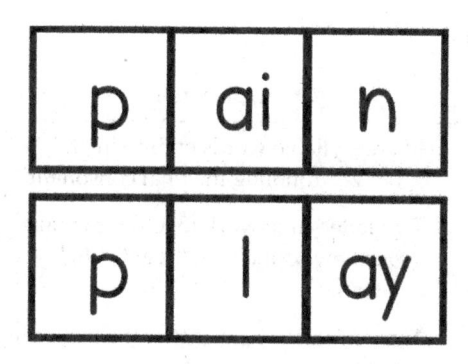

FIGURE 6.5 Vowel teams in one sound.

"igh" represents the long "i" sound and can appear in the middle of a word ("light") or at the end of a syllable ("highlight").

Understanding when to use vowel teams like "ee" and "ea" is often trickier because there is no universal rule for when to use one over the other. For instance, words like "sea" and "see" sound the same but are spelled differently, making homophones a useful tool for teaching these vowel teams. By connecting the spelling patterns to vocabulary lessons, students can begin to internalize these tricky distinctions (see Table 6.1).

Table 6.1 Phonics Rules and Patterns

Phonics Rule/Pattern	Explanation	Examples
CVC	A consonant vowel consonant structure where the vowel makes its short sound	cat, bed, pin
Open syllable	A syllable that ends in a vowel, making the vowel sound long	go, he, flu
Closed syllable	A syllable where a vowel is followed by a consonant, making the vowel sound short	cat, run, hop
Final "-ck" rule	In one-syllable words with a short vowel sound, the /k/ sound is spelled with "-ck" at the end	back, duck, sick

(Continued)

Table 6.1 (*Continued*)

Phonics Rule/Pattern	Explanation	Examples
Floss rule	In one-syllable words ending in "f," "s," or "z," doubling the final consonant	buzz, pass, fill
Digraphs	Two letters that work together to make one new sound ("ch," "sh," "th," "wh")	ship, chat, thin
Initial blends	Two or more consonants at the beginning of a word where each retains its sound.	bl (blue), st (stop)
Final blends	Two or more consonants at the end of a word where each retains its sound	nd (band), st (best)
Schwa sound	An unstressed vowel sound that often sounds like "uh," common in the middle of words	about, taken, pencil
Nasals	Consonants where air passes through the nose ("m," "n," "ng")	man, ring, sun
Silent "e" (CVC"e")	The final "e" at the end of a word making the preceding vowel say its name (long vowel)	cape, bike, hope
Soft "c" and "g"	"C" and "g" make a soft sound when followed by e, i, or y.	city, gem, giraffe
"R"-controlled vowels	A vowel followed by an "r," changing its sound (neither long nor short)	car, bird, fur
Vowel teams	Two vowels working together to represent one long vowel sound ("ai," "ay," "ee," "ea")	rain, play, team
Trigraphs	Three letters working together to make one sound ("tch," "dge")	watch, badge, catch
Diphthongs	A sound formed by the combination of two vowels in a single syllable ("oi," "oy," "ou," "ow")	boil, toy, house, cow
Consonant digraphs	Two consonants that create a new sound	wh (when), ph (phone), gh (laugh)

Table 6.1 (*Continued*)

Phonics Rule/Pattern	Explanation	Examples
Consonant trigraphs	Three consonants together making one sound ("tch," "dge").	catch, badge
Double consonants (doubling rule)	Double the final consonant when adding "-ing" or "-ed" to words with a short vowel and single consonant.	hop → hopping run → running
Final "-le" syllables	A separate syllable formed when a consonant is followed by "-le" at the end of a word	table, apple, candle
Silent letters	Letters that are not pronounced but appear in the word for historical or linguistic reasons	knee, write, comb

The Importance of a Scope and Sequence in Phonics Instruction

A well-designed scope and sequence is the foundation of systematic and explicit phonics instruction. As educators, our role is to break down the complexities of the English language in a way that supports students' development from simple to more complex patterns.

THE SCOPE and sequence serves as a road map, guiding what phonics skills should be introduced and in what order. This ensures that students gradually build their knowledge, mastering foundational skills before progressing to more advanced concepts.

THE ENGLISH language consists of 26 letters, which combine to create 44 unique sounds—20 vowel sounds and 24 consonant sounds. Each of these sounds can be represented in multiple ways, which makes learning to read and spell particularly challenging for young learners.

A scope and sequence help mitigate this challenge by organizing these sounds into manageable instructional units. For instance, rather than overwhelming students by introducing all the possible representations of the letter "a" at once (as in "a," "ai," "ay," "ea"), the scope and sequence enables educators to introduce the most common form of that letter and build on that foundation.

An important element of the scope and sequence is assessment. After evaluating a student's current phonics skills, educators can use the scope and sequence to determine the appropriate starting point for instruction. This not only helps address the individual needs of each student but also ensures that no student is left behind or rushed through content they have not mastered. The scope and sequence provides a grade-level road map and a differentiated small-group instructional tool. This enables teachers to meet students where they are and provide instruction in that area.

Collaboration across grade levels is another vital aspect of using a scope and sequence effectively. Teachers should engage in discussions with colleagues in the grades above and below their own to ensure continuity in instruction.

For example, kindergarten teachers should communicate with first-grade teachers to understand what skills their students need to master by the end of the year and what first-grade teachers would like their incoming students to know. This type of coordination creates a cohesive learning path for students, helping them build on what they have learned in previous grades.

Finally, the scope and sequence align high-frequency words (heart words—words with irregular or partially irregular spellings that require some memorization) with phonics skills. By strategically pairing these words with the phonics skills students are learning, the scope and sequence ensures that students learn to decode new words while recognizing and remembering the irregular parts of heart words. This approach helps students build a sight word vocabulary through both decoding and meaningful exposure. This careful alignment supports students in applying their phonics knowledge in meaningful reading and writing activities. We will chat more about this in Chapter 7. In summary, a scope and sequence are essential for providing students with a structured and systematic phonics education. It is the starting point. We cannot begin phonics instruction without this critical road map to guide us. It enables us to introduce skills logically and assess and place students at the appropriate point in instruction.

Consistent Routines in Phonics Instruction

PHONICS INSTRUCTION should follow a predictable routine. When we have a consistent routine for our students, we reduce the cognitive load, enabling students to focus on applying the phonics skills being taught rather than learning new activities every day.

Incorporate a few core phonics activities and rotate them regularly. Consistency enables students to predict what comes next and stay focused on the phonics patterns rather than the mechanics of the activity itself.

Incorporate Review of Previously Taught Skills

Revisiting previously taught skills is a core component of effective phonics instruction.

PHONICS BUILDS layer on layer, and students need consistent opportunities to review and consolidate previously learned sounds and words as they move on to new content.

Whether through decodable texts, fluency grids, or dictation, building a review component into every lesson strengthens students' ability to retain and use phonics skills effectively. Begin each phonics lesson with a brief review of sounds and words previously taught. Use visual and auditory drills, reread decodable texts, and apply phonics patterns in short writing tasks to help students strengthen their recall. Without consistent review, students are likely to forget previously taught phonics patterns. Regular review strengthens the neural pathways associated with reading and ensures students understand foundational skills before tackling more complex words.

Important Components of a Phonics Lesson

A well-structured phonics lesson is the cornerstone of effective reading instruction. By incorporating key components such as phonemic awareness warm-ups, cumulative review, explicit teaching of a focus skill, and opportunities for application, teachers can create an engaging learning experience. These elements work together to build students' decoding skills, reinforce previously taught concepts, and provide practice in meaningful contexts. A consistent and systematic approach ensures that every student develops the confidence and skills needed to become a successful reader.

Phonemic Awareness Warm-Up

A short, targeted phonemic awareness warm-up allows for students to prime their brains for what's to come during the phonics portion of the lesson. Research shows that three minutes of oral practice daily is sufficient to solidify students' foundational skills (see Figure 6.6). Phonemic awareness involves working with sounds orally. This part of the lesson should include blending and segmenting tasks. Blending and segmenting are closely linked to reading and writing. It is important to note that the words we choose for this portion of the lesson should be tightly connected to the phonics skill we are working on during that lesson.

3 Minute Phonemic Awareness Warm-Up
short o

	Teacher cue…	Teacher cue…	Teacher cue…	Teacher cue…	Teacher cue…
Monday	Can you guess my word? m-o-p	Can you guess my word? n-o-t	Can you tap the sounds you hear in my word? fog	Can you tap the sounds you hear in my word? log	Can you tap the sounds you hear in my word? lot
Tuesday	Can you guess my word? t-o-p	Can you guess my word? n-e-t	Can you tap the sounds you hear in my word? Tom	Can you tap the sounds you hear in my word? hog	Can you tap the sounds you hear in my word? mom
Wednesday	Can you guess my word? c-o-t	Can you guess my word? m-o-b	Can you tap the sounds you hear in my word? sob	Can you tap the sounds you hear in my word? dot	Can you tap the sounds you hear in my word? pop
Thursday	Can you guess my word? h-o-p	Can you guess my word? p-o-t	Can you tap the sounds you hear in my word? job	Can you tap the sounds you hear in my word? bob	Can you tap the sounds you hear in my word? not
Friday	Can you guess my word? b-o-g	Can you guess my word? d-o-g	Can you tap the sounds you hear in my word? got	Can you tap the sounds you hear in my word? top	Can you tap the sounds you hear in my word? won

© Literacy Edventures with Amie 2021

FIGURE 6.6 Three-minute phonemic awareness warm-up.

The Three-Part Drill/Cumulative Review

Review is critical to reinforcing previously taught skills and should be integrated at the beginning of each lesson. This can be done through visual or auditory drills or vowel-intensive drills. This ensures that students build automaticity with their phonics skills. Regular cumulative review prevents "learning decay" (Blevins, 2016) by revisiting foundational skills.

The three-part drill consists of three essential pieces:

Auditory drill. The purpose of the auditory drill is to review previously taught phonics patterns by asking students to produce the corresponding sound for a phoneme by writing it. For example, the teacher might say the sound /a/ and ask the students how to spell it. The auditory drill supported cumulative review by reinforcing past learning and strengthening students' ability to link sounds to their corresponding graphemes (see Figure 6.7).

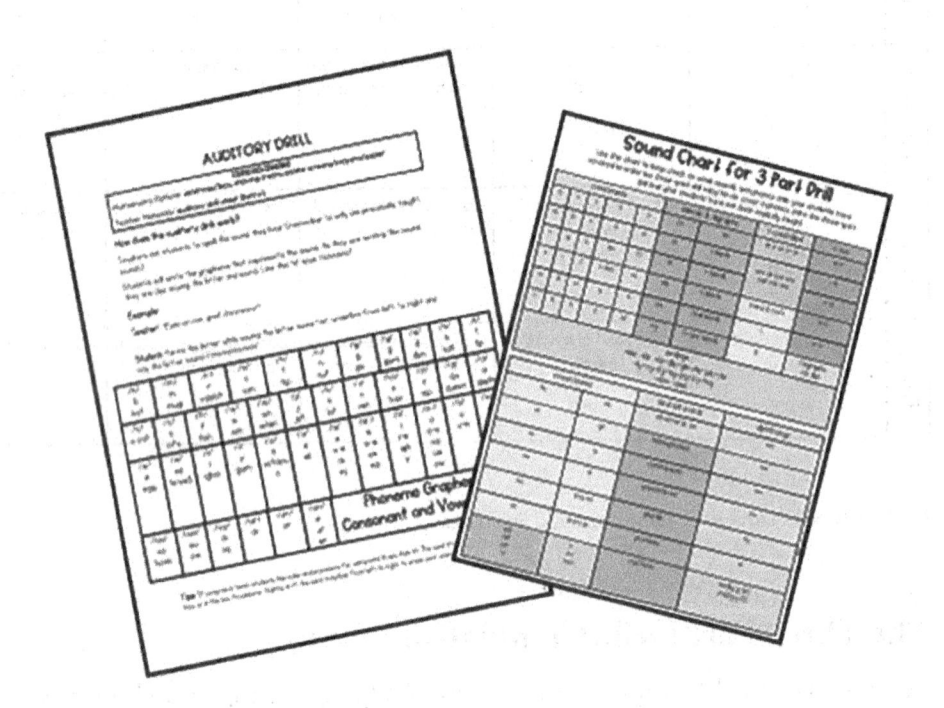

FIGURE 6.7 Auditory drill chart.

Visual drill. Flashcards help students recognize graphemes and connect them to sounds. Students practice rapid and accurate recognition of these visual representations of sounds. Repeated practice like this builds recognition automaticity with letter sounds (see Figure 6.8).

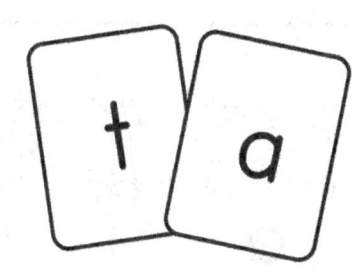

Building Strong Readers Through Systematic Phonics 149

FIGURE 6.8 Visual drill cards.

Blending drill. This drill involves students blending sounds into words, developing their ability to decode. For example, students might be asked to blend the sounds /t/ /a/ /p/ to make "tap." This helps students practice combining phonemes into words. A blending drill is often done as a group. As the teacher touches and says each sound, the students participate chorally (see Figure 6.9).

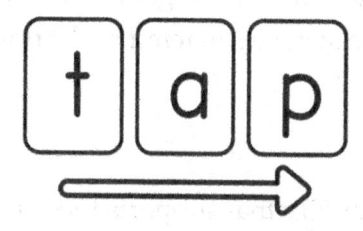

FIGURE 6.9 Blending drill.

Vowel intensive. A vowel-intensive drill is a focused activity designed to reinforce students' understanding and mastery of vowel sounds, which can often be tricky. This can be done using vowel charts where students clip or point to the correct vowel sound when the teacher says a word. It can also involve practicing vowel discrimination through word reading or syllable work, such as identifying the vowel sound in "bat" versus "bit." This drill strengthens vowel recognition and helps students better understand how vowels function in words (see Figure 6.10).

FIGURE 6.10 Vowel-intensive strip.

Explicit Teaching of a Focus Skill

After spending time reviewing the text, the next logical step is to introduce the new phonics skill. Explicit phonics instruction focuses on teaching new phonics skills or patterns. During this phase, activities should align with the specific skill being taught (e.g., word chaining or phoneme grapheme mapping). These activities help students to see, manipulate, and understand how sounds come together to form words.

Following are some activities to reinforce learning during this portion of the lesson.

Word Chaining

Word chaining is an activity that supports the connection between phonemes (sounds) and graphemes (print). Students begin to understand that changing just one sound can change the word and its meaning. For example, "big" can be changed to "bag" by switching the medial vowel sound. This process enables students to see the connection between phonemes (individual sounds) and the letters that represent them, encode, and decode words (see Figure 6.11).

Word Reading

Word reading practice is essential for students learning to connect sound to print. It enables students to read words that contain the phonics pattern they are working on. It serves as a scaffold to longer text. Students

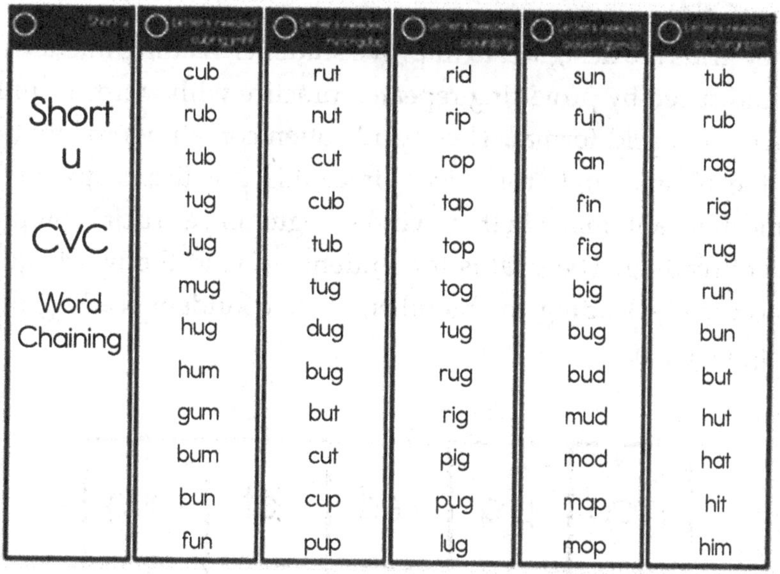

Building Strong Readers Through Systematic Phonics

Short u CVC Word Chaining					
	cub	rut	rid	sun	tub
	rub	nut	rip	fun	rub
	tub	cut	rop	fan	rag
	tug	cub	tap	fin	rig
	jug	tub	top	fig	rug
	mug	tug	tog	big	run
	hug	dug	tug	bug	bun
	hum	bug	rug	bud	but
	gum	but	rig	mud	hut
	bum	cut	pig	mod	hat
	bun	cup	pug	map	hit
	fun	pup	lug	mop	him

FIGURE 6.11 Word chaining card.

may also need to work at the phrase level before moving to longer texts that will boost fluency and confidence. Research shows that phrased reading supports fluency (see Figure 6.12)!

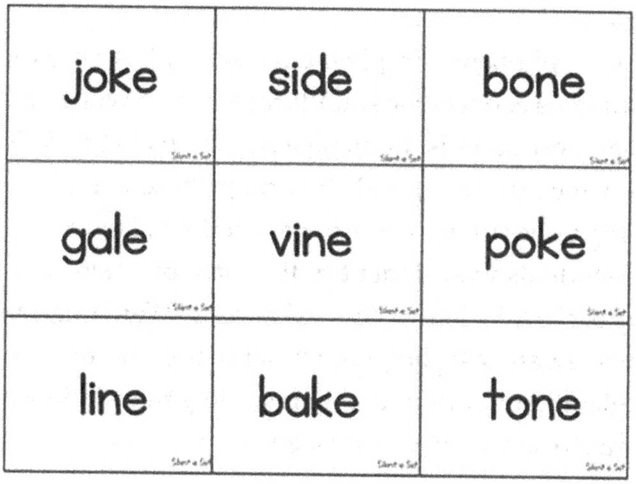

joke	side	bone
gale	vine	poke
line	bake	tone

FIGURE 6.12 Word reading cards.

Fluency Grids

Fluency grids are designed to improve students' reading fluency, accuracy, and speed by providing repeated practice with words or phrases arranged in a grid format. These grids often contain words that align with the phonics patterns. Over time, this practice helps students become more automatic in their word recognition, a crucial component of fluent reading. The goal is for students to read the words quickly and accurately, leading to smoother, more confident reading overall (see Figure 6.13).

map	pig	red	lot	mug
lot	mug	pig	map	red

FIGURE 6.13 Fluency grid.

Word Mapping

Word mapping (phoneme grapheme mapping) is a structured activity that helps students connect the sounds they hear in words and the letters that represent those sounds. In this activity, students break down a word into its phonemes (sounds) and then map those sounds to the corresponding graphemes (letters or groups of letters). For example, with the word "cat," students would identify the three phonemes /c/, /a/, and /t/ and map each to the letters "c," "a," and "t." Word mapping strengthens phonemic awareness, helping students become more proficient in decoding unfamiliar words and understanding the relationship between spoken language and written text (see Figure 6.14).

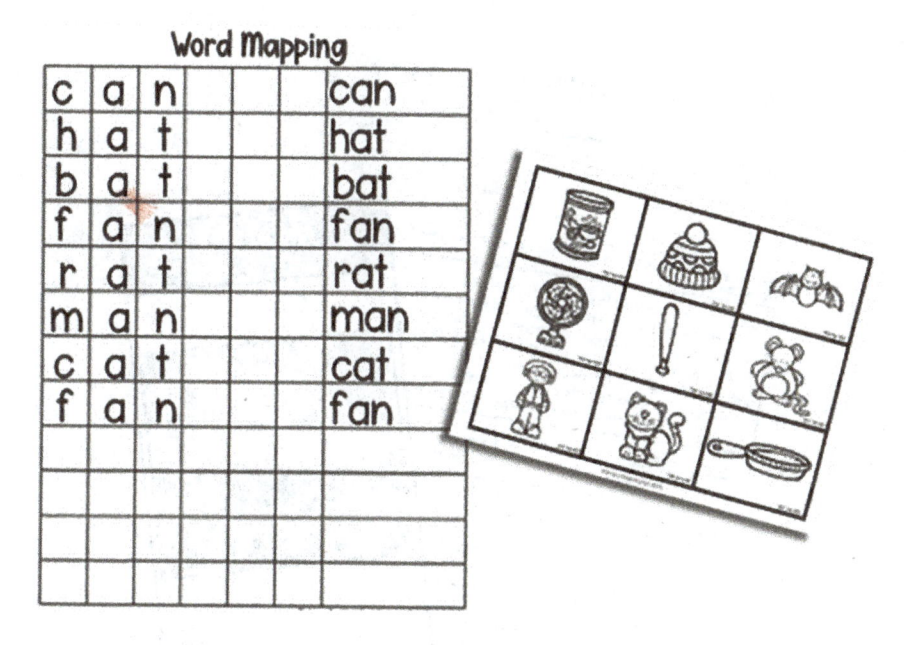

FIGURE 6.14 Word mapping.

Application of Skills: Connected Texts and Dictation

THE APPLICATION phase is critical, moving students from working on isolated skills to applying those skills in context.

This may involve reading decodable texts, which are carefully sequenced to match the phonics skills students have learned. Decodable text enables students to practice reading in a way that reinforces phonics instruction by focusing on the phonics patterns they are currently mastering and asking for skills that are being reviewed (see Figure 6.15).

Dictation supports the encoding process of the phonics skills students are currently mastering.

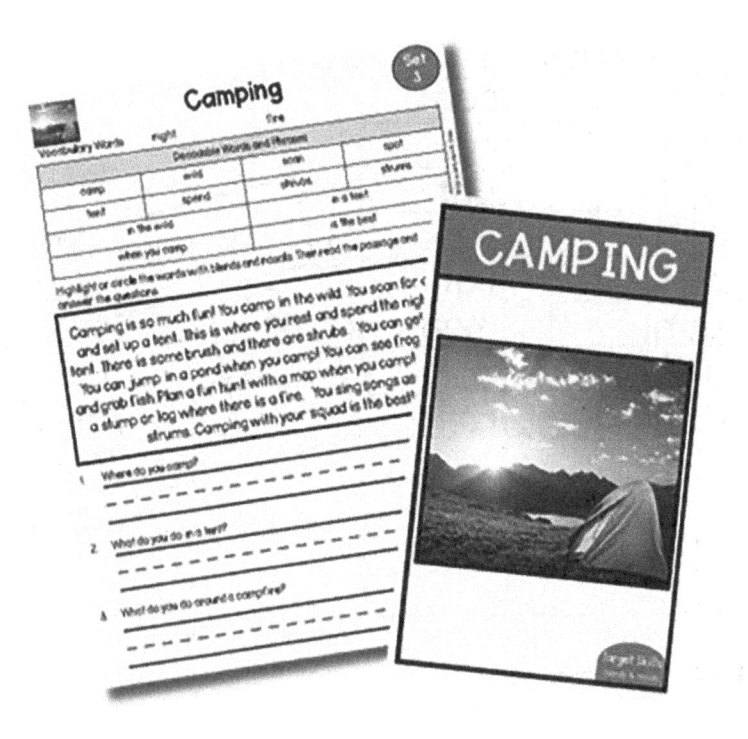

FIGURE 6.15 Decodable text sample.

DICTATION ENABLES students to take the skills they are learning through decoding and apply those skills to print.

During dictation, the teacher dictates a sound, word, or sentence, and students write it. For example, if the lesson focuses on short vowels, the dictated sentence might be "The big cat ran fast." To write the sentences, students must take their knowledge of phoneme grapheme correspondence and apply it to writing (see Figure 6.16).

In Chapter 8, we will learn more about using decodables and dictation in your phonics lessons.

Effective phonics instruction hinges on a strong understanding of how our language works along with a structured scope and sequence to guide learning. By consistently reinforcing these concepts through routines, practice activities, and application in connected texts, we equip our students with the tools they need to become confident, skilled readers.

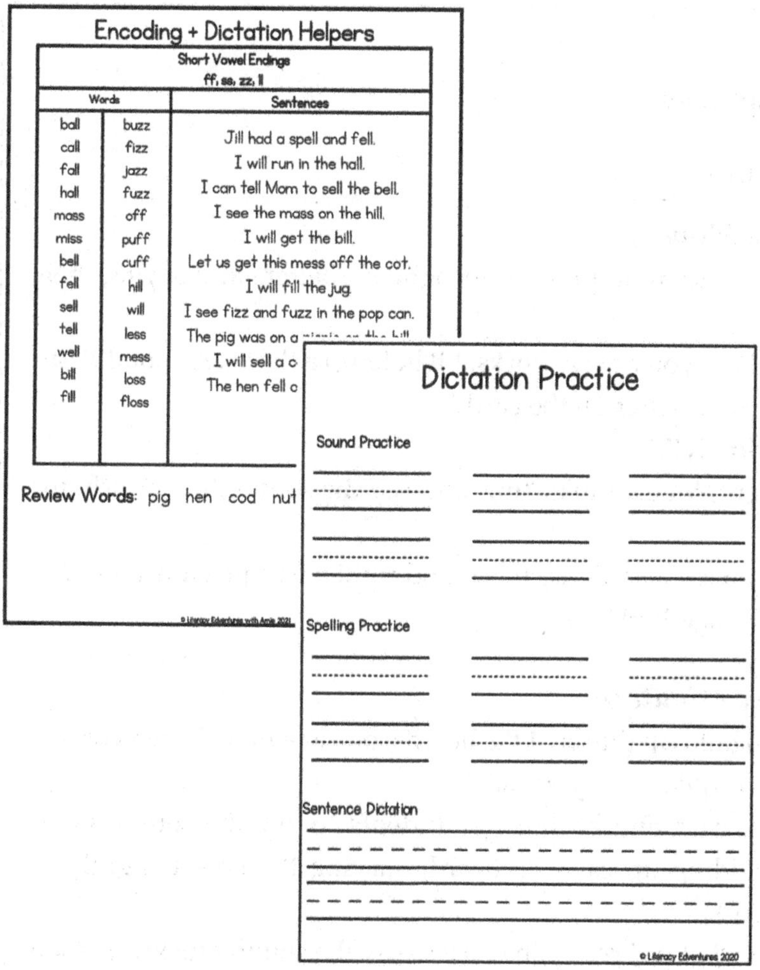

Building Strong Readers Through Systematic Phonics

Encoding + Dictation Helpers

Short Vowel Endings
ff, ss, zz, ll

Words		Sentences
ball	buzz	Jill had a spell and fell.
call	fizz	I will run in the hall.
fall	jazz	I can tell Mom to sell the bell.
hall	fuzz	I see the mass on the hill.
mass	off	I will get the bill.
miss	puff	Let us get this mess off the cot.
bell	cuff	I will fill the jug.
fell	hill	I see fizz and fuzz in the pop can.
sell	will	The pig was on a picnic on the hill.
tell	less	I will sell a c…
well	mess	The hen fell o…
bill	loss	
fill	floss	

Review Words: pig hen cod nut

Dictation Practice

Sound Practice

Spelling Practice

Sentence Dictation

FIGURE 6.16 Dictation practice.

Classroom Implementation Actionable Steps

Lesson Plan 1   Visual Drill

Objective

Students will strengthen their grapheme recognition by identifying letters and their sounds.

(Continued)

Materials Needed
- Flashcards with graphemes

Scripted Lesson Plan

1. Introduction (One Minute)
Teacher: "Today, we are going to practice recognizing letters and saying their sounds quickly! "

Teacher: "Let me show you how it works. I'll hold up a flashcard, and I'll say the sound that matches the letter on the card."

Teacher: "Watch closely!"

(Hold up a flashcard, for example, "m," and say the sound /m/ clearly for the class.)

Teacher: "When you see a card, say the sound right away, just like I did. Let us get ready to try this together!"

2. Visual Drill (Three Minutes)
Teacher: "I'm going to hold up different flashcards, one at a time. When you see a letter, say its sound as quickly as you can."

(Hold up the first card and encourage students to say the sound aloud together. Continue holding up each flashcard, varying the speed slightly to keep students engaged.)

Teacher: "Great job! Let us keep going. Try to say the sound quickly as soon as you see the letter."

(Go through several cards, mixing in a combination of new and previously taught letters to reinforce both familiar and newer sounds.)

Teacher: "Awesome! Remember to say the sound right away when you see the letter. Let us do a few more together."

(Continue holding up cards, offering gentle corrections if needed and encouraging students to stay focused on quick, accurate responses.)

3. Conclusion (One Minute)
Teacher: "You all did a fantastic job recognizing those letter sounds quickly! Knowing these sounds instantly helps us read and spell more easily."

> Teacher: "Can anyone share one sound they practiced today that felt a little faster or easier this time?"
>
> (Have a few students share one of the sounds they practiced, reinforcing positive progress.)
>
> Teacher: "Great work, everyone! Keep practicing these sounds, and soon you'll recognize them instantly. This will make reading even smoother!"

Lesson Plan 2   Auditory Drill

Objective
Students will identify sounds and corresponding phonemes through listening.

Materials Needed
- Sand tray or whiteboard

Scripted Lesson Plan

1. Introduction (One Minute)

Teacher: "Today, we are going to practice listening for sounds and writing them.

Teacher: "I'll say a sound, and when you hear it, you'll write the letter that matches the sound. Watch as I show you an example."

(Demonstrate by saying a sound, such as /m/, and writing the letter "m" in the sand tray or on the whiteboard. As you are writing the letter say "the sound /m/ says /mmmmm/.")

Teacher: "Now that you have seen how it works, you'll get to try it out with the sounds I say."

(Continued)

2. Auditory Drill (Three Minutes)

Teacher: "Let us get started! I'll say a sound, and I want you to write the letter that makes that sound. Remember to listen carefully."

(Say the sound /m/ and wait for students to write "m," saying the sound as they write it.)

Teacher: "Nice work! Let us keep going. Listen carefully to each sound, and write the letter that matches."

(Continue with other sounds such as /s/, /a/, and /t/. Provide feedback as students write each letter.)

Teacher: "For some sounds, like /k/, there are different letters that can represent the sound. If you hear /k/, try writing down all the letters that make that sound, like 'c' and 'k.' Let's try it together."

(Say the sound /k/. Tell students that they know two ways to make this sound and encourage students to write both "c" and "k," repeating "/c/ says /c/ and /k/ says /k/." Students will eventually add graphemes like /ck/ as they come up in the scope and sequence.)

Teacher: "Great! We're focusing on the sounds we have learned before, so see if you can remember each one quickly. Let us do a few more!"

(Continue with a mix of sounds, reinforcing quick and accurate responses.)

3. Conclusion (One Minute)

Teacher: "You did an excellent job listening for sounds and writing the matching letters. Practicing sounds like this helps us get even better at reading and spelling words."

Teacher: "Can anyone repeat one sound we practiced today and tell us the letter or letters that make that sound?"

(Have a few students share one sound they practiced, along with the letter or letters that correspond to it, and provide positive reinforcement.)

Teacher: "Great work, everyone! Remember, listening carefully to sounds and connecting them to letters is an important step in becoming strong readers."

Lesson Plan 3   Vowel-Intensive Drill

Objective
Students will solidify their understanding of vowel sounds in different contexts.

Materials Needed
- Vowel chart
- Clothespins or markers for students to mark vowels

Scripted Lesson Plan

1. Introduction (One Minute)
Teacher: "Today, we are going to focus on practicing vowel sounds. Vowels are really important because they help us read and understand words better. Every word we read and write must have a vowel."

(Point to the vowel chart.)

Teacher: "Let us start by looking at the vowel 'a.' I'll say the sound it makes: /a/. Now, let us all say it together: 'a' says /a/."

(Encourage students to point to the vowel "a" on their charts and say the sound aloud.)

Teacher: "Now, let us touch each vowel on our charts and say its sound. Remember, I'll be saying sounds or words, and when you hear the vowel, point to it and say its sound. Let us practice listening for vowels together!"

2. Vowel Drill (Three Minutes)
Teacher: "We're going to practice with three levels today. I'll start by saying a vowel sound, a word part, or a syllable."

Teacher: "Listen carefully, and when you hear the vowel sound, point to it on your chart and say it."

(Continued)

Level 1: Vowel Sound Practice

Teacher: "The sound is /a/. Point to 'a' on your chart and say, '"a" says /a/.'"

(Students respond by pointing to "a" on their charts and saying, "'a' says /a/.")

Teacher: "Great! Let us do a few more vowel sounds."

(Repeat for other vowel sounds, encouraging students to identify and say each vowel sound as they point to it.)

Level 2: Rime Practice

Teacher: "Now let us practice with a rime. The syllable is "et." Listen for the vowel sound in /et/."

(Students respond by pointing to "e" on their charts and saying, "'e' says /e/.")

Teacher: "Good job! Let us practice with other rimes."

(Continue with other rimes, asking students to identify the vowel in each and repeat its sound.)

Level 3: Syllable Practice

Teacher: "For this level, we'll practice with full syllables. The syllable is 'sub.' Which vowel do you hear in 'sub'?"

(Students respond by pointing to "u" and saying, "'u' says /u/.")

Teacher: "Excellent! Let us practice a few more syllables."

(Go through a few additional syllables, helping students to identify and vocalize the vowel in each.)

3. Conclusion (One Minute)

Teacher: "You all did a great job listening for vowel sounds today. Recognizing these vowel sounds helps us read and write words more easily!

Can anyone share one vowel sound they practiced today and tell us the vowel it matches?"

(Have a few students share an example, reinforcing positive feedback.)

Teacher: "Great work, everyone! Remember, every word must have a vowel."

Lesson Plan 4 Explicit Introduction of a New Skill Using Sound Boxes

Objective
Students will learn the digraph "sh" through explicit instruction and practice mapping words by writing sounds in sound boxes.

Materials Needed
- Sound boxes (drawn on student paper or whiteboards)
- Whiteboard and markers

Scripted Lesson Plan

1. Introduction (One Minute)
Teacher: "Today, we are going to learn a new sound: the /sh/ sound. This sound is called a *digraph*. A digraph is when two letters come together to make one sound."

(Demonstrate by writing "s" and "h" on the board.)

Teacher: "When I put 's' and 'h' together, they make a new sound: /shhhhhh/. It's a soft, quiet sound, like this: /shhhhhh/. Can you try it with me?"

(Encourage students to hold up their two index fingers as if putting "s" and "h" together and practice saying the /sh/ sound.)

Teacher: "Let us do it together: 's' 'h' makes /shhhhhh/. Great job!"

2. Skill Practice (Three Minutes)
Teacher: "Now that we know the /sh/ sound, let us practice mapping a word with it. We'll use sound boxes to help us see how each sound fits into the word. Remember, because 'sh' makes only one sound, it will go in one box."

(Draw three sound boxes on the board and write "sh" in the first box, "i" in the second box, and "p" in the third box.)

(Continued)

Teacher: "Let us map out the sounds in 'ship' together. We'll say each sound as we go. For the first box, we have /sh/—that's just one sound, so it goes in one box. Next, /i/ goes in the second box, and /p/ goes in the last box. Let us say each sound as we blend it together: /sh/.../i/.../p/, 'ship.'"

Teacher: "Now, let us try another one together. Let us map the word 'shop.' I'll guide you through it."

(Draw three sound boxes on the board again. Write "sh" in the first box, "o" in the second box, and "p" in the third box. Blend the sounds together with students, saying /sh/.../o/.../p/, 'shop.')

3. Independent Practice (Two Minutes)

Teacher: "Now it's your turn! I'll give you some words, and I want you to write the sounds in the sound boxes, just like we did together. Remember, 'sh' is a digraph, so it goes in one box."

(Sample words: "wish," "fish," "shin," "shack," "shed")

(Have students practice mapping each word by writing the sounds in sound boxes. Walk around to provide guidance, reminding students to blend each sound smoothly and use one box for "sh.")

4. Conclusion (One Minute)

Teacher: "Great work today, everyone! Remember, a digraph is when two letters come together to make one sound. We practiced the /sh/ digraph by putting it in one sound box."

Teacher: "Who can tell me which two letters come together to make the /shhhh/ sound?"

(Have a few students to answer and reinforce the concept of the "sh" digraph.)

Teacher: "Excellent! Keep practicing, and soon you'll be reading and mapping 'sh' words with confidence."

Lesson Plan 5   Word Chaining

Objective
Students will practice manipulating phonemes to form new words through word chaining, focusing on beginning, medial, and ending sound changes using short vowels.

Materials Needed
- Whiteboard and markers or letter cards

Scripted Lesson Plan

1. Introduction (One Minute)
Teacher: "Today, we are going to practice something called *word chaining*. This means changing just one sound in a word to make a new word. It helps us hear how even a small change can make a big difference."

(Demonstrate on the board or with letter cards.)

Teacher: "Let us start with the word 'bat.' Watch as I change just one sound to make a new word. Now it says 'bit.' See how changing just one sound makes a completely different word!"

Teacher: "Now it's your turn to try!"

2. Word Chaining Practice (Three Minutes)
Teacher: "We'll start with the word 'bat,' and I'll call out a new word. Each time, change just one sound to make the new word. Remember to touch and say each sound and blend it to read the word after each change."

(Write "bat" on the board or display it with letter cards.)

1. Word part: "bat" → "bit"
   - Teacher: "Change one sound to make the new word 'bit.' Touch each letter, say the sounds: /b/…/i/…/t/, blend to say 'bit.'"

(Continued)

2. Word part: "bit" → "sit"
   - Teacher: "Change one sound to make the new word 'sit.' Touch each letter and say the sounds: /s/…/i/…/t/, blend to say 'sit.'"
3. Word part: "sit" → "sip"
   - Teacher: "Change one sound to make the new word 'sip.' Touch each letter, say the sounds: /s/…/i/…/p/, blend to read 'sip.'"
4. Word part: "sip" → "sap"
   - Teacher: "Change one sound to make the new word 'sap.' Touch each letter and say the sounds: /s/…/a/…/p/, blend to say 'sap.'"
5. Word part: "sap" → "map"
   - Teacher: "Change one sound to make the new word 'map.' Let us read 'map' by touching each letter: /m/…/a/…/p/, then blend to read 'map.'"
6. Word part: "map" → "mat"
   - Teacher: "Change one sound to make the new word 'mat.' Touch each letter, say the sounds: /m/…/a/…/t/, blend to say 'mat.'"
7. Word part: "mat" → "mot"
   - Teacher: "Change one sound to make the new word 'mot.' Let us read 'mot' by touching each letter: /m/…/o/…/t/, then blend to read 'mot.'"
8. Word part: "mot" → "pot"
   - Teacher: "Change one sound to make the new word 'pot.' Touch each letter, say the sounds: /p/…/o/…/t/, blend to say 'pot.'"
9. Word part: "pot" → "pop"
   - Teacher: "Change one sound to make the new word 'pop.' Touch each letter, say the sounds: /p/…/o/…/p/, blend to read 'pop.'"

10. Word part: "pop" → "pup"
    - Teacher: "Change one sound to make the new word 'pup.' Touch each letter, say the sounds: /p/.../u/.../p/, then blend to read 'pup.'"

Teacher: "Each time, we changed just one sound and practiced touching and saying each sound to blend the new word. This helps us see how letters and sounds work together to make words!"

3. Conclusion (One Minute)
Teacher: "Awesome job, everyone! You just made a whole chain of words by changing one sound at a time. Who can share a few words they created during our practice?"

(Have students share some words they worked with and provide positive feedback.)

Teacher: "Remember, changing even one letter in a word can make a brand new word. This is a great way to get better at reading and spelling!"

Teacher: "Excellent work today. Keep practicing, and soon you'll be able to change sounds to make lots of new words!"

Additional Sample Word Chains for Teachers
Here are some sample word chains focusing on various phonics patterns, including digraphs, blends with short vowels, CVC"e" words, "r"-controlled words, vowel teams, and diphthongs. These can be used to further develop students' phonemic awareness and blending skills.

Word Chain with Digraphs
1. ship → chip → chop → shop → shot → shut
2. thin → then → them → shem* → shed → she

(Continued)

Word Chain with Blends (Short Vowels Only)
1. clap → slap → slat → slit → slip → slop → stop
2. slop → stop → shop → slop → slap

Word Chain with CVC "e" (Silent "E")
1. cape → tape → tame → time → tile → mile → mice
2. hope → rope → ripe → ride → wide → wise → wine

Word Chain with "R"-Controlled Words
1. car → far → for → form → farm → harm → hard
2. her → here → hire → fire → fir → fur → far

Word Chain with Vowel Teams
1. wait → bait → boat → boot → hoot → heat → meat
2. team → teem → seem → seed → heed → heel → feel

Word Chain with Diphthongs
1. coin → join → joint → point → paint → pant → plant
2. boil → foil → soil → soar → roar → rear → fear

These chains help students practice various phonics rules systematically, reinforcing patterns in English spelling and sound structure.

Lesson Plan 6   Word Mapping

Objective
Students will map phonemes to graphemes to reinforce sound-symbol connections.

Materials Needed
- Phoneme grapheme mapping mats
- Letter tiles

Scripted Lesson Plan

1. Introduction (One Minute)
Teacher: "Today, we are going to practice mapping sounds in words. This means listening carefully to each sound and matching it to the letter that represents that sound. We'll put each letter in its own box to show how each sound in a word has a specific letter."

(Demonstrate by writing or placing letter tiles for the word "dog" on a mapping mat, one letter in each box as you say the sounds.)

Teacher: "Watch and listen as I map the word 'dog.' Each sound in 'dog' gets its own box. First, I'll say the sound /d/ and place the 'd' tile in the first box. Next, I say the sound /o/ and put the 'o' tile in the next box. Finally, I say the sound /g/ and place the 'g' tile in the last box. When I put these sounds together, I can read the word 'dog.' This helps us hear and see every sound in the word."

2. Word Mapping Practice (Three Minutes)
(Give each student a mapping mat and letter tiles.)

Teacher: "Now it's your turn to practice word mapping. I'll say a word, and I want you to listen to each sound, then place the letter tiles in the boxes on your mat."

(Continued)

1. Word: "vet"
   - Teacher: "Our first word is 'vet.' Say the sounds with me: /v/…/e/…/t/. Now, map each sound by placing a letter tile in the correct box on your mat. Touch each box and say the sound as you go."

   (Allow time for students to map "vet" and check that each student places "v," "e," and "t" in separate boxes.)
2. Word: "pet"
   - Teacher: "Next, let us map the word 'pet.' Say each sound with me: /p/…/e/…/t/. Place each letter tile in its box, just like we practiced."
3. Word: "med"
   - Teacher: "Now let us map the word 'med.' Listen and say the sounds: /m/…/e/…/d/. Place a letter tile in each box to match each sound."
4. Word: "pen"
   - Teacher: "Next word is 'pen.' Say each sound as you place the tiles: /p/…/e/…/n/. Fill each box with the correct letter tile."
5. Word: "web"
   - Teacher: "Let us map the word 'web.' Say the sounds: /w/…/e/…/b/. Make sure each box has the correct sound tile."
6. Word: "ten"
   - Teacher: "Our last word to map is 'ten.' Say each sound with me: /t/…-/e/…/n/. Place each sound in its own box."

3. Conclusion (One Minute)

Teacher: "Great job mapping sounds today! Each letter you placed in a box represented a sound you heard. This helps us read and spell by making sure we hear and see every sound in a word."

> Teacher: "For our final word, let us map 'pen' together one more time as a group. Say each sound with me as we place each tile: /p/.../e/.../n/."
>
> (After mapping "pen," provide positive reinforcement and encourage students to keep practicing word mapping to strengthen their reading and spelling skills.)

Five Key Takeaways from Chapter 6

- **Systematic and explicit instruction is key.** Research highlights that phonics instruction must be direct, systematic, and cumulative, ensuring students master simpler phonics patterns before progressing to more complex ones.

- **The importance of cumulative review.** Consistent review of previously taught phonics skills helps prevent learning decay and solidifies students' phonics knowledge, aiding retention and long-term mastery.

- **Phonemic awareness is a foundation.** Phonemic awareness, the ability to hear and manipulate sounds, is critical for building decoding skills. It should be integrated into phonics lessons to connect auditory recognition of sounds with their corresponding letters.

- **Code-based instruction produces better outcomes.** Research supports prioritizing phonics-based (code-based) instruction over meaning-based approaches in early reading development. Mastering decoding first lays the foundation for later reading comprehension.

- **A well-structured scope and sequence is essential.** A systematic progression from simple to complex phonics skills, guided by a clear scope and sequence, ensures students build strong foundational decoding skills, leading to reading fluency. Regular assessments ensure students are placed at the correct instructional level.

CHAPTER SEVEN

Teaching High-Frequency Words

This chapter explores the critical role of high-frequency words (HFWs) in early literacy. HFWs are those words that children encounter most frequently in the text—words like "the," "and," "to," "said"—and recognizing these words instantly can significantly improve reading fluency and comprehension. Historically, these words have been taught through rote memorization, recalling the word as a whole unit or visual shape. However, recent research tells us this approach is not as practical as once believed. Instead, by focusing on connecting sounds (phonemes) to letters (graphemes), students can store words more effectively in their long-term memory, reducing the need for repeated memorization.

What the Research Says

HFWs are often misunderstood as words that must be memorized visually, but research tells a different story. Studies by leading experts like Share, Ehri, and others have shown that acquiring HFWs is rooted in phonics instruction and orthographic mapping. This process involves connecting sounds to letters, enabling students to store these words in their long-term memory for instant recognition. By integrating HFWs into phonics lessons and emphasizing phoneme-grapheme connections, teachers can equip students with the tools they need for fluent and efficient reading. This section explores the key research supporting this approach and its implications for effective literacy instruction.

David Share's (2004) study delved into the self-teaching hypothesis, exploring how children acquire orthographic knowledge—learning the spelling of words—through minimal exposure. His research highlighted that when children decode unfamiliar words by sounding them out, they build a mental lexicon of word patterns. This process is essential for fluent reading development. Share emphasized that phonological decoding is not just about recognizing unfamiliar words but also a fundamental part of how children learn to recognize words instantly over time. This ability to decode unfamiliar words independently leads to efficient reading fluency and comprehension, making it a key milestone in literacy development.

Linnea Ehri's (2014) research fundamentally reshaped our understanding of how children acquire sight words. Contrary to the common belief that sight words are memorized visually, Ehri's work demonstrated that students learn them by connecting sounds (phonemes) to letters (graphemes), a process known as *orthographic mapping*. For this process to happen effectively, students need three critical skills: phoneme awareness, letter-sound knowledge, and the ability to connect sounds to letters meaningfully. By mastering these skills, children can quickly and accurately decode words, enabling them to store these words in long-term memory for fluent reading. This process is critical to building a strong sight word vocabulary, supporting reading proficiency.

In their 2019 study, Miles, McFadden, and Ehri investigated the connections among language skills, literacy skills, and sight word learning in both native English and non-native English-speaking kindergartners. They discovered that phonological awareness and knowledge of letter-sound relationships were crucial for sight word acquisition, with native speakers generally benefiting more from these skills. However, non-native English speakers, who often face additional challenges due to language barriers, still showed significant progress when given structured, explicit phonics instruction. The study emphasized the importance of recognizing the role of language proficiency in early literacy development and suggested that non-native speakers may require extra support to ensure they build the necessary foundations for successful reading.

These studies highlight the importance of teaching sight words through phonics instruction, focusing on phoneme-grapheme mapping rather than relying solely on visual memorization. For teachers, this means integrating sight words into phonics lessons and providing repeated exposure to reinforce learning.

Wrap-Up of the Research

Ehri. (2014). "Orthographic Mapping in the Acquisition of Sight Word Reading, Spelling Memory, and Vocabulary Learning."

- **Importance of phoneme-grapheme connections.** Students do not learn sight words by memorizing the whole word visually. Instead, they link sounds (phonemes) to letters (graphemes), which helps them store words in their long-term memory.
- **Three essential skills:**
  - **Phoneme awareness.** Students must recognize and manipulate sounds in words.
  - **Letter-sound knowledge.** Students need to know how letters correspond to specific sounds.
  - **The study of words.** Students learn to connect sounds to written letters, forming mental pictures of words.

Share. (2004). "Orthographic Learning at a Glance."

- **Self-learning through repetition.** When students encounter new words, they use their phonics skills to decode them, and through repeated exposure, they store these words for automatic retrieval. This process enables students to grow their sight word vocabulary independently.

(Continued)

- **Key concept.** The more students read, the more words they can learn without explicit instruction, as they become proficient in decoding and internalizing new words.

Miles et al. (2019). "Associations Between Language and Literacy Skills and Sight Word Learning for Native and Nonnative English-Speaking Kindergartners."

- **Visual versus phonics instruction.** Although non-native speakers initially rely more on visual memorization of words, all students benefit from phoneme-grapheme instruction, which helps them store sight words long-term.
- **Crucial insight.** Phonics-based instruction is necessary to help students—both native and non-native—effectively retain HFWs, making them more fluent readers over time.

Practical Tips for Implementation

Over the years, the approach to teaching HFWs has evolved significantly. Traditionally, many teachers relied heavily on rote memorization, asking students to repeatedly rehearse word lists until they could recognize them by sight. However, with the rise of the science of reading and new research into orthographic mapping and phonemic awareness, educators are now questioning whether this method is truly effective. There is growing interest in phonics-based strategies, like the heart word method, which helps students map words based on their sound and spelling patterns rather than memorizing their visual shapes. This shift has sparked numerous questions among teachers about how best to balance phonics instruction with HFW teaching, whether tracking progress is necessary, and how to ensure students retain these critical words for reading fluency. The following section will dive into practical tips to address these questions and implement effective HFW instruction.

Understand the Terminology

Before diving into tips for implementing sight word instruction, let us clarify some commonly confused terms. Once we have a solid understanding of terms that are frequently used interchangeably, we will dive into tips and tricks for implementation.

- **Sight words.** These are words students can recognize automatically. Every reader has a unique sight word vocabulary, which develops through repeated exposure. For instance, as an educator, your sight word vocabulary might include words like "phonemes" and "morphology." Medical terms like "Pneumonoultramicroscopicsilicovolcanoconiosis" may not be in your sight vocabulary. Sight words can be either regular or irregular, but they are recognized automatically.
- **HFWs.** These frequently appear in written texts, such as "the," "is," "and." Learning them early helps with fluency, and they can be regular or irregular.
- **Irregular words.** These words do not follow typical phonics patterns and cannot be easily decoded. They make up about 4% of English words. Words like "eye," "are," and "of" fall into this category.
- **Temporarily irregular words.** These words appear irregular to students until they learn more advanced phonics rules. For example, "like" may seem irregular until the student learns the silent "e" rule.
- **Phonetically regular words.** These words follow predictable phonics rules and can be decoded easily. Words like "cat," "dog," and "jump" are examples of regular words.
- **Heart words.** Heart words are high-frequency or irregular words that cannot be fully decoded using phonics rules. Students learn these words by heart, focusing on the regular sounds and memorizing the irregular parts.

Now that we have clarified these essential terms, you are better equipped to understand the nuances of sight word instruction. By recognizing the differences among sight, high-frequency, and irregular words, you can tailor your teaching strategies to meet the diverse needs of your students. In the next section, we'll dive into practical tips and techniques to help you implement effective sight word instruction that builds fluency and confidence in your young readers.

Understanding the Process of Orthographic Mapping

How do we learn words if we do not learn them by sight? The answer lies in how our brains process words through orthographic mapping.

> **RATHER THAN** memorizing words as whole units, we use our understanding of how sounds correspond to letters—to anchor words in our long-term memory efficiently (see Figure 7.1).

What Is Orthographic Mapping?

Orthographic mapping is the process by which readers connect a word's spelling (its orthography) to its pronunciation (its phonology) and

Reading and the Brain

PHONOLOGICAL PROCESSOR
speech and sound awareness

PHONOLOGICAL ASSEMBLY
connects speech to print

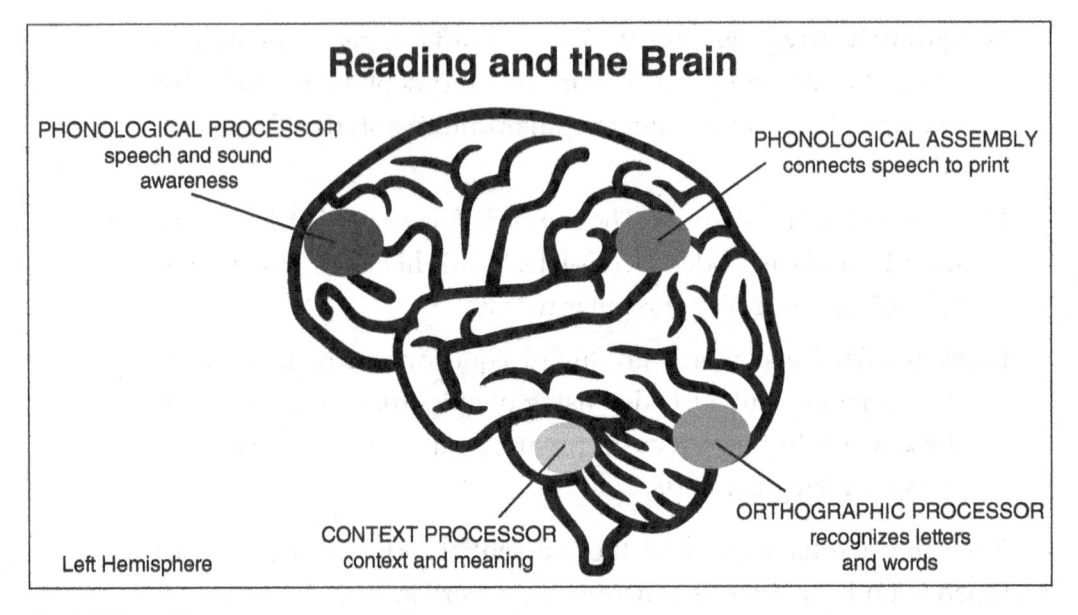

CONTEXT PROCESSOR
context and meaning

ORTHOGRAPHIC PROCESSOR
recognizes letters and words

Left Hemisphere

FIGURE 7.1 The parts of the brain responsible for reading.

meaning (its semantics). When we encounter a new word, our brain does not memorize it as a picture. Instead, we break it down by its sounds (phonemes) and associate those sounds with the letters (graphemes) that represent them. This letter-sound relationship helps us map the word into our memory.

Through repeated encounters with the word in different contexts—both in reading and writing—we strengthen its mapping, enabling us to store it for instant recognition. This is what we call "sight word reading," but unlike rote memorization, the word is deeply connected to its phonological structure.

Why Does Orthographic Mapping Matter?

Orthographic mapping is a critical process because it enables readers to become fluent without having to memorize thousands of individual words. Instead of learning every word by sight, readers use the decoding strategies they have learned (through phonics) to break down new words, which makes the word more memorable.

> **ONCE THE** word is stored through this process, the brain can retrieve it quickly and effortlessly in the future.

This is why teaching phonics and letter-sound correspondence is so essential. By understanding how letters and sounds work together, readers can map words orthographically and store them for fast, automatic recognition. The more words a reader maps, the more fluent they become, which enables them to decode unfamiliar words with ease.

How Orthographic Mapping Develops

The process of orthographic mapping starts early and evolves with practice:

1. **Phonemic awareness.** The foundation is hearing, identifying, and manipulating phonemes (sounds in words). Students can begin mapping sounds to print if they have the ability to segment and

blend sounds and knowledge of the letters that represent those sounds.

2. **Phonics instruction.** It is crucial to explicitly teach the relationships between letters and sounds. When students understand how graphemes (letters or letter combinations) represent phonemes, they can begin to map words efficiently.

3. **Repeated exposure.** The more often students encounter a word, the faster it becomes mapped. This is why early exposure to HFWs is helpful. However, the goal is not to have students memorize these words as wholes but to connect their knowledge of letter-sound patterns to recognize the word quickly.

4. **Instant recognition.** Over time, through orthographic mapping, students will store many words in their long-term memory for instant retrieval. These words become part of their sight vocabulary, which is not the result of memorization but of a deeper understanding of how letters and sounds combine.

The Power of Orthographic Mapping for Decoding and Fluency

Once a word is mapped, it is stored for automatic retrieval. The beauty of orthographic mapping is that it not only helps with familiar words but also enables the reader to recognize chunks or parts in unknown words. This means that as students begin to build their sight word vocabulary, the process of learning new words becomes easier and easier because they begin making these connections.

Implications for Instruction

When we consider the orthographic mapping process, we can easily see how important it is to focus on teaching explicit and systematic phonics instruction. It's not about encouraging students to memorize words as whole units but also about ensuring they can break words down into sounds and understand how they map to letters. When this foundation is in place, students can independently map words and grow their reading fluency over time. Thus, mapping words as whole units.

Bridging the Gap Between Spoken and Written Language

Orthographic mapping is also critical for helping students connect spoken language with written language. Most early learners come to school with a sizable spoken vocabulary, but they need explicit instruction to recognize these words in their written form. HFWs, such as "said," "have," and "could," may be common in spoken language, but students often struggle to recognize or spell them in writing.

It used to be believed that sight words were best taught in isolation, separate from phonics instruction. However, now that we understand the importance of connecting letters to sounds, we know that sight words should be integrated into daily phonics lessons. When thinking about how to do this effectively, there are several important considerations.

Teach Two to Three Words per Week

The ideal number of sight words to teach per week can vary depending on your students' readiness, but typically, teaching two to three words per week is a manageable pace. This allows for enough repetition and reinforcement without overwhelming students.

It's important to note that some HFWs are entirely decodable and align well with the phonics skills students are learning. These words, such as "can," "man," and "sit," follow phonics rules and can be taught alongside the phonics patterns being introduced. These fully decodable words are taught in addition to the irregular or partially irregular words, like "the" or "said," which do not follow regular phonetic patterns. This balance allows for phonics skills and sight word recognition to develop simultaneously.

Start with a Small Bank of Words

When starting sight word instruction, more than rote memorization is needed for long-term learning.

> **ALTHOUGH SOME** argue that teaching students to memorize *any* words could disrupt their ability to decode or encourage guessing, no research supports these claims.

In fact, starting with a small number of HFWs in early kindergarten will enable students to gain a bank of words for early reading and writing tasks and boost confidence as they learn how our language works.

Words like "the," "come," "have," and "said" are frequently seen in early texts, and teaching them directly helps students connect written language to spoken language, even when spelling-to-sound complexities exist.

These words are very common in the English language and I start with them as soon as possible.

a	I	is	of	do
to	the	and	for	you
my	like	can	see	look
we	go	at	as	said

Connect HFWs to Phonics Skills

When teaching sight words, aligning them with the phonics patterns students learn is essential. Some HFWs are entirely decodable, meaning they can be sounded out based on the phonics skills students are mastering. For example, words like "can," "man," and "sit" align well with short vowel sounds and can be taught alongside these phonics patterns. These fully decodable words should be integrated into irregular or partially irregular words, like "the" or "said," which do not follow standard phonics rules.

You can organize the first 100 HFWs by phonics patterns and integrate them into your phonics scope and sequence. For instance, teach decodable words like "can" and "man" during lessons on short vowel sounds and introduce words like "she" and "me" when working on open syllables. This approach enables students to connect decoding skills with word recognition, reinforcing both skills systematically. Figure 7.2 shows a sample of words you might introduce aligning with the phonics skills that you are teaching.

Interactive and Multisensory Approaches to HFW Instruction
Engaging students in interactive activities is another effective way to teach HFWs. Multisensory techniques that involve sight, sound, movement, and touch help reinforce orthographic mapping and make learning more memorable. For example, students can trace words in sand, use magnetic letter tiles to build words, or use mini erasers to push out the sounds they hear in each word.

Incorporating multisensory activities makes learning fun and helps students stay motivated, especially when paired with phonics

| Short a CVC | Decodable Words: am, at, an, can, ran, dad, had, bag, pat, had, cat, Heart Words: has*, as*, have* want, any *indicates temporary irregular words | Short u CVC | Decodable Words: us, up, but, cut, run, upon, cub, fun Heart Words: was, put, some, from, look*, book* *indicates temporary irregular words |

FIGURE 7.2 Organizing HFWs.

FIGURE 7.3 Mapping a heart word.

instruction. This approach builds memory and reinforces the letter-sound connections necessary for orthographic mapping (see Figure 7.3).

Using HFWs in Context: Reading and Writing Integration

Although phonics and multisensory activities are crucial, it is equally important that students see and use HFWs in meaningful contexts.

> **LEARNING THESE** words in isolation or through drills alone does not provide the depth of understanding that reading and writing in context offers.

Students should frequently encounter these words in books, decodable texts, and daily writing exercises to reinforce their learning.

Practice makes perfect, and early readers need lots of it. In the next section, I share some of my favorite ways to practice sight words after mapping them.

Classroom Implementation Actionable Steps

Lesson Plan 1   Shake, Shake, Rattle, and Drop

Objective

Students will reinforce their knowledge of sight words by building them with magnetic letters in a multisensory game.

Materials Needed

- Magnetic letters ("s," "a," "i," "d") for each student
- Container for each student to shake letters in

Scripted Lesson Plan

1. Introduction (One Minute)

Teacher: "We've been working hard on the word 'said.' We know that there are parts of this word, like 'a' and 'i,' that do not follow the usual sounds, so we have to remember them by heart. Now that we know that, it's time to get faster at spelling and reading 'said'!"

Teacher: "Today, we are going to play a game called 'Shake, Shake, Rattle, and Drop' to help us get quick with the word 'said.' Here's how it works."

(Demonstrate by putting the letters for "s," "a," "i," and "d" into a container. Shake it, rattle it a bit, and then drop the letters onto a flat surface. Arrange the letters to spell "said" and read the word aloud.)

Teacher: "Now it's your turn! You'll each have your own container with the letters for 'said,' and we'll practice this three times together."

2. Game Instructions (Three Minutes)

Teacher: "Let us start! Everyone take your container of letters—'s', 'a', 'i', and 'd.'"

Teacher: "First, give the container a good shake!"

(Continued)

Teacher: "Now, rattle it a little bit so the letters move around."

Teacher: "Drop the letters onto your desk or table. Look at the letters that landed and arrange them to spell the word 'said.'"

Teacher: "Once you have built the word, say it out loud: 'said.' Great job!"

(Allow students a moment to complete each step and provide guidance if needed.)

Teacher: "Fantastic! Let us shake, rattle, drop, build, and read again!"

(Repeat the process twice more, encouraging students to complete each step smoothly and read the word each time.)

3. Conclusion (One Minute)

Teacher: "Wonderful work, everyone! Who would like to share how many times they were able to build and read the word 'said'?"

(Have a few students share their experience, providing positive reinforcement.)

Teacher: "Practicing with games like this makes it easier to remember sight words. By shaking, rattling, dropping, and building the word, we are practicing in a fun way that helps us remember 'said' more easily."

Teacher: "Keep practicing, and soon you'll be reading and spelling sight words even faster!"

Lesson Plan 2   Mystery Word

Objective

Students will practice identifying missing letters in sight words, reinforcing their phonemic awareness and spelling skills.

Materials Needed

- Whiteboard and markers
- Individual student whiteboards and markers

Scripted Lesson Plan

1. Introduction (One Minute)

Teacher: "Today, we are going to play a game called 'Mystery Word.' This game will help us think about each letter in a word and where it belongs. I'm going to write a word on the board, but I'll leave out one or two letters. Your job is to figure out which letters are missing to complete the word!:

Teacher: "Let us start with a word we have been working on: 'have.' I'll write it on the board but leave out one letter."

(Write "h __ ve" on the board and draw a blank line for the missing letter.)

Teacher: "Can anyone guess which letter is missing in this word?"

2. Game Instructions (Three Minutes)

Teacher: "The word is 'have.' Think about each sound in the word. What letter goes in the blank spot?"

(Allow students a moment to think and respond. Encourage them to sound out the word if needed.)

Teacher: "Yes, the missing letter is 'a.' Let us say the whole word together: 'have.'"

Teacher: "Now, on your own whiteboards, I want you to write the complete word: 'have.' Make sure you have each letter in the correct place."

(Wait for students to write the word on their boards. Walk around and provide guidance as needed.)

Teacher: "Great job! Let us try another one. This time, I'll leave out two letters."

(Write "h __ __ e" on the board and draw two blank lines. Go through the same process, encouraging students to identify the missing letters and write the complete word.)

Teacher: "Let us do one more round, with the word 'have' missing different letters each time. Remember to think about each sound and where the letters belong."

(Continued)

3. Conclusion (One Minute)

Teacher: "Excellent work, everyone! Who would like to share the completed word they wrote today?"

(Have a few students share and provide positive reinforcement.)

Teacher: "By finding the missing letters, we practiced how to spell words and got to know the letters in 'have' even better."

Teacher: "Keep looking out for those tricky letters in sight words, and soon you'll know them by heart!"

Teacher: "Great job! We'll keep practicing to make reading and spelling these words easier every day."

Lesson Plan 3   Beat the Teacher

Objective

Students will improve their speed and accuracy in writing sight words by competing against the teacher in a fun, fast-paced game.

Materials Needed

- Whiteboard and markers
- Individual student whiteboards and markers

Scripted Lesson Plan

1. Introduction (One Minute)

Teacher: "Today, we are going to play a game called "Beat the Teacher." In this game, you'll try to write sight words faster than I can! This is a fun way to practice writing words quickly, which helps us become faster readers and writers."

Teacher: "I'm going to call out a sight word, and we'll see if you can write it faster than me. Let us see if you can beat me!"

2. Game Instructions (Three Minutes)

Teacher: "Take out your whiteboards and markers. I'm going to draw four boxes on my whiteboard, and I want you to do the same on yours."

Teacher: "When I call out a word, your job is to write it in each box as quickly as you can, just like me! Let us see if you can finish writing it four times before I do."

(Call out a sight word, such as "said," and begin writing it in each of the four boxes while students race to do the same. You may pause to provide encouragement and check for accuracy.)

Optional Extension for Teachers

If students are just starting with sight words, have them write the word once in one box while you write it four times, gradually increasing to four as their confidence grows. For an extra challenge, call out a short sentence for students to write and race against the teacher.

3. Conclusion (One Minute)

Teacher: "Wow, you all did such an amazing job! I think some of you definitely beat me a few times today."

Teacher: "Who wants to share a word or sentence they wrote really quickly?"

(Have students share and celebrate their efforts.)

Teacher: "Practicing our sight words quickly helps us become more confident when reading and writing. Keep practicing, and soon you'll be able to write these words in no time!"

Teacher: "Great job, everyone! Let us play "Beat the Teacher" again soon!"

Lesson Plan 4 Bang

Objective
Students will practice reading sight words in a game where they can win or lose cards based on their accuracy.

Materials Needed
- Sight word cards
- Bang cards
- Optional: Decodable sentence cards with sight words for an advanced version of the game

Scripted Lesson Plan

1. Introduction (One Minute)
Teacher: "Today, we are going to play a game called "Bang!" This game is all about reading your recently learned sight words accurately. Each of you will take turns drawing a card from the pile. If you can read the word correctly, you get to keep it."

Teacher: "But be careful! Some of these cards say 'Bang!' If you draw a 'Bang' card, you have to put all your cards back in the pile. The goal is to collect as many cards as possible by reading the words correctly."

(Another alternative to this game is to swap the cards for decodable phrases or sentences with sight words embedded.)

2. Game Instructions (Three Minutes)
Teacher: "Let us start! We'll take turns, and each of you will draw a card from the pile. When you draw a card, read the word aloud, or if it's a sentence card, read the whole sentence."

> (Demonstrate by drawing a sight word card from the pile, reading it out loud, and setting it aside to keep it. Draw a sentence card next to show how to read the sentence aloud and emphasize the sight word within the sentence.)"
>
> Teacher: "If you read the word or sentence correctly, you get to keep the card. But if you cannot read it, the card goes back into the pile."
>
> Teacher: "Remember, if you draw a 'Bang' card, you have to put all your cards back into the pile. Be careful and read accurately!"
>
> Teacher: "We'll keep going until all the sight words and sentences have been drawn, or until time is up."
>
> **3. Conclusion (One Minute)**
> Teacher: "Wow, great job, everyone! Let us see who collected the most cards."
>
> (Have students share their totals and celebrate the student with the most cards.)

Five Key Takeaways from Chapter 7

- **Orthographic mapping is key.** Rather than memorizing words visually, students store HFWs by mapping sounds (phonemes) to letters (graphemes), building a stronger foundation for fluency and retention.

- **Integrating phonics and HFWs.** Teaching HFWs should be part of daily phonics lessons to ensure students connect their decoding skills to word recognition.

- **Cumulative review reinforces learning.** Once students have mapped words successfully, repeated practice through games, flashcards, and contextual reading and writing activities helps solidify these words in their long-term memory.

- **Interactive, multisensory learning strengthens retention.** Engaging students in hands-on, multisensory activities—such as tracing letters

in sand or using laser pointers to write—builds stronger connections and keeps learning fun and memorable.
- **Context matters.** Students should regularly see and use HFWs in context, whether in decodable texts or their own writing. This approach deepens understanding and aids fluency and comprehension, especially as they encounter more complex texts.

CHAPTER EIGHT

Making Phonics Stick
Application Is Key

The previous chapters have explored the importance of building a solid foundation for our students. Many components must support students in these early literacy years to help them become strong, confident readers. Thus far, we have laid the groundwork for decoding, and now it is time to help students apply that knowledge in context through reading and writing. Although this chapter will lean more heavily into decodable texts to strengthen decoding skills, we will also discuss the importance of encoding—decoding's sister skill—and how it can be reinforced through activities like dictation. Together, these two practices will help students connect and solidify their phonics knowledge in the context of reading and writing. This will ensure they can apply what they have learned meaningfully.

Before we begin this chapter, I would like you to do an exercise with me. You will need a pencil.

Read the text in Table 8.1 and use your phonics knowledge to identify the phonics skills within the text. You can record them along the side. This exercise will help you sharpen your phonics skills and keep a tally of every phonics skill you notice with the text.

Let us examine what you noticed (see Table 8.2).

Now, I would like you to pretend that you are a first-grade teacher using this book to follow up on your short vowel phonics lesson. Is this book decodable? Could students probably read this with picture

Table 8.1 Phonics Pattern Tally

The dog is big and brown. It likes to run fast in the yard. The dog sees a ball and chases it. Can the dog catch the ball? Yes! The dog can catch the ball. The dog will play with the ball all night. Now, the dog is sleeping.	Short vowels	
	Blends/digraphs	
	Floss/ending ck	
	CVC"e" "r"-controlled	
	Vowel teams	
	Diphthongs	
	Other skills	

Table 8.2 Phonics Pattern Analysis

Text	Short Vowels	Blends/ Digraphs	Floss/Ending "ck"	CVC"e""r"- Controlled	Vowel Teams	Diphthongs	Other
The dog is big and brown.	dog, big, and	brown, *the		yard		brown	*is
It likes to run fast in the yard.	it, run, in	fast, *the		likes, yard			*to
The dog sees a ball and chases it.	dog, it, and	*the chases	ball	sees, chases	sees		*a chas<u>es</u> see<u>s</u>
Can the dog catch the ball?	dog, can	*the	ball				ca<u>tch</u>
Yes! The dog can catch the ball.	yes, dog, can	*the	ball				ca<u>tch</u>
The dog will play with the ball all night.	dog	*the, with, play	ball, all, will		night, play		
Now, the dog is sleeping.	dog	*the			sleeping	now	sleep<u>ing</u> *is
Total	8	7	4	4	3	2	3

support? Could they read it without picture support? What if I told you that this text is a level D equivalent to the end of kindergarten? What are your thoughts?

Let us examine another text (see Tables 8.3 and 8.4).

Table 8.3 Phonics Pattern Tally in a Leveled Text

My mom got me a big hot dog. She put it on my lap. I like hot dogs. But my cat likes hot dogs. I see him look at my hot dog. He can get it! I pat his leg. "No, cat. It is not for you. Sit, cat." I run to sit on the box. Yum, I like the hot dog, but my cat is mad at me.	Short vowels	
	Blends/digraphs	
	Floss/ending ck	
	CVC"e" "r"-controlled	
	Vowel teams	
	Diphthongs	
	Other skills	

Table 8.4 Phonics Pattern Analysis in a Leveled Text

Text	Short Vowels	Blends/ Digraphs	Floss/ Ending "ck"	CVC"e""r"- Controlled	Vowel Teams	Diphthongs	Other
My mom got me a big hot dog.	mom, got, big, hot, dog						*my, *me, *a
She put it on my lap.	it, on, lap	*she					*she, *put, *my
I like hot dogs.	hot, dogs						* I, *like dog<u>s</u>
But my cat likes hot dogs.	but, cat, hot, dogs						*my, dog<u>s</u> *likes
I see him look at my hot dog.	him, at, hot, dog,						*I, *see, *look, *my
He can get it.	can, get, it						*he

Text	Short Vowels	Blends/ Digraphs	Floss/ Ending "ck"	CVC"e" "r"- Controlled	Vowel Teams	Diphthongs	Other
I pat his leg.	dog, pat, leg						*his, *I
"No, cat. It is not for you. Sit cat."	cat, it, not, you, sit						*no *for
I run to sit on the box.	run, sit, on, box						*I, *the
Yum, I like the hot dog, but my cat is mad at me.	yum, hot, dog, but, cat, mad, at						*like, *the, *my, *is, *me
Total	24	1					15

This time, pretend you are a first-grade teacher using this book to follow up on your short vowel phonics lesson. Is this book decodable? Given the skills and high-frequency words (assume you have taught these), would they be able to read this? What are your thoughts?

I love doing this exercise so educators can see the difference between using leveled readers versus decodable readers in early literacy and understanding that decodable texts are like training wheels that provide the bridge to more authentic text. As we work through this chapter, I encourage you to remember this exercise. Now, let us dive in.

The Research

Beverly et al. (2009) investigated the reading gains of first-grade students following enrichment programs that focused on different types of reading materials. The study compared two primary groups: one received phonics instruction paired with decodable texts and the other read authentic literature aloud. The study used the Gray Oral Reading Test Fourth Edition and the Preventing Academic Failure benchmark to measure fluency, accuracy, and comprehension improvements.

The study's findings are of utmost importance as they support the effectiveness of decodable texts in helping children build foundational reading skills. Students in the decodable text group made notable gains in fluency and decoding accuracy, and the authentic literature group demonstrated greater improvement in reading comprehension. These findings provide educators with valuable insights into the benefits of both text types, enhancing their knowledge and understanding of early literacy instruction.

The research highlights the importance of including both decodable texts and authentic literature in early reading instruction. Decodable texts are essential for helping students build fluency and phonics skills through structured practice. Simultaneously, reading authentic literature aloud to children exposes them to richer language and narrative structures, supporting their comprehension and vocabulary development. By integrating both text types, teachers can provide a well-rounded literacy experience that equips students with the skills and understanding needed to engage independently with diverse texts.

Heidi Anne Mesmer (2000) reviewed the effectiveness of decodable texts in early reading instruction. The study synthesized the available research and explored how decodable texts that are designed to align with phonics instruction can be an essential tool for beginning readers. Mesmer argues that decodable texts are critical at specific developmental stages, as they help students to practice decoding skills in a controlled, structured environment where most words follow regular phonetic patterns.

Mesmer's study highlights several key points regarding the effectiveness of decodable texts in early reading instruction. First, decodable texts are crucial for supporting fluency and phonics application. By closely matching the phonics rules that students are taught, these texts enable young readers to apply their knowledge in a controlled setting, helping them build confidence and fluency in their reading. Additionally, the study emphasizes the importance of phonetically regular words, where consistent letter-sound relationships are key to solidifying decoding skills, which are essential for early reading development. Finally, the study suggests that once students achieve a certain level of fluency with decodable texts, they can gradually transition to authentic texts, which offer richer language experiences and help broaden their knowledge and vocabulary. This balanced approach ensures students develop both technical reading skills and the ability to engage with more complex texts as they advance.

Mesmer's review concludes that decodable texts are critical in helping students develop their foundational decoding skills. However, they should be complemented with authentic literature for broader language exposure as students advance their reading abilities.

Wrap-Up of the Research

Beverly et al. (2009). "First-Grade Reading Gains Following Enrichment."

- **Study focus.** Investigated reading gains in first-grade students using two different approaches: decodable texts with phonics instruction and authentic literature read aloud.
- **Key findings:**
  - **Decodable texts** improved fluency and decoding accuracy, supporting the idea that decodable texts help build foundational reading skills.
  - **Authentic literature** showed better comprehension, highlighting the benefit of exposure to complex language structures.
- **Takeaway.** Decodable texts are crucial for developing fluency and decoding, but comprehension and vocabulary are best supported by reading authentic texts aloud. Including both text types helps students grow.

(Continued)

> **Mesmer. (2000). "Decodable Text."**
> - **Study focus.** Reviewed the role of decodable texts in early reading instruction, especially for building phonics and decoding skills.
> - **Key findings:**
>   - Decodable texts provide controlled practice for applying phonics rules, helping students develop confidence and fluency.
>   - It is important to use phonically regular words to reinforce decoding skills.
>   - Once fluency with decodable texts is achieved, students should transition to authentic texts for broader language experiences.
> - **Takeaway.** Decodable texts are highly effective for early readers in building technical skills, but they need to be complemented with authentic literature to ensure students also develop comprehension and vocabulary.

Decodable texts are excellent tools for teaching phonics and building fluency. They provide structured practice that helps students become confident in sounding out words and applying their phonics knowledge. However, authentic literature plays a crucial role in enhancing comprehension and vocabulary. Reading authentic stories aloud to children exposes them to richer language, enabling them to understand meaning better as they listen. A combined approach is ideal—using decodable texts when students are learning to read while incorporating authentic texts through read-aloud sessions to boost understanding and vocabulary. Together, these strategies ensure that students receive a well-rounded reading development experience.

Practical Tips for Implementation

We know that reading and writing go hand in hand and are essential for building a solid literacy foundation. Explicit and systematic instruction is critical to helping students become fluent readers and writers. Before expecting students to read a book or write a sentence using specific phonics patterns, we must ensure they have been taught them.

One powerful way to reinforce phonics instruction is through dictation. Dictation enables students to hear sounds, words, or sentences and write them down. This process helps to strengthen their understanding of letter-sound relationships and their ability to apply phonics rules in writing. Dictation also enables teachers to model the necessary writing skills, such as proper handwriting, spelling, and sentence structure.

Decodable texts are another critical component to applying phonics skills through reading. Decodable texts are controlled texts that align with phonics skills students have learned or are learning. This controlled text provides a space for students to practice the phonics skills they have been learning and helps to boost their confidence as young readers. The structured nature of decodable texts ensures that students experience success as they apply their phonics skills to actual reading tasks.

WE USE dictation and decodable texts to create an all-encompassing approach to reinforcing phonics instruction and connecting them in context.

Dictation strengthens writing, and decodable texts support reading, ensuring students build fluency in both areas.

We will soon examine decodable texts and their critical role in reinforcing phonics instruction. Decodable texts offer students structured opportunities to apply knowledge, gradually building fluency and decoding skills. But before we can dive in, we need to understand some critical vocabulary.

Leveled Text

Leveled texts are books or passages often labeled with letters or numbers (e.g., A–Z or 1–70). These levels are typically determined based on factors such as sentence complexity, vocabulary, and text structure;

however, the criteria can vary widely between systems and are not always grounded in evidence-based practices. In many cases, assigning levels is a subjective process that prioritizes text predictability over phonics alignment, which can inadvertently encourage guessing strategies. As a result, although leveled readers are frequently used to gauge a student's independent reading ability by matching texts to their perceived reading level, their reliance on predictable patterns and limited emphasis on phonics may not accurately reflect a student's decoding skills or overall reading proficiency.

Using leveled texts when students are learning to decode and attack words can be particularly detrimental when paired with instructional strategies tied to the theory of three-cueing. Three-cueing, a popular but controversial approach in early reading instruction, encourages students to rely on meaning, visual cues, and structure to identify unknown words. These strategies are often explicitly promoted, encouraging students to look at pictures, use the first letter of a word, or guess based on what would make sense in the context. Although this may help students navigate leveled, predictable texts with strong picture support, it does not equip them with the decoding skills necessary to tackle unfamiliar words independently.

This focus on meaning and context over letter-sound correspondence bypasses the critical process of orthographic mapping, where our brains store words for automatic recognition. Orthographic mapping requires students to attend to each grapheme in a word to build accurate and efficient word recognition. By relying on the three-cueing system, students develop habits that interfere with this process, like looking at pictures, predicting based on the first letter, or asking themselves, "What word would make sense here?"

Breaking these habits is often challenging because many students have been taught to read this way. However, reading research (Ehri, 2004) tells us that to support orthographic mapping, students must focus on decoding each word by its letter-sound correspondences rather than guessing or relying on context. This shift in instruction is essential for helping students move beyond guessing strategies and toward becoming fluent, confident readers.

Decodable Text

Decodable texts are specifically designed to align with the phonics skills that students are learning. These texts contain words that follow consistent phonics patterns, enabling students to practice decoding based on the rules they have been taught.

> **A DECODABLE** text is only as decodable as the phonics knowledge of the child reading it—meaning, its effectiveness depends on whether the student has been taught the specific phonics patterns that appear in the text.

For example, a decodable text for students learning short vowels will focus on words like "cat" or "bat," reinforcing the phonics skills they are mastering. Decodable texts help students build confidence and fluency by providing controlled reading opportunities where they can successfully apply their phonics knowledge.

By contrast, leveled readers often encourage students to rely on guessing strategies, such as looking at pictures or using the first letter of a word. These texts frequently feature repetitive sentences like "We can see the dog" or "We can see the cat." Although this predictability can make the text easier for students to memorize or guess, it does not provide opportunities for them to apply specific phonics patterns. Decodable texts, however, focus solely on the phonics code students are learning, reducing reliance on guessing and encouraging students to sound out words based on their phonics knowledge.

Decodability

Decodability refers to the degree to which a text aligns with a student's phonics knowledge, making it easier for them to decode words.

Decodability can be seen as a spectrum, with some texts being highly decodable, containing almost all familiar phonics patterns. By contrast, others may have more challenging words that students have not yet learned. The goal is to select texts that match each student's current phonics abilities, enabling them to decode words successfully while building fluency.

The Power of Decodable Texts

Decodable texts are intentionally designed to reinforce the specific phonics skills students are currently learning. For example, when students are introduced to vowel teams, a decodable text might include words like "play" or "stain," providing targeted practice in decoding these patterns. By aligning with the phonetic structure students are studying, these texts help bridge instruction and application in a meaningful way.

Researcher Heidi Anne Mesmer (2000) provides valuable insights into how we should think about decodable texts. She suggests viewing decodability as a meter, with some texts being more decodable than others based on how many words match the reader's phonics knowledge. Mesmer emphasizes the importance of lesson-to-text match, where the phonics patterns in the text should align with what students have recently been taught. She also highlights that decodable texts offer students the joy of decoding words for the first time—a milestone comparable to riding a bike without training wheels. This decoding process supports orthographic mapping, helping students store words in their long-term memory for automatic recognition.

A KEY point Mesmer raises is that there is not a strict research-backed standard for how decodable a text should be. Instead, it's essential to consider the text's decodability relative to the reader's knowledge.

For instance, a text that is 70–90% decodable might be appropriate for one student, and another student may benefit from a text that is

95% decodable. This flexibility enables educators to tailor the level of decodability based on each student's progression through their phonics journey.

Building Fluency Through Rereading

Teachers can use various strategies, such as choral reading or echo reading, to support students during reading. Encouraging rereading is essential, as repetition builds fluency and confidence. Teachers should also offer immediate corrective feedback to help students self-correct and reinforce proper decoding strategies. For example, if a student misreads a word, the teacher can guide them back to it, have them sound it out again, and reread the sentence. I love using these decodable helpers. These provide an excellent visual for students and encourage them to sound the word out rather than guess.

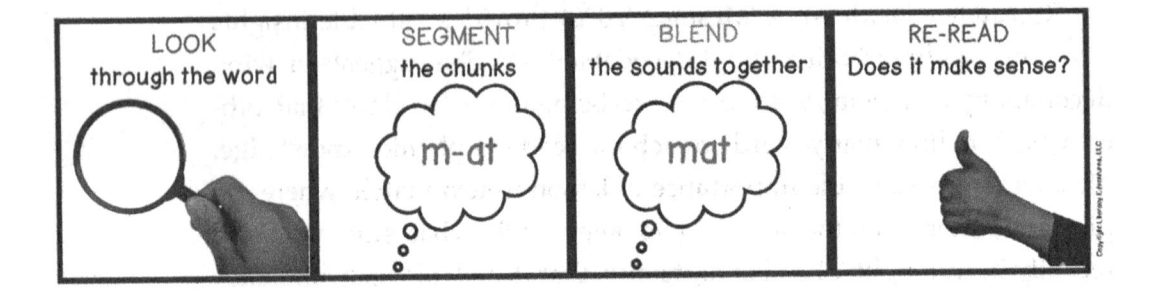

LOOK through the word	SEGMENT the chunks	BLEND the sounds together	RE-READ Does it make sense?
	m-at	mat	

Scaffolding Decodable Texts for Struggling Readers

For struggling readers, decodable texts can be overwhelming without proper scaffolding. Start by having students decode individual words in isolation. Once they are comfortable with this, introduce sentence-level decoding using tools like sentence pyramids. These pyramids enable students to decode one word at a time, gradually building up to reading complete sentences. This approach helps build confidence and reduces the overwhelm students might feel when faced with a full text.

Making Phonics Stick 203

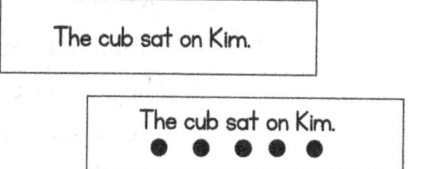

After mastering sentences, students can move on to full decodable texts. It is essential to preview the text with students, highlight high-frequency words, and review any phonics skills they'll encounter. This builds background knowledge and prepares students for success as they move into reading the full text.

Decodables as a Stepping Stone

Decodable texts are a temporary but essential stepping stone in a student's literacy journey. They help readers learn to attack unknown words and build fluency. Once students build fluency and automaticity with phonics patterns, they can transition to more complex texts.

> **THE GOAL** is to develop readers who can decode efficiently and comprehend more complex language as they progress.

Unfortunately, there is no magic time to transition students to more authentic texts, but here are some indicators that they might be ready.

- **Mastery of phonics patterns.** Students should have a firm grasp of phonics skills within their scope and sequence. They should be able to decode words and easily apply their knowledge of letter-sound relationships.
- **Fluency.** Students read decodable texts with accuracy, appropriate speed, and expression. Their reading should sound smooth rather than choppy or robotic, indicating that decoding is becoming more automatic.
- **Increased word recognition.** Students should have a growing sight word vocabulary, meaning they can recognize high-frequency and irregular words effortlessly without needing to decode each.

Comprehension. Students can focus on understanding their reading rather than spending most of their mental energy on decoding. They should be able to retell stories, answer comprehension questions, and make connections between the text and their own experiences.

Confidence and motivation. Students show increased confidence in their reading abilities and may express interest in reading more complex or diverse texts. This motivation can strongly indicate that they are ready for a new challenge.

Ability to decode multisyllabic words. Once students can decode multisyllabic words using their knowledge of syllable types and patterns, they will likely transition to more authentic texts that contain longer, more complex words.

Instructional Routines for Decodable Texts

Using decodable texts effectively requires a structured instructional routine. This routine typically includes a warm-up, time in text, and a follow-up activity:

- **The warm-up.** Begin with phoneme-grapheme practice, review of high-frequency words, and vocabulary introduction. This helps prepare students for the reading task ahead.

- **Time in text.** Have students do the work during this time. Decoding is essential, and students need lots of practice. It may be slow and labored at first, but with practice and repeated reading, students will begin to build fluency.

- **The follow-up.** After reading, focus on comprehension questions. Remember, although the goal of a decodable is to practice reading and build fluency, we can also address comprehension. We can also encourage lots of partner reading and repeated reading to continue building fluency.

Using Decodable Texts for Comprehension

Although the primary purpose of decodable texts is to build decoding skills, this doesn't mean that we don't also address comprehension. After reading, students can answer questions about the text or retell the story. This helps them connect phonics skills to meaning and reinforces their ability to understand what they are reading. Teachers can also extend reading with writing activities, encouraging students to use the phonics patterns they have learned in their written responses.

Building Vocabulary and Background Knowledge

Before students begin reading a decodable text, it's important to introduce any irregular words and unfamiliar vocabulary. This builds background knowledge and prepares students for words they may otherwise struggle with. For example, if the text includes the word "brisk," the teacher can explain its meaning before students encounter it in the text.

Moving Beyond Decodables

As students become more proficient readers, they will eventually move beyond decodable texts. It is important to note that students become proficient readers by learning *how* to read. Decodable texts are an essential foundation in this process. They provide the practice students need to become fluent and confident readers. Once students have mastered phonics and decoding, they can transition to more complex texts, focusing more on comprehension and vocabulary development.

The Role of Read-Alouds in Early Literacy

Although decodable texts are crucial for developing phonics and fluency, we must remember the other important components of reading. Reading authentic literature aloud to our students is also critical. When we do this, we expose students to more complex language structures, helping them develop a deeper understanding of language.

> **BY ENSURING** that we are hitting all essential components of reading, we are ensuring that the foundation is strong from the ground up.

In summary, decodable texts are an invaluable tool for early reading instruction. When paired with systematic phonics lessons and scaffolded effectively, decodable texts help students build the decoding skills they need to become fluent readers. By combining decodable texts with read-aloud and writing activities, teachers can ensure students develop the technical and comprehension skills they need for long-term reading success.

Dictation

Dictation in phonics is a teaching strategy in which students listen to spoken sounds, words, or sentences and then write them down. This process helps reinforce letter-sound relationships, spelling patterns, and phonics rules by requiring students to encode (or spell) the sounds they hear. Dictation strengthens students' phonics skills and provides a direct connection between hearing sounds and writing them, supporting reading and writing development. It is essential for reinforcing phonemic awareness, spelling accuracy, and proper sentence structure.

Practical implications of dictation in phonics instruction are essential to bridging the gap between reading and writing.

> **DICTATION PROVIDES** a structured opportunity for students to actively apply phonics skills in a guided, hands-on manner, strengthening their encoding abilities—also known as spelling—while reinforcing what they have learned in reading.

Following are some critical practical applications of dictation and how they support emerging readers and writers.

Application of Phonics Skills in Writing

Dictation enables students to transfer their phonics knowledge from decoding (reading) to encoding (writing). As students listen to a sound, word, or sentence and write them down, they actively participate in sound-symbol correspondences. This active engagement between letters and sounds is crucial. Research indicates that phonics skills stick when practiced during authentic reading and writing tasks.

Structured and Systematic Practice

Dictation follows a systematic approach that gets more complex as students grow in their skills. For younger students or those just starting, it might begin with individual letter sounds or simple consonant vowel consonant (CVC) words. As they progress, dictation includes sentences that blend new phonics patterns with skills they have already learned. This mix, known as *interleaving* (Agarwal & Bain, 2019), helps students strengthen their understanding by practicing both new and familiar concepts together. It's a great way to help students build confidence while reinforcing what they have already mastered, all without feeling overwhelmed.

Immediate Feedback and Self-Correction

One of the most important things to remember regarding dictation is to provide students with immediate feedback. When students finish writing, it's vital to have them check their work for mistakes and then offer feedback on mistakes the students do not catch. With both dictation and independent writing, I use this graphic organizer to support students in organizing their thoughts and ensuring their writing is clear and accurate. After students finish writing, I ask them to reread their sentences twice. During the first read, they focus on checking for spelling accuracy and whether their sentences make sense. During the second read, they check for proper capitalization, punctuation, and neat handwriting. This process reinforces self-monitoring skills and encourages attention to detail in their writing.

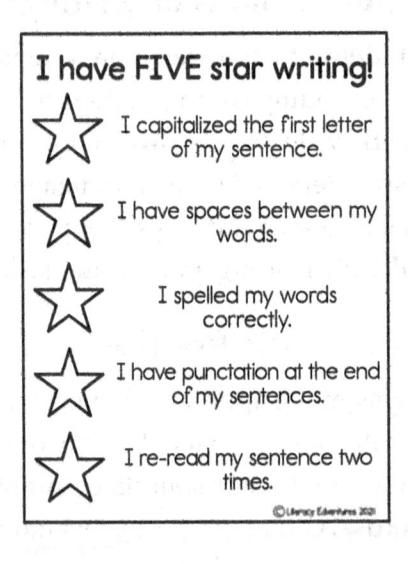

I have FIVE star writing!

☆ I capitalized the first letter of my sentence.

☆ I have spaces between my words.

☆ I spelled my words correctly.

☆ I have punctation at the end of my sentences.

☆ I re-read my sentence two times.

© Literacy Edventures 2021

ENCOURAGING SELF-CORRECTION fosters independence and helps students recognize their errors, an essential part of mastering spelling and phonics.

Cumulative Review and Reinforcement

Dictation is not just about practicing new phonics skills; it also reinforces skills learned in previous weeks. A solid dictation routine includes a balance of skills students are currently working on and those they have previously been taught. This ensures that students retain and apply skills over time, helping to prevent learning decay and solidifying students' long-term understanding of sound-spelling correspondences.

Phonemic Awareness and Orthographic Mapping

When students participate in dictation, they practice writing and strengthen their phonemic awareness, as they must hear, segment, and reproduce the sounds they are learning. Additionally, students engage in orthographic mapping by connecting the sounds they hear to the letters they write. This process helps them store words in their long-term memory, making them easier to recognize and spell in the future.

Supporting Struggling Students

As teachers, we can use several strategies to support students during dictation. For example, you can segment the sounds of a word out loud to help break it down, use manipulatives for word mapping, or give extra practice with shorter, more straightforward sentences for those who might find dictation challenging. By adjusting the exercises' difficulty and pace, you can ensure all your students get the support they need, no matter where they are in their learning journey.

Enhancing Handwriting and Sentence Structure

Dictation also provides a chance to teach and reinforce proper handwriting, punctuation, and sentence structure. As students write sentences during dictation practice, teachers can model and correct these aspects of writing, helping students transfer their phonics knowledge into well-formed written language.

By incorporating dictation into regular phonics instruction, we can create a powerful learning experience that connects reading and writing, giving students the tools they need to succeed in both areas. Dictation is a critical part of phonics instruction, ensuring that students can decode words when reading and encode them when writing.

Classroom Implementation Actionable Steps

Lesson 1   Pre-reading Activity for Decodable Texts

Materials Needed
- Decodable text (aligned with current phonics skills)
- Whiteboard and markers
- Flashcards with high-frequency words
- Word list with target phonics skill (e.g., short vowel "a" or "i")

Activity: Introduction (One Minute)
Explain that before reading a new text, students will review some of the sounds and words they have been practicing. This will help them get ready to read the book and understand it better.

Pre-reading (Three Minutes)

1. Phoneme-Grapheme Practice
Write a few CVC words that align with the phonics skill (e.g., "bat," "pin") on the board and model blending them. Then have the students echo you and blend the words.

2. High-Frequency Word Review
Review a few high-frequency words they will encounter in the text. Map them if necessary.

3. Discuss Vocabulary
Discuss vocabulary words students might encounter while reading the text.

4. Book Walk
Flip through the decodable text without reading it. Ask students to identify words on each page that they recognize and can decode. Focus on words that use the target phonics skill.

Conclusion (One Minute)
Explain that now that they have reviewed the words, they are ready to read the story using their phonics knowledge to help them decode.

Lesson 2   Blending Lines Practice

Materials Needed
- Blending lines sheet (words with the specific phonics skill)
- Whiteboard and markers

Activity: Introduction (One Minute)
Tell students that today they'll practice blending words to get faster and more accurate at reading.

Blending Lines (Three Minutes)
1. Display a list of words that align with the phonics skill you are focusing on.
2. Model how to blend the words by saying each sound slowly, then smoothly blend them together.

(Continued)

3. Have students echo you. Then, repeat the process a few times, blending the words more quickly with each pass.
4. After practicing, have students try blending the words on their own.

Conclusion (One Minute)
Explain how reading words in isolation can help warm our brains up for reading longer texts.

Lesson 3   Decodable Text Staggered Reading

Materials Needed
- Decodable text (aligned with current phonics skill)

Activity: Introduction (One Minute)
Explain to students that instead of taking turns reading one at a time (round robin), they will use staggered reading to practice the decodable text.

Staggered Reading (Five Minutes)
1. Ask students to place their finger on the title of the book. Remind students that they may begin whisper reading the text when you touch their book. Begin to the right of your table and touch student number one's book. As they start reading, skip over the person beside them and touch the next student's book. Continue this process until all students are whisper reading.
2. Lean in and listen to different students as they read and offer support and immediate feedback.

Conclusion (One Minute)
Discuss the text and tricky words. Model good reading that you notice. Example: "I noticed that Sarah used her decoding helper when she came to a difficult word. She sounded out the word and read it again to make sure it made sense."

Lesson 4   Dictation of Words and Sentences

Materials Needed
- Paper and pencils
- Whiteboard and markers
- Word list with target phonics skill (e.g., short vowel "a" and "i")

Activity: Introduction (One Minute)
Tell students that today, they will practice writing words and sentences using the phonics patterns they have learned. This will help them connect their reading to writing.

Dictation Routine (Five Minutes)
(Note you can easily choose to do just a sound, word, or sentence or a combination. Decide what your students need. Use the following samples.)

1. **Row 1—sounds.** Say a sound (e.g., /a/, /i/) and have students echo it. Then, they write the letter that represents the sound.

2. **Row 2—words with new skill.** Say a word with the target phonics pattern (e.g., "cat," "sit"). Have students echo the word and then write it down.

3. **Row 3—review words.** Say a word that uses a previously taught phonics skill (e.g., "dog," "pig") and have students write it down after echoing the word.

4. **Row 4—sentence.** Dictate a simple sentence that includes the new and review skills (e.g., "The cat is on the mat."). Have students write the entire sentence.

Conclusion (One Minute)
After students finish, have them read their sentence aloud and check for any mistakes. Provide corrective feedback as needed, and encourage students to self-correct.

Five Key Takeaways from Chapter 8

- **Decodable texts are crucial for fluency.** Decodable texts provide structured opportunities for students to apply their phonics knowledge in reading and help them build fluency and confidence.
- **Encoding is just as important as decoding.** Spelling is a powerful activity that reinforces phonics by enabling students to practice spelling the sounds they are learning in reading.
- **Orthographic mapping supports long-term retention.** Both decodable texts and dictation contribute to orthographic mapping, helping students store words in long-term memory for automatic recognition.
- **Cumulative review is key.** Effective phonics instruction includes regular cumulative review of previously taught skills, ensuring long-term mastery and preventing learning decay.
- **Immediate feedback enhances learning.** During dictation, offering immediate corrective feedback and encouraging self-correction helps students solidify their understanding and build independence in both reading and writing.

CHAPTER NINE

Background Knowledge and Vocabulary

In any classroom, students arrive with a wide range of experiences and knowledge about the world, significantly affecting their ability to understand new topics. Some students come with rich vocabulary and background knowledge, and others may have had fewer opportunities to develop these skills. It's important to remember that every child enters our classrooms with different levels of background knowledge and varying vocabularies, and it's our job to build on that foundation, no matter where they start.

Although this book emphasizes early literacy skills like phonemic awareness and phonics—crucial components for learning to read—these foundational skills alone are insufficient for ensuring success. Suppose we focus solely on helping students decode words. In that case, we risk neglecting an equally important part of reading comprehension: the ability to understand and make sense of those words in context. That's why we must also prioritize building vocabulary and background knowledge, which is essential for students to comprehend what they read.

Think of it as balancing both sides of Scarborough's Reading Rope: one strand represents word recognition skills, like decoding and phonics, and the other represents language comprehension, where background knowledge and vocabulary come in. If we only focus on one side, we leave our students with gaps in their reading abilities, making it harder for them to comprehend texts later on. The ultimate goal is for our students to read fluently and deeply understand and engage with what they are reading. To do that, we must reinforce comprehension through read-alouds and conversations until our students are able to read and comprehend on their own.

Understanding Background Knowledge and Vocabulary

Background knowledge refers to the facts, concepts, and ideas that students have already learned from their experiences at home, in school, and in the world around them, as they relate to the texts they'll be encountering. Nancy Hennessy draws a slight distinction between background knowledge and prior knowledge, emphasizing that background knowledge is text-specific (Hennessy, 2020). This knowledge enables students to connect their reading to what they already know, helping them make sense of new texts. Even a skilled decoder may struggle to comprehend a text without sufficient background knowledge, as they'd lack the context needed to understand what the words mean in a particular situation.

Vocabulary is the collection of words students know and can use to communicate. The more words a student knows, the better they can understand what they read and hear. An extensive vocabulary opens up new opportunities for making connections between ideas and grasping deeper meanings in texts. Research has consistently shown that having a strong vocabulary is one of the most significant predictors of reading comprehension.

However, not all vocabulary words hold equal weight and importance.

Tier 1 Vocabulary: Everyday Words

These are the common words that most children acquire through daily conversation and interactions, such as "play," "mom," "happy," or "school." These words rarely need direct instruction because students are frequently exposed to them daily.

Tier 2 Vocabulary: Stronger Everyday Words

Tier 2 words are high-utility, academic words that appear across many subjects but may not be used in everyday conversation. Words like "purposeful," "worthy," or "encourage" fall into this category. Teaching these words explicitly is crucial because they appear frequently in texts across various content areas and are critical for academic success.

Tier 3 Vocabulary: Content-Specific Words

Tier 3 words are specialized words typically encountered in specific content areas, such as "precipitation" in science or "civilization" in social studies. Although these words are essential for understanding specific topics, they are less likely to be encountered in everyday contexts. Tier 3 words are usually taught in focused instruction when students explore particular subjects.

Building Vocabulary and Background Knowledge Alongside Phonics

As we teach students how to decode words through phonics and phonemic awareness, we must simultaneously work to build their background knowledge and vocabulary. This ensures that when students become fluent readers, they are not simply decoding words—they are also making sense of those words in a meaningful way.

Imagine a student who can easily read the word "precipitation" but does not understand what it means in the context of weather. This student might be able to pronounce the word perfectly, but their comprehension will suffer without the background knowledge to understand it. However, a student with a rich vocabulary and strong background knowledge about weather can decode, understand, and engage with a text about storms or climate change.

This chapter will explore practical, research-based strategies to help build vocabulary and background knowledge, ensuring that we develop both sides of the literacy equation. As our students master foundational reading skills, they will also gain the tools to comprehend texts and thrive as readers in all content areas.

What the Research Says

Effective literacy instruction requires a comprehensive understanding of how children develop reading skills. Although systematic phonics is a critical foundation for decoding, research underscores that phonics alone is not enough. To become proficient, confident readers, students also need content-rich curricula that build background knowledge and vocabulary, as well as instruction that foster fluency and comprehension. The power of vocabulary instruction lies in its ability to bridge the gap between decoding and understanding, equipping students to make meaningful connections with texts. The following studies delve into these essential components, highlighting how decoding, background knowledge, and vocabulary collectively contribute to reading success.

Castle et al. (2018) delved into the "reading wars," which have long debated the merits of phonics versus whole-language approaches. Their research concluded that systematic, explicit phonics instruction is essential for early reading success, particularly for learning to decode unfamiliar words. However, they also emphasized that phonics instruction alone is not enough. Students need to integrate phonics with vocabulary development, fluency, and comprehension to become proficient readers. This balanced approach not only aids in decoding but also supports overall reading comprehension. They argue that expert readers are formed by combining these instructional components, highlighting the importance of decoding skills and broader language comprehension.

Hirsch's (2004) work stresses the role of background knowledge and vocabulary in reading comprehension. He argues that although phonics is essential for decoding, students also need broad knowledge to understand what they read. Hirsch points out that having a strong vocabulary and rich background knowledge equip students to connect with new texts, deepening their comprehension. His research supports the idea that content-rich curricula, filled with opportunities to build general knowledge across subjects, are critical in the early years of learning to read. By developing vocabulary and background knowledge early, children are better prepared for the academic demands of later reading.

In a comprehensive meta-analysis of vocabulary intervention studies, Shapiro (2004) examined how vocabulary instruction affects reading comprehension. Shapiro's findings indicate that vocabulary interventions significantly enhance vocabulary acquisition, especially when integrated into read-alouds and explicit teaching. The meta-analysis suggests that when teachers focus on vocabulary in context—through read-alouds, discussions, and explicit instruction—students are more likely to grasp and retain new words. The study reinforces the importance of structured vocabulary instruction as a critical component of literacy development and reading comprehension.

To help guide instruction, Beck et al. (2002) introduced a framework in *Bringing Words to Life* that categorizes vocabulary into three tiers: Tier 1 (basic words), Tier 2 (high-utility, academic words), and Tier 3 (domain-specific terms). Their research emphasizes the importance of prioritizing Tier 2 words, as these are versatile and critical for comprehension across various texts. Beck and her colleagues highlight that effective vocabulary instruction involves rich, engaging discussions and multiple exposures to new words in meaningful contexts, enabling students to integrate these words into their broader language use and comprehension.

Wrap-Up of the Research

Castle et al. (2018). *Ending the Reading Wars.*

- **Phonics and vocabulary.** Students need systematic phonics instruction to decode words but they also require broader vocabulary and comprehension activities to develop full reading proficiency.
- **Balanced approach.** The most successful readers are those who combine decoding skills with broader language comprehension, which helps them transition from novice to expert readers.

Hirsch. (2004). *The Knowledge Deficit.*

- **Vocabulary is a key to comprehension.** Reading comprehension depends on understanding words, and students who have strong vocabularies and background knowledge can better understand what they read.
- **Building knowledge.** Introduce diverse topics and rich content across subjects to develop vocabulary and prepare students for reading comprehension success.

Shapiro. (2004). "A Meta-Analysis of Vocabulary Intervention Studies."

- **Vocabulary builds comprehension.** When students are taught vocabulary explicitly and through engaging contexts like read-alouds, their reading comprehension improves.
- **Practical instruction.** Provide vocabulary instruction in context, and encourage active engagement with new words to make sure students retain them for future reading success.

Beck et al. (2002). *Bringing Words to Life.*

- **Three tiers of vocabulary.** Vocabulary words are categorized into three tiers: Tier 1 (basic words), Tier 2 (high-utility academic words), and Tier 3 (domain-specific terms). Prioritizing Tier 2 words is key for enhancing comprehension across texts.
- **Effective strategies.** Robust vocabulary instruction involves teaching words in context, engaging students in rich discussions, and providing multiple exposures to ensure long-term retention and application in comprehension.

Practical Tips for Implementation

Building vocabulary and background knowledge is a cornerstone of effective literacy instruction, and it's most impactful when explicitly taught and integrated into everyday teaching practices. This section provides practical, research-based strategies that teachers can use to enhance their students' vocabulary and deepen their understanding of the world around them.

From leveraging content-rich lessons in science and social studies to creating thematic units and using interactive read-alouds, these tips offer actionable ways to make vocabulary instruction meaningful and connected to real-world contexts. By embedding new words in engaging, cross-curricular experiences, educators can help students retain and apply vocabulary in powerful ways.

Content-Rich Lessons: Integrating Science and Social Studies

One powerful strategy for building both vocabulary and background knowledge is to integrate science and social studies into your literacy block. This cross-curricular approach exposes students to content-rich lessons that provide real-world contexts for new vocabulary. For example, during a unit on ecosystems, incorporating fiction and nonfiction texts about habitats and animal adaptations helps students connect words to concepts they are exploring in other subjects. According to Nell Duke (2000), content-area instruction—especially in science and social studies—supports vocabulary development by embedding new words in meaningful, relevant contexts. This makes it easier for students to retain and apply new vocabulary to various academic situations.

Interactive Read-Alouds

Another effective approach is using interactive read-alouds, which provide students with rich opportunities to hear, discuss, and apply new vocabulary. During these sessions, pausing to explain key vocabulary, asking questions, and making connections enables students to engage actively with the text. This interactive process deepens their understanding and helps anchor new words in their long-term memory. Research by Wasik and Bond (2001) highlighted the value of this method, showing that children who participate in interactive read-alouds experience significant gains in vocabulary when meaningful discussions are integrated into the reading experience.

Thematic Units

Thematic units provide another valuable approach to building vocabulary and background knowledge. By immersing students in a focused topic across different content areas, teachers can help students develop a deep understanding of both the vocabulary and the content itself. For instance, a thematic unit on space might include reading books about the solar system, creating models of planets, and writing reports about astronauts, enabling students to engage with words like "orbit," "gravity," and "astronaut" in a hands-on, meaningful way. Cervetti et al. (2009) demonstrated that thematic teaching fosters vocabulary retention by connecting new words to real-world applications, making them easier to learn and remember.

Multiple Texts on the Same Topic

Using multiple texts on the same topic is also an effective way to reinforce vocabulary and deepen background knowledge. When students encounter the same words in varied contexts—through fiction, nonfiction, and multimedia—they are better able to understand and remember the vocabulary. For example, a unit on weather could involve reading different texts about storms, climate, and meteorology, all of which reinforce key vocabulary such as "forecast," "temperature," and "storm." Research by Nagy et al. (1987) emphasized the importance of repeated exposure to vocabulary in varied contexts, demonstrating that encountering words across different texts and situations strengthens understanding and fosters deeper connections with new vocabulary.

Multiple Exposures to Vocabulary

Finally, multiple exposures to vocabulary across different contexts are essential for ensuring long-term retention. Students need to hear and use new words repeatedly throughout the day to fully grasp their meanings. For example, after introducing the word "observe" during a science lesson, teachers can encourage students to use it during a reading activity or a class discussion, reinforcing the word's meaning through various applications. Stahl and Fairbanks (1986) showed that repeated exposure to vocabulary across multiple settings significantly improves retention, emphasizing the importance of using new words consistently in different contexts.

Classroom Implementation Actionable Steps

Now that we have a clearer understanding of vocabulary and comprehension—their importance, how they support reading development, and effective ways to teach them—let us explore practical strategies you can start incorporating into your classroom tomorrow!

Lesson Plan 1: Room on the Broom—Vocabulary and Read-Aloud

Grade level: K–2
Focus skills: Vocabulary and comprehension
Book: *Room on the Broom* by Julia Donaldson, illustrated by Axel Scheffler
Message/lesson: Friendship
Time: 45–60 minutes (split into two 30-minute sessions)

Part 1   Activity Title: Schema Connection Web

Objective

Students will use their schema (prior knowledge) to make meaningful connections with a story and visually represent those connections in a web.

Materials Needed

A fiction picture book (*Room on the Broom*)

- Large chart paper or whiteboard
- Markers
- Sticky notes or index cards for each student
- Optional: a large schema web template drawn on chart paper

Activity Instructions

1. Introduction (Five Minutes)

Teacher: "Alright, friends, today we are going to do a fun activity where we make a 'schema connection web!' Remember, your schema is all the things you already know that help you understand a story better. As we read, we'll connect the story and our own lives, using our schema to build a giant web of ideas!"

2. Read-Aloud and Sticky Notes (10–15 Minutes)

Read the chosen fiction book aloud to the class. At specific points in the story (predetermined by you), pause and ask students to think about any connections they can make to their own lives:

- "Has something like this ever happened to you?"
- "Does this remind you of another book or story you have read?"
- "How do you think the character is feeling? Have you ever felt like that?"

As students share their connections, they write them down on sticky notes or index cards. Encourage them to think broadly—about family, feelings, events, or even things they have seen in movies or TV shows.

3. Build the Schema Web (10 Minutes)
After reading the book, gather the students in a circle around the large chart paper or whiteboard. Write the title of the story in a big bubble at the center of the paper (this will be the center of the web).

Invite students to come up individually and stick their schema (sticky note or index card) around the central bubble. As they do, they'll explain their connection to the class. Draw lines connecting each student's schema to the story, forming a web of ideas that shows how everyone's prior knowledge connects to the book.

4. Discuss and Reflect (Five Minutes)
Once all the connections are on the web, lead a class discussion by asking these questions:

- "Look at how our schema helped us understand the story better!"
- "Did anyone else have the same connection? Why do you think that is?"
- "What are some ways our schema helped us understand what the characters were feeling?"

5. Closure (Three Minutes)
Teacher: "Wow! Look at all the connections we made! Our schema helps us connect stories to our lives, and that helps us understand the book so much better. Every time you read, think about what the story reminds you of, just like we did today!"

Part 2   Vocabulary

Objective

Students will learn and understand two key vocabulary words from *Room on the Broom*: "bounded" and "glint."

- Students will engage in activities to deepen their understanding and use the words in context.

Materials Needed

- Chart paper/whiteboard
- Sticky notes
- Vocabulary picture cards ("bounded," "glint")
- Exit cards

Vocabulary Instruction

1. *Introduction (One Minute)*

Teacher: "Today, we are going to learn two new words from our story. These words help us understand the story better and make it more exciting! First, I'll tell you the words, then we will learn what they mean, how they are used in the book, and we'll practice using them in our own sentences."

"Our two words today are 'bounded' and 'glint.' Let's say them together: 'bounded,' 'glint.'"

(Pause and have students repeat.)

2. *Introduce the Words and Definitions (Five Minutes)*

Teacher: "Let's start with our first word: 'bounded.' Listen carefully—'bounded' means to leap, jump, or hop. Let's say it together: 'bounded.'"

(Pause for students to repeat.)

Teacher: "Now, let's act it out! Stand up and show me what it looks like to bound across the room. Imagine you're a dog running excitedly to your owner or a rabbit hopping in the grass!"

(Give students a moment to act out the motion.)

Teacher: "Great! Now, let's talk about our second word: 'glint.' Listen carefully—'glint' means a small flash or gleam of light. Say it with me: 'glint.'"

(Pause for students to repeat.)

Teacher: "Let's imagine we are holding a shiny ring in the sunlight. Tilt it back and forth. Do you see how the light catches it for just a moment? That little flash is a glint!"

3. Examples and Nonexamples (Five Minutes)

Teacher: "Now, let's look at some examples and nonexamples of our words. This helps us really understand what they mean."

- "Bounded"
  - Example: "If I see a squirrel run across the yard really fast, I can say it bounded across the grass!"
  - Nonexample: "If the squirrel walks slowly across the grass, is it bounding? No! That would be walking."

Teacher: "Let's try another one! If a dog jumps up to catch a frisbee, is it bounding? Yes! But if the dog is lying down and resting, is it bounding? No!"

- "Glint"
  - Example: "If the sun shines on the water and you see tiny sparkles, that is a glint."
  - Nonexample: "If you are in a dark room with no light, would you see a glint? No, because there's no light to reflect."

(Continued)

Teacher: "Let's try one more. If a clean car is parked in the sun and you see little flashes of light on it, does it have a glint? Yes! But if the car is covered in dirt and looks dull, would it have a glint? No!"

4. Sentences and Context in the Story (Five Minutes)
Teacher: "Now, let's see how these words are used in *Room on the Broom*! I'm going to read a sentence from the book, and I want you to listen for our words."

- "Bounded" (page 6): "Then out of the bushes on thundering paws / There bounded a dog with the hat in his jaws."

Teacher: "The dog isn't just walking—he is so excited to bring the hat back that he jumps and bounds toward the witch!"

- "Glint" (page 16): "The dragon drew near with a glint in his eyes."

Teacher: "The dragon's glint tells us he is excited and determined. He sees something he wants, and his eyes flash with light!"

Teacher: "Let's talk about why the author chose these words. What does 'bounded' tell us about the dog? Would it be as exciting if the book said the dog 'walked' out of the bushes? No! And what does 'glint' tell us about the dragon's eyes? Does it make him seem happy or a little scary?"

5. Check for Understanding (Five Minutes)
Teacher: "Now it's your turn to use our words! I'm going to ask you some questions, and I want you to think carefully before answering."

Teacher: "Can you think of a time when you bounded somewhere quickly? Maybe you ran to get ice cream or jumped to catch a ball!"

(Give students time to respond.)

Teacher: "What is something that might have a glint?"

(Guide students toward answers like jewelry, the sun on the ocean, or a flashlight shining on something reflective.)

Background Knowledge and Vocabulary

6. Vocabulary Picture Cards (10 Minutes)
Teacher: "Now let's create our own vocabulary picture cards. Each of you will get a blank card with one of our words: 'bounded' or 'glint.' You can draw a picture to match the word or write a sentence using it!"

(Pass out vocabulary picture cards and allow students to illustrate or write.)

Teacher: "Before we finish, let's share a few examples. Who would like to show their picture and tell us about it?"

(Choose a few students to share.)

Part 3 Read-Aloud

Objective
Students will engage with the story *Room on the Broom* through guided questions, focusing on comprehension and story structure.

Materials Needed
- Copy of *Room on the Broom*
- Sticky notes

Lesson Plan
1. Pre-reading (Five Minutes)
Teacher: "Today, we are going to read about a witch and her friends who go on an exciting journey. Remember the words we learned: 'bounded' and 'glint.' Let us listen for them in the story!"

2. During Reading (20 Minutes)
Read *Room on the Broom* aloud to the class. Pause at the following points to ask comprehension questions:

(Continued)

- Page 2: "Where do you think they are going?"
- Page 6: "Do you think they'll let the dog on the broom?"
- Page 10: "What (or who) might they find in the bog?"
- Page 12: "How is the witch showing empathy?"
- Page 18: "Do you notice anything about the beast?"
- Page 22: "How has the broom changed from the beginning to the end?

As you come across the words "bounded" and "glint," remind students of their meanings and how they are used in the story:

- "Bounded" (page 6): "Then out of the bushes on thundering paws/There bounded a dog with the hat in his jaws."
- "Glint" (page 16): "The dragon drew near with a glint in his eyes."

3. After Reading (Five Minutes)

- Retell the story together as a class.
- Ask: "How did the characters help each other? What was the theme of the book?"
- Reinforce the use of the vocabulary words: "Can anyone explain how the word 'bounded' was used in the story?"

Extension Activity (Optional for Independent Practice)

- **K–1 activity.** Students will cut out and paste the characters from the story in the order they were found. Then, they will write a sentence using "bounded."
- **Grades 2–3 activity.** Students will write down examples of repetition and rhyming in the book. Then, they will fill in the plot diagram to summarize the story, using the word "glint" in one of their sentences.

> *Assessment*
> - Vocabulary use on exit cards
> - Participation in the read-aloud comprehension questions

Lesson Plan 2: Nonfiction Vocabulary and Read-Aloud

Grade level: Kindergarten–second grade
Focus skills: Vocabulary and comprehension
Book: *Over and Under the Pond* by Kate Messner, illustrated by Christopher Silas Neal
Theme: Exploring nature while learning about the habitats and animals of a pond
Time: 45–60 minutes (split into two 30-minute sessions)

Part 1   Activity Title: Schema Activation and Background Knowledge

Objective
Students will activate their schema (prior knowledge) to make connections with the topic of ponds and visually represent their ideas in a web.

Materials Needed
A nonfiction picture book (*Over and Under the Pond*)
- Large chart paper or whiteboard
- Markers

(Continued)

- Sticky notes or index cards for each student
- Optional: large schema web template drawn on chart paper

Activity Instructions

1. Introduction (Five Minutes)
Teacher: "Friends, today we are going to learn about ponds! Ponds are small bodies of water with so much life—plants, animals, and even insects live there. Let us make a web of ideas to show what we already know about ponds. This is called 'activating our schema,' or all the things we already know that help us understand new information better."

2. Brainstorm (Five to Seven Minutes)
- Write "pond" in a big bubble in the center of the chart paper.
- Ask guiding questions:
  - "What kinds of animals might live in a pond?"
  - "What do ponds look like?"
  - "What do animals need to live in a pond?"
- Write student ideas around the word "pond," connecting them with lines to form a web.

3. Turn and Talk (Five Minutes)
- Students turn and talk with a partner to share any personal experiences with ponds.
- Invite a few students to share their connections aloud, adding to the web.

4. Discuss and Reflect (Three Minutes)
Teacher: "Look at all the things we already know about ponds! This will help us as we read and learn even more."

Part 2 Vocabulary

Objective
Students will learn and understand two key vocabulary words: "surface" and "glide."

Materials Needed

- Chart paper or whiteboard
- Sticky notes
- Vocabulary picture cards ("surface," "glide")
- Exit cards

Vocabulary Instruction

1. Introduction (One Minute)
Teacher: "Today, we're going to learn two new words that will help us describe what we see and how things move. These words are important because they help us picture what's happening when we read or talk about nature."

Teacher: "Our words today are 'surface' and 'glide.' Let's say them together: 'surface, glide.'"

(Pause and have students repeat.)

2. Word and Definition (Five Minutes)
(Write the words and definitions on the board.)

Teacher: "Let's start with our first word: 'surface.' Listen carefully—'surface' means the top layer of something, like water. Let's say it together: 'surface.'"

(Pause for students to repeat.)

Teacher: "Imagine looking at a lake. The very top of the water where the ducks swim—that's the surface. But if you dive under, you are no longer on the surface!"

(Continued)

Teacher: "Now, let's learn our second word: 'glide.' 'Glide' means to move smoothly and quietly. Say it with me: 'glide.'"

(Pause for students to repeat.)

Teacher: "Think about an ice skater. When they move across the ice without stopping, they glide. Can you show me with your hands how something might glide?"

(Model a smooth hand motion, then encourage students to do the same.)

3. Examples and Nonexamples (Five Minutes)

Teacher: "Now, let's look at some examples and nonexamples to help us really understand these words."

- "Surface"
  - Example: "The top of a calm pond is the surface."
  - Nonexample: "The muddy bottom of the pond is NOT the surface because it is underneath."

Teacher: "If I say 'the surface of a table,' where am I pointing? Yes, the very top! But if I look underneath, is that the surface? No, because the surface is always the top!"

- "Glide"
  - Example: "A duck moves across the water without making waves—it glides."
  - Nonexample: "A fish jumps out of the water. Is it gliding? No! Because gliding means moving smoothly, and jumping is fast and bumpy."

Teacher: "If you ride a bike and stop every few seconds, are you gliding? No! But if you ride down a hill without pedaling and move smoothly, that's gliding!"

4. Sentences and Context in the Story (Five Minutes)

Teacher: "Now, let's see how these words are used in sentences. Listen carefully and think about what these words help us picture."

- "Surface": "The surface of the pond reflects the sky above."

    Teacher: "What does this sentence tell us? If the surface reflects the sky, that means it's smooth and clear, like a mirror."

- "Glide": "The heron glides over the water, looking for fish."

    Teacher: "Does the heron flap its wings fast and make a lot of noise? No! It moves smoothly through the air. That's what it means to glide."

    Teacher: "Let's talk about these words. Why do you think the author used the word 'surface' instead of just saying 'the water'? How does the word 'glide' help us imagine how the heron moves?"

5. Check for Understanding (Five Minutes)

Teacher: "Now it's your turn to think about these words! I'm going to ask you a few questions. Can you think of something else that moves smoothly or glides?"

(Guide students toward answers like ice skaters, a paper airplane, or a snake slithering.)

Teacher: "What do you see when you look at the surface of the water?"

(Encourage answers like reflections, ripples, or floating leaves.)

6. Vocabulary Picture Cards (10 Minutes)

Teacher: "Now let's create our own vocabulary picture cards. Each of you will get a blank card with one of our words: 'surface' or 'glide.' You can draw a picture to match the word or write a sentence using it!"

(Pass out vocabulary picture cards and have students to illustrate or write.)

Teacher: "Before we finish, let's share a few examples. Who would like to show their picture and tell us about it?"

(Choose a few students to share.)

Part 3 Nonfiction Read-Aloud

Objective
Students will engage with the story *Over and Under the Pond* through guided questions, focusing on vocabulary and comprehension.

Materials Needed
- *Over and Under the Pond* by Kate Messner, illustrated by Christopher Silas Neal
- Sticky notes

Activity Instructions
1. Pre-reading (Five Minutes)
Teacher: "Today, we are going to read about a pond and the amazing plants and animals that live there. Listen carefully for the words 'surface' and 'glide.' Think about how the story shows what happens above and below the pond!"

2. During Reading (20 Minutes)
Read the book aloud, pausing to discuss key moments and vocabulary:
- Page 5: "What do you think lives under the surface of the pond?"
- Page 9: "How does the heron move across the pond?"
- Page 13: "What do the fish need to live under the water?"
  Reinforce vocabulary in context as the words appear in the text.

3. After Reading (Five Minutes):
Discuss these questions:
- "What new things did we learn about ponds today?"
- "How do animals move on the surface or under the water?"
  Retell the story together, focusing on what happens over and under the pond.

Extension Activities

1. K–1 Activity

- Students cut and paste images of animals into categories: Over the Pond, Under the Pond.
- Write one sentence using "surface" or "glide."

2. Grades 2–3 Activity

Students create a mini-booklet about pond animals, including their own sentences with vocabulary words.

Assessment

- Vocabulary use on exit cards
- Participation in the schema web and comprehension questions during the read-aloud

While teaching foundational skills like phonics and decoding is critical to early reading success, building vocabulary and background knowledge is equally important to ensure students can fully comprehend what they read. By recognizing and addressing the varied experiences and knowledge students bring to the classroom, we can bridge the gap and create a more equitable learning environment. Integrating strategies that support vocabulary development, such as interactive read-alouds, thematic units, and cross-curricular lessons, ensures students can engage meaningfully with texts and deepen their understanding. Ultimately, fostering both sides of Scarborough's Reading Rope—word recognition and language comprehension—equips students with the tools they need to become fluent, thoughtful readers.

Five Key Takeaways from Chapter 9

- **Importance of background knowledge and vocabulary.** Students come to class with varying levels of background knowledge and vocabulary, which significantly affects their ability to comprehend texts. It is essential to build on this foundation to help students make sense of what they read.

- **Balance in reading instruction.** Although phonics and decoding are crucial for early reading, focusing solely on these skills is not enough. Vocabulary and background knowledge are equally important for comprehension, as they enable students to understand the context of the words they decode.
- **Foster both sides of Scarborough's Reading Rope.** The process of learning to read can be visualized as two strands of a rope—word recognition (decoding) and language comprehension (background knowledge and vocabulary). To ensure students become proficient readers, it's essential to nurture both strands equally, integrating explicit instruction in decoding with rich opportunities to build background knowledge and expand vocabulary.
- **Understand the three tiers of vocabulary:**
  - **Tier 1.** Common, everyday words that children typically pick up naturally through regular conversations and experiences (e.g., "play," "mom," "happy").
  - **Tier 2.** Academic words that are versatile and frequently used across different subjects but may not come up in casual conversations (e.g., "purposeful," "encourage"). These words are essential for academic achievement and benefit from explicit instruction.
  - **Tier 3.** Subject-specific, technical terms often tied to particular areas of study (e.g., "precipitation" in science or "civilization" in social studies). These words are best introduced and explored within the context of the subject matter.
- **Knowledge building and vocabulary in context:** Building vocabulary is most effective when students encounter new words in meaningful contexts. Strategies like read-alouds, discussions, and thematic units enable students to see and use vocabulary in real-world scenarios, which helps with retention and understanding. Engaging with vocabulary through varied contexts helps solidify comprehension and long-term retention.

CHAPTER TEN

Bringing It All Together
Fostering a Love for Reading and Creating Lifelong Readers

In this book, we have covered the foundations of literacy instruction, from phonemic awareness and phonics to the role of dictation and decodable texts. Along the way, we have explored what research tells us about how children learn to read and the importance of using evidence-based strategies in the classroom. Now, it's time to pull everything together with one ultimate goal: creating lifelong readers who not only read because they can but also because they love to. To make this vision a reality, we must leverage both the power of the classroom and the support of the home.

THE JOY of reading is something we want every child to experience.

Fostering a Love for Reading in the Classroom

As educators, our ultimate goal is not just to teach students how to read and write but to foster a lifelong love for literacy that brings joy and fulfillment. Katie Egan Cunningham, coauthor of *Shifting the Balance 3–5*, beautifully emphasizes this in her book *Start with Joy: Designing Literacy Learning for Student Happiness* (Cunningham, 2019). Cunningham bridges literacy instruction with the science of happiness, highlighting how literacy experiences can contribute to students' overall well-being.

In her work, Cunningham outlines seven pillars of joy that can transform literacy instruction: connection, choice, challenge, play, story, discovery, and movement. These pillars remind us that fostering a joyful classroom goes hand-in-hand with creating effective, engaging learning environments. For example, integrating *choice* into literacy activities—such as allowing students to select books that resonate with their interests—can significantly increase motivation and engagement. Similarly, *story* serves as a powerful tool for building empathy and making learning memorable, while *play* and *discovery* encourage creativity and curiosity (Cunningham, 2019).

Incorporating these principles into structured literacy practices enriches the learning process and builds a foundation of happiness and intrinsic motivation. For instance, when we use decodable texts to reinforce phonics skills, we can also tap into discovery by exploring how these skills unlock the magic of reading. When teaching vocabulary, we can enhance connection by tying new words to students' lives and experiences, making them more meaningful and memorable (Cunningham, 2019).

Cunningham's framework reminds us that literacy instruction is not just about developing skills; it's about nurturing whole learners. By embedding joy into literacy instruction, we empower students to see reading and writing as tools for exploration, self-expression, and connection—skills that will serve them both academically and personally for a lifetime.

Here are a few key ways to bring research into the classroom while fostering that joy for reading:

- **Interest-driven engagement.** Research highlights that students are more engaged when their personal interests are incorporated into their learning. Although data should guide our instruction, we can also tap into students' curiosities and preferences to foster a deeper connection to reading. For example, allowing students to explore topics they find fascinating—whether through decodable texts, nonfiction picture books, or engaging stories—creates opportunities for meaningful reading experiences. Encouraging students to share their favorite discoveries or insights from what they have read builds a sense of ownership and enthusiasm for learning, while also cultivating a supportive classroom community rooted in shared interests (Guthrie & Wigfield, 2000).

- **Celebrate progress.** Everyone loves to be celebrated, and students are no different. Recognizing small wins—like decoding a tricky word or finishing a book—can make a big difference in students' learning. Celebrating these moments helps students feel successful and motivates them to keep going, even when tasks get harder.

  Research supports the importance of celebrating progress. In *How Learning Works: Seven Research-Based Principles for Smart Teaching*, Ambrose et al. (2010) explained that motivation is key to learning, and positive reinforcement—like acknowledging small achievements—boosts intrinsic motivation. When students see how their efforts lead to success, they are more likely to persist in challenging tasks.

  By celebrating progress, we show students that reading is not just about finishing a book—it's about getting better and enjoying the process. This simple practice helps create confident, motivated learners who are excited to grow.

- **Make reading fun.** Research shows that when learning is enjoyable, students are more likely to participate actively and retain what they learn. Guthrie and Wigfield (2000) emphasize the importance of motivation and engagement in reading, finding that when students experience reading as meaningful and enjoyable, they are more likely to improve their reading achievement. Bringing fun into the literacy block—through read-alouds, interactive activities, or even reading games—helps make reading feel less like a chore and more like an adventure. When students enjoy the process, they are more likely to stick with it and, over time, develop a lifelong love for reading.

Gaining At-Home Support

The power of classroom instruction is strengthened when it is reinforced at home. Family engagement plays a critical role in extending learning beyond the school day, and research shows that when families are involved in their child's literacy development, children tend to have higher reading achievement (Epstein, 2001). Although we recognize that not all families are able to provide the same level of support, we can encourage and guide caregivers who are able and offer resources to help bridge the gap for those who need additional support.

Explain the Why

Parents are more likely to be involved in at-home literacy when they understand the importance of their role. Short, easy-to-read newsletters or videos that explain the benefits of reading for fun—building vocabulary comprehension and fostering a love of learning—can motivate parents to prioritize reading. Once parents see that reading is about more than homework, they are more likely to make it part of their daily routine.

By equipping families with practical strategies and accessible tools, we can create opportunities for meaningful literacy growth both inside and outside the classroom. Here's how we can help:

- **Read aloud for 10 minutes a night.** Encourage families to set aside a short, consistent time for reading together, whether it's a bedtime story or a favorite book.
- **Play literacy-based games.** Share simple games like rhyming matching, alphabet scavenger hunts, or word bingo that make learning fun.
- **Provide decodable books.** Offer books that align with the phonics skills being taught in class so children can practice decoding words with confidence.

- **Discuss stories together.** Suggest that families ask open-ended questions after reading, like "What was your favorite part?" or "What do you think will happen next?" to boost comprehension.
- **Label items at home.** Encourage families to label common household objects (e.g., "chair," "door," "lamp") to help younger children connect words with their meanings.
- **Listen to audiobooks.** Recommend audiobooks for car rides or quiet time to expose children to new vocabulary and fluent reading.
- **Create a word jar.** Families can write new or interesting words they come across and add them to a jar to revisit and discuss.
- **Sing songs and nursery rhymes.** Suggest incorporating literacy into daily routines through songs that build phonemic awareness and rhythm in language.
- **Visit the library.** Encourage families to take advantage of free resources by borrowing books, attending story times, or exploring community literacy events.
- **Celebrate reading milestones.** Remind families to acknowledge small wins, like finishing a book or mastering a tricky word, to motivate and build their child's confidence.

Build a Home-School Connection with a Literacy Night

Building a strong home-school connection is essential for fostering student success, particularly in literacy. Hosting a literacy night is an effective and engaging way to bring parents and students together to celebrate learning and strengthen literacy skills.

Set up a welcoming and cozy environment with reading nooks, pillows, and soft lighting to make the evening enjoyable for families. Let students take the lead during the event, showcasing what they are learning through demonstrations of phonics games or practicing letter sounds. This gives parents a hands-on view of the skills their children are developing and offers insight into how they can support literacy learning at home.

To make the event more interactive, set up simple literacy stations where families can rotate through activities like phonemic awareness games, decoding practice, and reading fluency exercises. Each station should have clear, simple instructions, making it easy for parents to replicate the activities at home.

At the end of the evening, provide take-home resources such as these:

- Phonics-aligned high-frequency word lists
- Tips for reading aloud
- Printable literacy games
- A suggested nightly reading routine calendar

Add fun, family-friendly elements like a reading bingo game or a book swap, where families can trade gently used books to encourage a love for reading. Include a brief question and answer session to give parents the chance to ask questions and learn more about how to support literacy development at home.

Wrap up the night with a community-building activity, such as a special story read aloud by you or a guest reader. Encourage parents to share tips and favorite children's books with one another, fostering a sense of connection and shared purpose.

By organizing literacy nights, you create a space where students can take pride in their learning, parents feel empowered, and families leave with practical tools to support literacy growth at home

As we bring this book to a close, it's clear that our ultimate goal goes beyond teaching students simply to read. We want to create lifelong readers who are passionate about reading because they can and love it. Throughout this book, we have examined the essential components of literacy instruction, including phonemic awareness, phonics, dictation, and the importance of decodable texts. Along the way, research has been our guiding light, showing us the most effective ways to support children's literacy development. But now it's time to turn all that knowledge into something more: a lifelong gift that students carry with them beyond the classroom.

Fostering a love for reading is not just about skills—it's about joy. We must create a classroom environment where students feel supported and inspired. Giving them choice and voice in what they read, celebrating every small victory, and making literacy instruction fun are just a few ways to nurture this love. By using research-based practices, we set students up for reading success and fuel their curiosity and confidence.

Equally important is the role of families. The partnership between home and school can amplify the power of classroom instruction. We extend learning far beyond the school day by providing parents with simple, actionable steps to support literacy at home. Hosting interactive events like reading nights brings families into the literacy journey and helps parents feel empowered to play an active role in their child's reading development.

We have the power to transform how students experience reading. By fostering a positive reading culture, partnering with families, and using research-based strategies, we can create confident, lifelong readers. This journey isn't about perfection—it's about progress. We start small, celebrate every milestone, and nurture a love for reading that extends beyond the classroom. When students see reading as an adventure rather than a task, they become readers for life. The work we do today will shape their futures, opening doors to knowledge, imagination, and endless possibilities. Now, let's make reading an experience every child will treasure for years to come. As educators, we are shaping the future, one reader at a time.

References

Adams, M. J. (1990). *Beginning to read: Thinking and learning about print*. MIT Press.

Agarwal, P. K., & Bain, P. M. (2019). *Powerful teaching: Unleash the science of learning*. Jossey-Bass.

Ambrose, S. A., Bridges, M. W., DiPietro, M., Lovett, M. C., & Norman, M. K. (2010). *How learning works: Seven research-based principles for smart teaching*. Jossey-Bass.

Beck, I. L., McKeown, M. G., & Kucan, L. (2002). *Bringing words to life: Robust vocabulary instruction*. Guilford Press.

Beverly, B., Giles, R. M., & Buck, K. (2009). First-grade reading gains following enrichment: Phonics plus decodable texts compared to authentic literature read aloud. *Reading Improvement, 46*(4), 191–199.

Blevins, W. (2016). *A fresh look at phonics: Common causes of failure and 7 ingredients for success*. Corwin.

Castle, J., Rastle, K., & Nation, K. (2018). Ending the reading wars: Reading acquisition from novice to expert. *Psychological Science in the Public Interest, 19*(1), 5–51. https://doi.org/10.1177/1529100618772271

Cervetti, G. N., Jaynes, C. A., & Hiebert, E. H. (2009). Increasing opportunities to acquire knowledge through reading. In E. H. Hiebert (Ed.), *Reading more, reading better* (pp. 79–100). Guilford Press.

Chall, J. S. (1996). *Learning to read: The great debate* (3rd ed.). Harcourt Brace.

Cunningham, A. & Rose, D. (2010). This is your brain on reading. Retrieved from https://www.hmhco.com/products/iread/pdfs/EdWeek_OpEd5_brain_on_reading.pdf

Cunningham, K. E. (2019). *Start with joy: Designing literacy learning for student happiness*. Stenhouse Publishers.

Duke, N. K. (2000). 3.6 minutes per day: The scarcity of informational texts in first grade. *Reading Research Quarterly, 35*(2), 202–224.

Ehri, L. C. (1995). Phases of development in learning to read words by sight. *Journal of Research in Reading, 18*(2), 116–125.

Ehri, L. C. (2004). What teachers need to know and do to teach letter-sounds, phonemic awareness, word reading, and phonics. In P. McCardle & V. Chhabra (Eds.), *The voice of evidence in reading research* (pp. 153–186). Brookes Publishing.

Ehri, L. C. (2014). Orthographic mapping in the acquisition of sight word reading, spelling memory, and vocabulary learning. *Scientific Studies of Reading, 18*(1), 5–21. https://doi.org/10.1080/10888438.2013.819356

Ehri, L. C., Nunes, S. R., Stahl, S. A., & Willows, D. M. (2001). Systematic phonics instruction helps students learn to read: Evidence from the National Reading Panel's meta-analysis. *Review of Educational Research, 71*(3), 393–447.

Epstein, J. L. (2001). *School, family, and community partnerships: Preparing educators and improving schools*. Westview Press.

Erbeli, F., Rice, M., & Paracchini, S. (2023). A meta-analysis on the optimal cumulative dosage of early phonemic awareness instruction. *Journal of Educational Psychology, 115*(2), 345–362. https://doi.org/10.1037/edu0000743

Foorman, B. R., Francis, D. J., Fletcher, J. M., Schatschneider, C., & Mehta, P. (1998). The role of instruction in learning to read: Preventing reading failure in at-risk children. *Journal of Educational Psychology, 90*(1), 37–55.

Gough, P. B., & Tunmer, W. E. (1986). Decoding, reading, and reading disability. *Remedial and Special Education, 7*(1), 6–10. https://doi.org/10.1177/074193258600700104

Graham, S., Harris, K. R., & Fink, B. (2000). Is handwriting causally related to learning to write? Treatment of handwriting problems in beginning writers. *Journal of Educational Psychology, 92*(4), 620–633.

Guthrie, J. T., & Wigfield, A. (2000). Engagement and motivation in reading. In M. L. Kamil, P. B. Mosenthal, P. D. Pearson, & R. Barr (Eds.), *Handbook of reading research* (Vol. III, pp. 403–422). Erlbaum.

Hennessy, N. (2020). *The reading comprehension blueprint: Helping students make meaning from text*. Brookes Publishing.

Hirsch Jr., E. D. (2004). *The knowledge deficit: Closing the shocking education gap for American children*. Houghton Mifflin Harcourt.

Hudson, N., Scheff, J., Tarsha, M., & Cutting, L. E. (2016). Reading comprehension and executive function: Neurobiological findings. *Perspectives on Language and Literacy, 42*(2), 31–35.

Keys to Literacy. (n.d.). *How the brain learns to read*. https://keystoliteracy.com/blog/how-the-brain-learns-to-read/

Mesmer, H. A. E. (2000). Decodable text: A review of what we know. *Reading Research and Instruction, 40*(2), 121–141. https://doi.org/10.1080/19388070109558338

Miles, K. P., McFadden, K. E., & Ehri, L. C. (2019). Associations between language and literacy skills and sight word learning for native and nonnative English-speaking kindergartners. *Reading and Writing, 32*, 1681–1704.

Moats, L. (2023). *Teaching phonemic awareness in 2023: A guide for educators*. Retrieved from https://louisamoats.com/wp-content/uploads/2023/02/Teaching-PA-in-2023_A-Guide-for-Educators_1.30.23.pdf

Nagy, W. E., Anderson, R. C., & Herman, P. A. (1987). Learning word meanings from context during normal reading. *American Educational Research Journal, 24*(2), 237–270. https://doi.org/10.3102/00028312024002237

National Institute of Child Health and Human Development. (2000). *Report of the National Reading Panel: Teaching children to read: An evidence-based assessment of the scientific research literature on reading and its implications for reading instruction* (NIH Publication No. 00-4769). US Government Printing Office.

Piasta, S. B., Purpura, D. J., & Wagner, R. K. (2010). Preschool-aged children's letter-sound acquisition: The role of instruction in letter names and sounds. *Journal of Experimental Child Psychology, 105*(4), 324–335. https://doi.org/10.1016/j.jecp.2010.01.002

Piasta, S. B., Wagner, R. K., & Torgesen, J. K. (2010). The role of phonological awareness in letter-sound acquisition: Evidence from kindergarten students. *Journal of Experimental Child Psychology, 105*(3), 324–344. https://doi.org/10.1016/j.jecp.2009.12.008

Ray, K., Dally, K., Rowlandson, L., long Tam, K., & Lane, A. E. (2022). The relationship of handwriting ability and literacy in kindergarten: A systematic review. *Reading and Writing, 35*, 1119–1155. https://doi.org/10.1007/s11145-021-10224-8

Rice, M., Erbeli, F., Thompson, C. G., Sallese, M. R., & Fogarty, M. (2022). Phonemic awareness: A meta-analysis for planning effective instruction. *Reading Research Quarterly, 57*, 1259–1289. https://doi.org/10.1002/rrq.473

Santangelo, T., & Graham, S. (2016). A comprehensive meta-analysis of handwriting Instruction. *Journal of Educational Psychology, 108*(4), 609–627. https://doi.org/10.1037/edu0000082

Scarborough, H. S. (2001). Connecting early language and literacy to later reading (dis)abilities: Evidence, theory, and practice. In S. B. Neuman & D. K. Dickinson (Eds.), *Handbook of early literacy research* (pp. 97–110). Guilford Press.

Shapiro, L. (2004). A meta-analysis of vocabulary intervention studies. *Reading Research Quarterly, 39*(3), 272–306. https://doi.org/10.1598/RRQ.39.3.2

Share, D. L. (2004). Orthographic learning at a glance: On the time course and developmental onset of self-teaching. *Journal of Experimental Child Psychology, 87*(4), 267–298.

Stahl, S. A., & Fairbanks, M. M. (1986). The effects of vocabulary instruction: A model-based meta-analysis. *Review of Educational Research, 56*(1), 72–110. https://doi.org/10.3102/00346543056001072

Stanovich, K. E. (1992). Speculations on the causes and consequences of individual differences in early reading acquisition. In P. B. Gough, L. C. Ehri, & R. Treiman (Eds.), *Reading acquisition* (pp. 307–342). Lawrence Erlbaum Associates.

Treiman, R., Pennington, B. F., Shriberg, L. D., & Boada, R. (2008). Which children benefit from letter names in learning letter sounds? *Cognition, 106*(3), 1322–1338. https://doi.org/10.1016/j.cognition.2007.07.007

Turkeltaub, P. E., Eden, G. F., Jones, K. M., & Zeffiro, T. A. (2002). Meta-analysis of the functional neuroanatomy of single-word reading: Method and validation. *NeuroImage, 16*(3), 765–780. https://doi.org/10.1006/nimg.2002.1131

Turkeltaub, P. E., Gareau, L., Flowers, D. L., Zeffiro, T. A., & Eden, G. F. (2003). Development of neural mechanisms for reading. *Nature Neuroscience, 6*(7), 767–773.

Wasik, B. A., & Bond, M. A. (2001). Beyond the pages of a book: Interactive book reading and language development in preschool classrooms. *Journal of Educational Psychology, 93*(2), 243–250. https://doi.org/10.1037/0022-0663.93.2.243

Webber, C., Patel, H., Cunningham, A., Fox, A., Vousden, J., Castles, A., & Shapiro, L. (2024). An experimental comparison of additional training in phoneme awareness, letter-sound knowledge and decoding for struggling beginner readers. *British Journal of Educational Psychology, 94*, 282–305. https://doi.org/10.1111/bjep.12641

Acknowledgments

To my husband, Evan, the steady force behind it all. Your unwavering belief in me is my greatest source of strength. Whether it is writing this book, building my reading program, or traveling to conferences, you never hesitate—you simply say, "You've got this," and make it possible. You step in, step up, and support me in ways big and small, always making sure I have what I need to keep moving forward.

You hold everything together at home, ensuring I have the time, space, and support to chase big ideas and make them happen. Your quiet sacrifices, steady encouragement, and ability to handle it all without question never go unnoticed. You make the hard days easier, the big decisions clearer, and the impossible feel within reach. This book is a testament to the dreams you help me pursue. I couldn't do any of this without you, and I wouldn't want to.

To my incredible children, Caleb and Nora, who inspire me every day with your curiosity, resilience, and joy. You remind me that learning is not just about the destination but the journey we take along the way. Watching you explore the world, asking big questions, and making sense of everything around you has been my greatest inspiration. You are a reminder that every child is more than a test score, more than a reading level, more than a grade—they are thinkers, dreamers, problem-solvers, and storytellers in the making.

Acknowledgments

This book is for you, and for every child who deserves the gift of literacy and the wonder it unlocks. It is for the students who see reading as a struggle but haven't yet discovered their breakthrough moment. It is for the children whose voices deserve to be heard, whose stories deserve to be told, and whose futures are waiting to be written. May they always know that reading is not just a skill but a gateway—to knowledge, to adventure, to endless possibilities.

To my wonderful parents—Mom and Dad, this book exists because of the foundation you built for me. You worked tirelessly to ensure that when I struggled to read, I had the support I needed. From tutors to extra reading programs, you opened the door to a world that once felt out of reach. The gift of literacy you gave me now enables me to help other struggling readers, passing on the same opportunity you fought to provide.

Beyond that, you have always been my greatest supporters—encouraging my dreams, lifting me up in moments of doubt, and reminding me of my purpose. Your love, sacrifices, and unwavering belief in me have shaped not only the educator I've become but also the person I am. I am forever grateful for all you have done and continue to do.

To Susan Brown—thank you for giving me the opportunity to make my dreams as a teacher a reality. You took a chance on me when no one else would, hiring me for my first teaching job and believing in me from the very start. Your encouragement and support laid the foundation for my journey as an educator, and I will always be grateful.

To Joe LeGault, my district leader—your belief in me has given me the confidence to take risks and grow. You have always been there to lift me up, offer encouragement, and remind me of my own capabilities when I've doubted them. Your unwavering support has been a steady force, giving me the strength to push forward. I truly couldn't have made this journey without your guidance and trust.

To Dr. Jennifer Jones Powell—your passion for literacy and dedication to your students left a lasting impact on me. As my professor and mentor, you not only deepened my understanding of reading instruction but also sparked a true love for literacy that continues to shape my work today. Your guidance, wisdom, and encouragement gave me the confidence to pursue this path, and I am forever grateful for the foundation you helped build. Thank you for believing in me and for inspiring me to carry that same passion into my own teaching and beyond.

To Rick and Shannon Fuhrman—Rick, my principal, and Shannon, my teacher—thank you for your steadfast belief in me during high school. Your constant support and encouragement gave me the confidence to pursue my dreams. You never stopped believing that I would grow up to accomplish amazing things, and that faith made all the difference. I am forever grateful for the impact you had on my journey. To Sally Cameron, Savannah Campbell, Jessica Farmer, Anna Geiger, Jenna Lyons, Sarah Paul, Stephanie Stollar, and Michelle Sullivan—thank you for your time, dedication, and thoughtful peer reviews of this book. Your expertise, insights, and invaluable feedback have strengthened its content in ways I couldn't have done alone. I am incredibly grateful for your willingness to lend your knowledge and perspective to this project. More than that, I feel so fortunate to be part of a community of educators who are as passionate and committed to literacy as you are. Your support means the world, and I deeply appreciate each of you. Finally, to the dedicated teachers: **You are the champions of literacy, shaping futures one child at a time.** Your work is more than teaching—it is unlocking potential, building confidence, and opening doors that will affect students for a lifetime.

This book is for you, not just as a resource but as a guide and companion on this journey. Together, we are turning research into practice, bridging the gap between what we know and what we do, and making a lasting difference in the lives of our students. The work you do each day matters, and I am honored to walk this path alongside you.

About the Author

Amie Burkholder has spent her career dedicated to helping teachers unlock the potential of every student through the power of evidence-based literacy practices. As a first-grade teacher, she knew she was in a critical role in her students' literacy journey—but something was missing.

Early in her teaching career, Amie thought she had it all figured out, relying on programs and balanced literacy methods. However, it quickly became clear that these approaches didn't work for all students. Determined to find better solutions, she pursued a master's degree in reading to become a reading specialist. Although this added knowledge helped, it wasn't the missing piece. The journey continued, leading to training in Orton-Gillingham and LETRS, where she began to connect the dots among practice, data, and the science of reading.

In 2019, Amie founded Literacy Edventures to support teachers beyond her school building, creating a community focused on actionable strategies and effective resources. Today, as a K–5 literacy coach, national speaker, and literacy consultant, she shares practical, tried-and-true activities and resources grounded in the science of reading through her Route2Reading Membership, Phonics Curriculum (approved under the Virginia Literacy Act), blog, and podcast.

Amie credits her own children with making her a better teacher. Seeing the world through their eyes inspired her to help other educators be the kind of teacher every child deserves—one who supports students both academically and emotionally.

When she's not working, Amie enjoys traveling to new places, spending time with her family, and seeking out little adventures along the way. But some of her favorite moments are the simple ones—relaxing on the couch with her favorite people and appreciating the joy of just being together.

Index

Page numbers followed by *f* and *t* refer to figures and tables, respectively.

A
academic words. *see* high-utility words
accuracy
    and decodable texts, 196, 203
    in fluency grids, 152
    games for, 186–9
    measurements for, 195
    and phonetic decoding, 21
    in reading, 23, 24
    scaffolding approach to, 119
    in spelling, 67, 207, 208
active engagement, 67, 104, 207, 220
alphabetic principle, 18, 21, 57, 62, 67, 85
Ambrose, S. A., 241
articulation
    and confusion, 107–8
    and decoding, 98
    exercises for, 105–9
    letter-sound instruction for, 97*f*
    of letter sounds, 99–100*t*, 99*f*, 103
    mouth movements for, 92
    teaching, 98–100, 99*f*
audiobooks, 243
auditory drills, 101, 105, 146–8, 148*f*, 157–8
authentic literature, 195–6, 197, 206
automaticity
    as brain function, 6
    daily practice for, 61, 117
    and decodable texts, 203
    of handwriting, 60
    in orthographic mapping, 24
    and phonetic decoding, 21, 23
    in three-part drills, 147
    in visual drills, 148

B
background knowledge, 215–38
    building, 206
    content-rich lessons in, 221
    definition of, 10
    exercises for, 223–37
    implementation of, 221
    interactive read-alouds in, 221–2
    multiple texts for, 222–3
    need for, 12
    phonics in, 217–18
    research on, 218–20
    role of, 26
    scaffolding for, 203
    schema activation and, 231–2
    thematic units in, 222
    understanding, 216–17
    see also vocabulary
Beck, I. L., 219

Index

blending
    consonant vowel, 115, 118–19, 122
    consonant vowel consonant, 120–2
    continuous, 115, 120–4, 126
    model, 116–17, 121, 210
    phoneme, 20–1
    successive, 115, 119–20
    vowel consonant, 115
    see also segmentation
blending drills, 149, 149*f*
blends, 112–13, 139, 139*f*, 165–6
Bond, M. A., 222
brain rewiring, 8–12
brain studies, 5–29
    imaging in, 5–8, 7*f*
    implementation of, 12–24
    orthographic mapping in, 24–7
    research in, 5–7
    Scarborough's Reading Rope in, 9–12
    Simple View of Reading in, 8–9, 11, 12
Bringing Words to Life (Beck, et al.), 219, 220

C

Castle, J., 218, 220
circle back letters, 70–1, 77–80
closed syllables, 137, 141*t*. *see also* open syllables
comprehension, 25–7
    background knowledge in, 26
    as reading journey end, 27
    vocabulary in, 26
consonant cousins, 92
consonant digraphs, 142*f*
consonant trigraphs, 143*f*
consonant vowel consonant (CVC) patterns
    in continuous blending, 120–2
    in dictation, 207
    in phoneme-grapheme practice, 210
    phonics instruction for, 113–14
    and short vowel sounds, 137
    in systemic phonics, 133
    transition to, 111, 130
    in word chains, 165–6
consonant vowel (CV) patterns, 114, 121. *see also* consonant vowel consonant patterns; CV blending
content-rich lessons, 218–19, 221
content-specific words, 217
continuous blending, 115, 120–4, 126
continuous sounds, 92, 94*t*, 96, 108
cross-curricular lessons, 221, 237
cumulative reviews, 101, 146–8, 209
Cunningham, Katie Egan, 6, 8, 239–40
CV blending, 115, 118–19
CVC blending, 122
CVC patterns. *see* consonant vowel consonant patterns
CVC picture cards, 42–7, 49–50, 52–3. *see also* picture cards

D

decodability, 200–2
decodable readers, 194. *see also* leveled readers
decodable texts, 200–6
    books as, 242
    for comprehension, 205
    dictation for, 198
    high-frequency words in, 182
    importance of, 194, 245
    instructional routines for, 204–5
    interest-driven engagement for, 240–1
    for phonics skills, 153, 240
    power of, 201–2
    pre-reading activity for, 210–11
    rereading in, 202
    research on, 194–7
    in review components, 145–6
    sample of, 154*t*
    scaffolding for, 202–3
    staggered reading exercise for, 212
    as stepping stones, 203–4
    vocabulary building in, 206
decoding, 111–31
    and articulation, 98

as brain function, 7
and comprehension, 11
continuous blending in, 120–2
CV blending in, 118–19
definition of, 10
dictation for, 154f, 207
and encoding, 191
exercises for, 122–30, 237, 244
of high-frequency words, 144, 181
learning through, 102
of leveled texts, 199
model blending in, 116–17
in orthographic mapping, 177–8
phonetic, 19–21, 137
phonological, 172
and rereading, 202
research on, 35–6, 111–13, 133, 136, 172, 218–20
Scarborough's Reading Rope for, 9–10, 215
sentence pyramids for, 202
sound boxes in, 115–16
strategies for, 113–22
successive blending in, 119–20
SVR model for, 8–9, 9f
VC blending in, 117–18
and vocabulary, 217
in word mapping, 152
see also encoding
dictation, 207–10
and connected texts, 153–4
CVC patterns in, 207
in decodable texts, 198
for decoding, 154f, 207
exercises for, 107, 213
graphemes in, 154
orthographic mapping in, 209
phonemes in, 154
for phonemic instruction, 207–10
for phonics patterns, 213
power of, 198
practice for, 155f
reviews for, 145

short vowel sounds in, 154
for spelling, 198, 207
spoken language in, 207
digraphs
blends vs., 139, 139f
consonant, 142f
definition of, 142t
exercises for, 161–2
research on, 112–13
in word chains, 165
diphthongs, 142t, 165–6
domain-specific terms, 219, 220
double consonants (doubling rule), 143t
drills
auditory, 101, 105, 146–8, 148f, 157–8
blending, 149, 149f
three-part, 147–53
visual, 101, 105, 148–9, 155–7
vowel-intensive, 101, 105, 147, 149, 150f, 159–60
Duke, Nell, 221
dyslexia, 8

E
Ehri, Linnea, 23, 112, 113, 118–19, 135, 136, 171–3
electroencephalograms, 5
encoding, 34, 57, 153, 191, 207. *see also* decoding
Ending the Reading Wars (Castle, et al.), 220
Erbeli, F., 112, 113
everyday words, 216–17
explicit instruction
exercises for, 161
in handwriting, 59, 61
in no sound cues, 88
and repetition, 174
research on, 219
in systemic phonics, 136
terminology in, 103
and word recognition, 179
explicit modeling, 59, 115–47

F

Fairbanks, M. M., 223
feedback
    exercises for, 73, 76, 79, 82, 158, 160, 165, 212–13
    for guided practice, 61
    importance of, 59
    and self-correction, 208
final blends, 142*t*
final "-ck" rule, 138, 141*t*
final "-le" syllables, 143*f*
fine motor skills, 58, 61, 62, 63
flashcards, 148, 155–6, 210
floss rule, 139, 142*t*
fluency grids, 145, 152, 152*f*
focus Skills, 146, 150, 223, 231
Foorman, B. R., 135, 136
frontal region of brain, 6
functional magnetic resonance imaging, 5

G

Gough, P. B., 8
Graham, S., 59, 60, 61
graphemes
    in auditory drills, 148, 157–8
    decoding, 30
    in dictation, 154
    in orthographic mapping, 177–8, 199
    phoneme connection with, 17–19, 22, 150, 171–3, 204, 210
    in phonemic awareness, 31, 41
    in sound boxes, 116
    in visual drills, 105, 148, 155–7
    in vowel-intensive drills, 159–60
    in word chaining, 150
    in word mapping, 152, 167–9
    see also phoneme-grapheme practice
graphophonic cues, 21
Gray Oral Reading Test, 195
Guthrie, J. T., 241

H

handwriting, 57–83
    cross-teacher consistency for, 65–6
    effective instruction of, 62
    exercises for, 67–82
    implementation of, 61–2
    instructional prerequisites for, 63
    letter formation in, 67
    in literacy, 57–8
    pencil grip routines for, 64
    research on, 58–61
    see also letter formation
handwriting lines, 63, 69
heart words, 144, 174, 175, 182*f*. *see also* irregular words
Hennessy, Nancy, 216
high-frequency words (HFWs), 171–90
    exercises for, 183–90
    implementation of, 174
    instructional implications of, 178–82
    multisensory approaches to, 181
    orthographic mapping in, 176–8
    research on, 171–4
    terminology of, 174–6
high-utility letters, 90, 95, 95*t*, 96
high-utility words, 217, 219, 220
Hirsch, E. D. Jr, 219, 220
How Learning Works (Ambrose et al.), 241
Hudson, N., 6

I

initial blends, 142*t*
instant recognition, 171, 177, 178
interactive activities, 181, 241
interest-driven engagement, 240–1
interweaving, 208
irregular spellings, 144
irregular words, 175, 179, 181, 203, 206. *see also* heart words

K

The Knowledge Deficit (Hirsch), 220

L

labeling, 15, 198, 243
language structures, 6, 11, 196, 206
learning decay, 147, 209
LETRS Early Childhood (LETRS EC), 62
letter characteristics, 87
letter formation
    and automaticity, 60
    consistency for, 65
    exercises for, 107 (*see also* handwriting)
    and fine motor skills, 61
    importance of, 57–8
    letter-sound instruction for, 97, 97*f*
    and literacy development, 67
    practicing, 83
    prerequisites for, 63
    in preschool, 62
letter formation chants, 65–6*t*
letter grouping, 95–6, 96*t*
letter name knowledge, 86, 87
letter-sound connections, 13, 15–16, 182
letter-sound knowledge, 85–110
    exercises for, 105–9
    implementation of, 88–96
    importance of, 112
    in orthographic mapping, 172
    research on, 35, 85–8, 113
    tips for teaching, 97–104
letter sounds
    activities for, 104
    articulation of, 98–100, 99*f*
    blending of, 114, 121
    and decoding, 111–31
    exercises for, 105–7
    and letter formation, 58
    letter grouping for, 96
    mouth positions for, 91–2
    and phonemic awareness, 17–19
    practice for, 207, 244
    research on, 86–8, 113, 135
    students' knowledge of, 102
    teaching, 37, 88–9, 97–104
    terminology of, 103
    transition to words, 130
    visual drills for, 148
leveled readers, 194, 199, 200
leveled texts, 193*t*, 198–200
libraries, 243
literacy knowledge, 11
literacy nights, 243–5
long vowel sounds, 138, 140. *see also* short vowel sounds
lowercase letters, 62, 106, 130

M

Mesmer, Heidi Anne, 195–7, 201
Messner, Kate, 231, 236
Moats, Louisa, 37
model blending, 116–17, 121, 210
mouth movements, 92*f*, 98. *see also* unvoiced sounds; voiced sounds
multiple texts, 222–3
multisyllabic words, 204

N

nasals, 142*t*
National Institute of Child Health and Human Development, 13–14, 40, 41, 133, 134, 136
National Reading Panel, 134, 136
Neal, Christopher Silas, 231, 236
nursery rhymes, 13, 243

O

occipital-temporal region of brain, 6–7
open syllables, 141*t*, 181. *see also* closed syllables
orthographic mapping, 24–7, 176–8
    and automaticity, 24–5
    and comprehension, 25–7
    and decodable texts, 201
    definition of, 176–7
    development of, 177–8
    in dictation, 209
    Ehri's work in, 172, 173
    and fluency, 30

orthographic mapping (*continued*)
  of high-frequency words, 171, 174
  importance of, 177–8
  in interactive activities, 181–2
  and phonemic awareness, 209
  power of, 178
  process of, 176
  in spoken and written language, 179–80
  and word recognition, 199
Over and Under the Pond (Messner and Neal), 231, 236
overcompensators, 22–3

P

parietal-temporal region of brain, 6–7
path to reading, 29*f*
pencil grip, 61–2, 63–4, 68
pencil grip routines, 64
phoneme addition, 33
phoneme deletion, 33
phoneme-grapheme mapping. *see* word mapping
phoneme-grapheme practice, 204, 210
phoneme isolation, 32
phoneme manipulation, 31, 33. *see also* sound manipulation
phonemes
  auditory drills for, 148, 157–8
  awareness of, 37
  blending drills for, 149
  blending of, 20–1, 32, 47, 49, 105
  in continuous blending, 120
  in CVC patterns, 114
  decoding of, 19–20, 24, 30
  in dictation, 154
  grapheme connection with, 17–19, 22, 150, 171–3, 204, 210
  in high-frequency words, 171
  in model blending, 116–17
  in orthographic mapping, 177–8
  in phonemic awareness, 16–17, 18*t*, 42
  in phonological awareness, 13–14
  scaffolding instruction for, 38, 39–40*t*, 39*f*
  sound boxes for, 115–16, 128–9
  in word chaining, 150, 163–6
  in word mapping, 152, 167–9
  see also phoneme-grapheme practice
phoneme segmentation, 17, 40*t*, 50–2, 115–16, 128–30. *see also* sound boxes
phoneme substitution, 34
phonemic awareness (PA), 31–55, 209
  definition of, 31
  exercises for, 41–54
  implementation of, 37–41
  importance of, 34
  layers of, 32–4
  in reading development, 16–17
  research on, 35
  warm-ups for, 146–7
phonemic focus skills, 150–3
  fluency grids in, 152
  word chaining in, 150
  word mapping in, 152–3
  word reading in, 150–1
phonemic instruction, 191–214
  decodable texts for, 200–6
  dictation in, 207–10
  exercises for, 210–13
  implementation of, 197–8
  leveled text for, 198–200
  read-alouds in, 206
  research on, 194–7
phonetically regular words, 175, 196, 197
phonetic decoding, 19–21. *see also* decoding
phonics-aligned high-frequency word lists, 244
phonics patterns
  analysis of, 192*t*, 193–4*t*
  in auditory drills, 148
  consistency in, 145–6
  in decodable text, 153, 200–1, 203, 205
  dictation for, 213
  fluency grids for, 152
  and interweaving, 208
  in irregular words, 175

and sight words, 180–1
  systemic approach to, 133
  teaching, 179, 198
  in vocabulary, 217–18
  in word chains, 165
  in word reading, 150
phonological awareness
  and CV blending, 118
  definition of, 10
  and letter-sound connections, 13–14, 86–7
  and phonemic awareness, 16, 30
  in reading development, 13–15
  and sight word acquisition, 172
  and sound cues, 88
  teaching of, 37–8
Piasta, S. B., 85–7
picture cards
  CVC, 42–7, 49–50, 52–3
  exercises for, 105–7, 109, 122–3, 177
  vocabulary, 226, 229, 233, 235
picture representation, 89–90, 98
posture, 61, 63–4, 68
Preventing Academic Failure benchmark, 195
printable literacy games, 244
prosody, 23, 25
Purpura, D. J., 85–7

R
Ray, K., 59, 60
"r"-controlled vowels, 140, 140*f*
  in word chains, 165–6
read-alouds
  of authentic texts, 197
  comprehension reinforcement through, 216
  in early literacy, 206
  exercises for, 223, 229–31
  fun through, 241
  interactive, 221–2
  nonfiction, 236–7
  and vocabulary acquisition, 26, 219, 220

reading brain, 5, 176*f*
reading development, 12–24
  blending and segmenting in, 20–1
  decoding in, 19–21
  graphemes in, 17–19
  letter sounds in, 15–16
  phonemes in, 17–19
  phonemic awareness in, 16–17
  phonological awareness in, 13–15
  three-cueing system in, 21–4
reading rate, 24–5
repeated exposure, 173, 175, 178, 222, 223
repetition, 101, 118, 122, 173, 179, 202, 230
rereading, 146, 202, 208
Rice, M., 35
Rose, D., 6, 8

S
Santangelo, T., 59, 60
scaffolding phoneme instruction
  for blending, 115
  in continuous blending, 119, 150
  of decodable texts, 202–3, 206
  flow chart of, 39–40*t*
  illustrated, 39*f*
  introduction to, 38–9
  in successive blending, 121
Scarborough, Hollis, 9, 11
Scarborough's Reading Rope, 9–12, 10*f*, 215, 237
schema activation, 224–5, 231–2, 237
schwa sound, 98, 103, 106, 142*t*
scope and sequence
  consideration of, 90
  for high-frequency words, 181
  importance of, 143–5
  in phonics instruction, 154, 203
  in strategic letter grouping, 95–6
segmentation
  of continuous and stop sounds, 92
  as critical skill, 28
  listening-only, 40
  oral, 34

segmentation (*continued*)
  in orthographic mapping, 177–8, 209
  as PA level, 32, 114
  phoneme (*see* phoneme segmentation)
  power of, 20
  practice for, 45–54, 146
  in reading development, 20–1
  sentence, 13
  sound, 116
  sound boxes for, 115–16, 128–30
  in successive blending, 119
  syllable, 13, 14, 30
  teaching of, 37, 38
  see also blending
self-correction, 208–9
semantic cues, 21
sentence pyramids, 202
sentence segmentation, 13
sentence structure, 11, 21, 198, 207, 209–10
Shapiro, L., 219–20
Share, David, 171–2, 173
Shifting the Balance 3–5 (Cunningham), 239
short lines, 71–4
short vowel sounds
  in closed syllables, 137
  and CVC patterns, 137–8
  in decodable texts, 191–4, 200
  in dictation, 154
  exercises for, 163, 165–6, 210, 213
  in high-frequency words, 181
  in VCE pattern, 140
  see also long vowel sounds
sight word acquisition, 10
sight word reading, 173, 177. *see also* word reading
sight words
  acquisition of, 172–3
  definition of, 175
  games for, 183–9
  memorization of, 22
  practicing, 182
  recognition of, 24, 203

  teaching of, 179–80
  vocabulary of, 144, 178
silent "e" rule, 140, 140*f*, 142*t*, 166, 175
silent letters, 143*t*
Simple View of Reading (SVR), 8–9, 9*t*, 11, 12
Simple View of Writing, 58
slanted lines, 69–71, 80–2
Soft "c" and "g," 142*t*
sound boxes, 115–16, 128–30, 161–2. *see also* phoneme segmentation
sound cues, 86–8
sound manipulation
  in continuous and sound stops, 92, 96
  as focus skill, 150
  and letter mapping, 112, 113
  in mouth movements, 92
  in orthographic mapping, 177
  in phonemic awareness, 14–17, 18*f*, 31, 173
  in phonological awareness, 10, 13, 30
  and sound boxes, 115–16
  and word mapping, 209
  see also phoneme manipulation
sound segmentation, 116
speech sound disorders, 87, 88
spelling
  blending and segmentation for, 20, 34, 92
  definition of, 10
  developmental, 87
  dictation for, 198, 207
  doubled consonants in, 138–9
  exercises for, 183–9
  feedback on, 208–9
  and handwriting fluency, 58–60
  irregular, 144
  and letter formation, 67
  orthographic mapping for, 172, 176
  patterns of, 141
  phonemic awareness for, 16, 41, 112, 113
  phonics instruction for, 135, 136, 174
  research on, 60–1
  teaching, 158, 165

-to-sound correspondences, 180, 209
in word chains, 166
in word mapping, 169
spoken language
   alphabetic principle of, 85
   in dictation, 207
   exposure to, 14
   phoneme isolation in, 32
   phonemic awareness in, 121
   segmenting of, 32
   sound manipulation in, 13, 16, 30
   and written language, 57, 59, 67, 152, 179–82
Stahl, S. A., 223
Start with Joy (Cunningham), 239
sticky notes, 50–2, 224–6, 229, 232, 233
stop sounds, 92, 94*t*, 96, 108
student knowledge, 102
successive blending, 115, 119–20
SVR (Simple View of Reading), 8–9, 9*t*, 11, 12
syllable segmentation, 13, 14, 30
syntactic cues, 21
systematic instruction
   effectiveness of, 58
   importance of, 21–2, 112
   models for, 11
   prioritizing, 23
   research on, 134–5, 136
   as routine, 101
   sequence of, 113
systematic phonics, 133–69
   blends in, 139–43
   CVC patterns in, 137–9
   and decodable texts, 206
   digraphs in, 139–43
   exercises for, 155–69
   focus skills in, 150–3
   implementation of, 137
   instruction of, 121
   lesson components of, 146–53
   research on, 111–14, 134–6, 218, 220
   scope and sequence in, 143–6
   short vowel sounds in, 137
   skills applications of, 153–5
   teaching of, 130, 178–9

T

tall lines, 74–6
temporarily irregular words, 175. *see also* irregular words
terminology, 103, 174–6
thematic units, 221, 222, 237
three-cueing system, 21, 22–3, 199
three-part drills, 147–53
Treiman, R., 86, 88
trigraphs, 140, 142–3*t*
Tunmer, W. E., 8
Turkeltaub, P. E., 6–7

U

unvoiced sounds, 90–2, 91*t*, 96, 139
uppercase letters, 62, 106

V

VC blending, 115, 117–18, 122, 124–6
VCE (vowel consonant "e") pattern, 140
VC (vowel consonant) patterns, 114. *see also* consonant vowel consonant patterns; VC blending
verbal reasoning, 11
visual clues, 21
visual drills, 101, 105, 148–9, 155–7
vocabulary, 215–38
   and authentic literature, 195–7
   building, 206
   content-specific words in, 217
   definition of, 10
   discussing, 211
   everyday words in, 216–17
   exercises for, 223–37
   and leveled texts, 198
   media for building, 242–3
   multiple exposures to, 223
   need for, 12
   non-fiction, 231–7

vocabulary (*continued*)
   phoneme-grapheme practice for, 204
   phonics in, 217–18
   and read-aloud, 223–37
   repetition in, 173
   research on, 218–20
   role of, 26
   sight words in, 144, 172, 175, 178, 203
   and spelling patterns, 141
   spoken, 179
   teaching, 240
   understanding, 216–17
   see also background knowledge
vocabulary picture cards, 226, 229, 233, 235. *see also* picture cards
voiced sounds, 90–2, 91*t*, 96, 139. *see also* mouth movements
vowel consonant (VC) patterns, 114. *see also* consonant vowel consonant patterns; VC blending
vowel-intensive drills, 101, 105, 147, 149, 150*f*, 159–60
Vowel Teams, 138, 140–1, 140*f*, 142*t*, 165–6, 201

W

Wagner, R. K., 86
Wasik, B. A., 222
Webber, C., 35
Wigfield, A., 241
word chaining, 41, 150, 163–6
word jars, 243

word mapping, 152–3, 153*f*, 167–9, 209
word reading
   in at-risk children, 122
   cards for, 151*f*
   importance of, 149–51
   research on, 59, 60, 112–13, 135–6
   systemic approach to, 90
   see also sight word reading
word recognition
   automatic, 23–4
   blending process in, 117, 118–19
   brain research on, 6–7
   in decodable texts, 203
   fluency grids for, 152
   of high-frequency words, 179, 181
   high-utility letters in, 96
   orthographic mapping of, 24, 109
   in Reading Rope, 10*f*, 11, 215, 237
   research on, 112
   skills for, 114
written language
   alphabetic principle of, 85
   in brain function, 6
   high-frequency words in, 175, 180
   letter-sound knowledge in, 112
   and letter sounds, 15
   mental pictures of, 173
   orthographic mapping of, 24
   phonemic awareness of, 67
   and sentence structure, 210
   and spoken language, 57, 59, 67, 152, 179–82